Current Issues in
Stuttering Research and Practice

CURRENT ISSUES IN STUTTERING RESEARCH AND PRACTICE

—— *Edited by* ——

NAN BERNSTEIN RATNER
University of Maryland

JOHN TETNOWSKI
University of Louisiana at Lafayette

2006

LAWRENCE ERLBAUM ASSOCIATES, PUBLISHERS
Mahwah, New Jersey   London

MW

Camera ready copy for this book was provided by the editors.

Copyright © 2006 by Lawrence Erlbaum Associates, Inc.

Lawrence Erlbaum Associates, Inc., Publishers
10 Industrial Avenue
Mahwah, New Jersey 07430
www.erlbaum.com

Cover design by Kathryn Houghtaling Lacey

Library of Congress Cataloging-in-Publication Data

Current issues in stuttering research and practice / edited by Nan
    Bernstein Ratner, John Tetnowski.
     p. cm.

Includes bibliographical references and index.

ISBN 0-8058-5201-8 (cloth : alk. paper)
ISBN 0-8058-5202-6 (pbk. : alk. paper)
1. Stuttering. I. Ratner, Nan Bernstein. II. Tetnowski, John.
RC424.C89 2005
616.85'54—dc22   2005043511
                       CIP

Books published by Lawrence Erlbaum Associates are printed on
acid-free paper, and their bindings are chosen for strength and
durability.

Printed in the United States of America
10 9 8 7 6 5 4 3 2 1

3/26/07

Acknowledgements

This volume was made possible by the hard work of contributors to the 2003 ASHA Special Interest Division 4 (Fluency and Fluency Disorders) Leadership Conference. The Steering Committee of the Division for 2003 consisted of Larry Molt (Coordinator), Bob Quesal (Associate Coordinator), Char Bloom, Bill Murphy and Scott Yaruss. We would like to additionally thank the program chairs for the Leadership Conference (Bob Quesal and Scott Yaruss), as well as members of the ASHA staff who helped to make the meeting possible, particularly Michelle Ferketic. In preparing this set of proceedings, the Division invited one contributor not on the original conference program to submit a chapter.

Additional heartfelt thanks are also due to Heather Barron, who ably and patiently served as our camera-ready compositor, and to Cathleen Petree of Lawrence Erlbaum Associates for her continued support of Special Interest Division conference proceedings.

Proceedings from the sale of this volume support ASHA's Special Interest Division 4.

– Nan Bernstein Ratner and John Tetnowski

CONTENTS

— 1 —

Stuttering Treatment in the New Millennium: Changes in the Traditional Parameters of Clinical Focus

Nan Bernstein Ratner
University of Maryland

John A. Tetnowski
University of Louisiana at Lafayette

A while back, there was a car commercial that boasted, "This is not your father's Oldsmobile." As we enter the new millennium, the same might be said of stuttering: from multiple perspectives, our view of stuttering, stuttering treatment, and appropriate preparation for those who provide stuttering treatment is changing. In this chapter, we discuss some challenges that face our discipline, to set the chapters that follow into current context.

Is there a growing disconnect between what SLPs actually do and what we *think* they do?

If one goes to the Internet to Ask Jeeves©, "What do speech pathologists do?", the top five answers might not seem surprising. According to the U.S. Department of Labor, Bureau of Labor Statistics:

> *Speech-language pathologists work with people who cannot make speech sounds, or cannot make them clearly;* **those with speech rhythm and fluency problems, such as stuttering;** *people with voice quality problems, such as inappropriate pitch or harsh voice; those with problems understanding and producing language; those who wish to improve their communication skills by modifying an accent; and those with cognitive communication*

1

impairments, such as attention, memory, and problem-solving disorders. They also work with people who have oral motor problems causing eating and swallowing difficulties. (U.S Department of Labor, retrieved from www.bls.gov/oco/pdf/ocos099.pdf)

Speech Pathology Australia answers the question, "Who do speech pathologists work with?" by answering:

A speech pathologist's workload might include {We provide here the first five answers}:
- *giving advice on feeding to a mother who has a baby with a cleft palate;*
- *working in a child care centre with a group of children who are hard to understand;*
- *working with a school child who can't understand what his teacher says;*
- ***working with a high school student who stutters;***
- *retraining a teacher who constantly loses her voice to use it more effectively...* (Retrieved from www.speechpathologyaustralia.org.au/library/11_FactSheet.pdf)

To provide some sense of how state speech-language-hearing associations view the profession, we went to the Illinois Speech-Language-Hearing Association (in tribute to Bob Quesal), and found an answer to the following question, "What Do Speech-Language Pathologists Do?":

Speech-language pathologists are specialists trained to evaluate, identify and remediate disorders of communication and swallowing. Speech-language pathologists work with people of all ages, from infants to elderly. Speech-language pathologists provide treatment to improve language, voice, stuttering, articulation, memory and swallowing. [Note the order of the disorders.] (Illinois Speech-Language-Hearing Association, retrieved from www.ishail.org)

A consumer-oriented pediatric health web site sponsored by the Pfizer company (Kidspeak) informs the public about what speech-language pathologists do:

*These healthcare professionals are educated and trained to help patients overcome speech, language, and swallowing disorders. {Children who see speech-language pathologists may or may not have hearing problems.} These specialists also help treat **stuttering**, voice, and pronunciation disorders.* (Retrieved from www.kidsears.com/kidspeak.html)

The same site prominently addresses the most common questions parents pose, including, "What should I do if my child stutters?"

Finally, our professional website (asha.org), in the area of the site providing information for prospective students, answers "Frequently Asked Questions about the Professions":

> *Some Basic Facts... Speech-Language Pathologists **help those who stutter to increase their fluency**; help people who have had strokes or experienced brain trauma to regain lost language and speech; help children and adolescents who have language disorders to understand and give directions, ask and answer questions, convey ideas, improve the language skills that lead to better academic performance; counsel individuals and families to understand and deal with speech and language disorders.* (American Speech-Language-Hearing Association; retrieved from www.asha.org/about/news/releases/faq_careers.htm)

IS THE ADVERTISING MISLEADING?

The point of what might seem like a tedious exercise in "Googling" is to note that stuttering treatment and work with people who stutter are broadly viewed as a primary focus of practice for speech-language pathologists (SLPs). Certainly a consumer seeking information about who to turn to for stuttering treatment is provided with a sense that fluency is a core professional activity. However, as we note, an emerging problem is the mismatch between perception and the statistics that characterize SLP practice. At the risk of proving the point made by a great anonymous author that, "Numbers are like people; torture them enough and they'll tell you anything," it is instructive to view the ASHA 2001 Omnibus Survey, specifically the caseload report for speech-language pathologists (American Speech-Language-Hearing Association, 2001a).

For SLPs in all settings combined, 65% see fluency cases. This proportion ranked above those who report treating aphasia (27%), dysphagia (37%), and voice (45%). In schools, the proportion of SLPs reporting that they have someone on the caseload who stutters rises to 78%, outranking the disorders just mentioned, as well as Specific Language Impairment (SLI), Pervasive Developmental Disorder (PDD), and children using Augmentative and Alternative Communication (AAC) devices. These numbers seem to provide support for the notion that stuttering is a disorder that SLPs commonly treat. But the numbers combine in interesting ways.

In any setting, if the absolute number of individuals seen for particular disorders is queried, the mean number of fluency clients seen *per SLP* falls to the absolute lowest of *all conditions that SLPs treat*, at 2.4% of each SLP's caseload (schools, 2.5%) of all disorders except "communication effective-ness" (whatever that is...). When viewed against caseload statistics, SLPs see more people with *hearing* disorders than persons who stutter.

WHAT DOES ALL THIS MEAN?

An emerging problem with the expanding scope of practice in speech-lan-guage pathology (American Speech-Language-Hearing Association, 2001b) is that the lay public *expects* SLPs to be able to treat fluency disor-ders: In job descriptions of SLPs, treatment of stuttering is often one of the top-listed responsibilities. And, in fact, most SLPs in practice do see people in need of treatment for fluency disorders. It is one of the top-ranked disor-ders seen by ASHA members. However, effective fluency treatment is not a skill that can be learned "on the job," since the absolute number of cases per clinician is among the lowest of all disorders that SLPs see, allowing lit-tle opportunity to hone skills. This is unfortunate because several surveys (e.g., Sommers & Carusso, 1995) have shown that stuttering is one of the least understood of all communicative disorders and that SLPs feel less com-fortable in treating this disorder than almost any other group. This makes some sense; stuttering is a relatively low-incidence disorder (approximately 1%; Andrews, Craig, Feyer, Hoddinott, Howie, et al., 1983; Bloodstein, 1995). But its effective treatment is complex, as many have noted, and as many of the chapters in this text emphasize. Thus, we have a disconnect between a kind of fiction and reality.

Some emerging realities of clinical training

Popular novelist Tom Clancy once made the comment, "The difference between fiction and reality? Fiction has to make sense." As noted earlier, the reality is that most SLPs are expected to, and can expect to, treat stut-tering. But there is an accompanying sense in graduate curricula that it is an uncommon disorder, and thus does not merit a prominent place in the curriculum and clinical training (Yaruss & Quesal, 2002). The standards for the Certificate of Clinical Competence (CCC) in speech-language pathology have progressively loosened the requirements that programs his-torically impose on their students to obtain clinical and coursework expert-ise in fluency. These changes have had measurable consequences (Yaruss & Quesal, 2002), and the revised CCCs do insist that programs document the ability of their students to competently provide fluency services. But these standards are amorphous, and their clear implementation is still a matter of some discussion (Yaruss & Quesal, 2002). In surveys conducted over the years, stuttering consistently falls among the least understood of all the areas that speech-language pathologists encounter (Brisk, Healey, & Hux, 1997; Sommers & Caruso, 1995). In this light, it is amazing that ASHA has chosen to remove any firm clinical requirement in stuttering for students graduating with master's degrees in speech-language pathology. It is indeed possible that a speech-language pathologist, with clinical credentials, could receive payment for treating a person who stutters without ever having had a single prior hands-on experience with stuttering. Perhaps this has contributed to the growth of the self-help movement in stuttering, where some consumers have avoided speech-language pathologists over the years and only recently are reinviting speech-language pathologists back to their groups (see Reeves, chap. 11, this volume). At this point, it is extremely unclear how competent the next generation of speech-language pathologists will feel in treating stuttering. It is evident that their predecessors, who supposedly received more rigorous training, have felt poorly equipped to work with children and adults who stutter (Brisk, Healey, & Hux, 1997; Sommers & Caruso, 1995; Quesal & Yaruss, 2002). Despite some recent improvements, stuttering remains an area of practice with which many speech-language pathologists feel less than comfortable.

Although the quality of training for speech-language pathologists to treat fluency disorders remains a serious problem, it is magnified by the emerging shortage of qualified teacher-researchers in fluency. One might ask where the new leadership in fluency treatment *research* will come from. A recent conference brought together most of the current Ph.D. students in fluency from throughout the country. At this conference, six doctoral students interested in fluency disorders participated and data showed that there were approximately 12 students seeking advanced degrees in fluency disorders (Eldridge, Kluetz, & Donaher, 2002). If this is an indicator of the next generation of leadership in fluency disorders in North America, consumer groups may very well start to consider alternatives to treatment by speech-language pathologists. Certainly 12 Ph.D.-level researchers will not be able to support the needs of more than 300 American SLP training programs.

One potential improvement in the U.S. model may emerge as a result of post-M.A., CCC specialization. However, it is unfortunate that there is still no compelling evidence that supports specialization as a factor in improving consumer care. In fact, the American Speech-Language-

Hearing Association, together with most professional health care organizations, still faces the challenge of documenting what we certainly feel to be a fact: that certified professionals achieve better outcomes than do those with lower credentials or less rigorous training. It is extremely difficult to obtain evidence that specialization training positively affects outcomes, and certain trade-offs have been observed in medicine.

As noted, this question is not specific to fluency disorders alone. Peach (2004) has shown this trend of "specialization" is emerging in other areas of speech-language pathology. As a matter of fact, he questioned the efficacy of "required" training and specialization for well-established programs, such as the Lee Silverman Voice Training (LSVT, Ramig, Countryman, O'Brien, Hoehn, & Thompson, 1995) and PROMPT therapy (Square-Storer & Hayden, 1989). Does the training and specialization really make a difference? Can we really endorse "specialization" without any data to back up the claim that specialists are better, more efficacious, or more efficient? In the medical literature, some evidence germane to this question is both reassuring and troubling. For example, Caron, Jones, Neuhauser, and Aaron (2004) reported that, in larger organizations (we might take as analogies school systems or large clinical settings), higher level emphasis on evidence-based, continuous quality improvement seems to exert a more favorable impact on outcomes than treatment by specialists alone. Donahoe (1998) performed a meta-analysis of outcomes reported in major medical journals and concluded that specialty training appeared to confer benefits in certain circumstances, but that generalized competency in the basic concepts underlying good care might have a greater impact on outcomes. For fluency, we might say that this could amount to the difference between knowing quite a bit about stuttering and fluency techniques, and having the clinical acumen to know when, how, and how best to provide effective therapy that best matches the patient's needs. Thus, despite the appealing notion that fluency specialization will improve care for those who stutter, is there any evidence that shows clinicians who hold specialty recognition in fluency disorders to be more competent than those who do not? Firmly documenting the value of fluency specialists through published research, or indeed, SLPs in the care of stuttering at all is but one more of the challenges that face future practitioners. Consumers, third-party payers, and school systems will justifiably continue to ask the question, "Does specialization really improve client care?"

This very question, as it relates to client care, outcomes, and treatment efficacy, is related to so many of the other issues that we face in the 21st century. The status of emerging therapies (e.g., electronic devices; see Bakker, chap. 9, this volume), the effectiveness of drug therapies for stuttering (for which SLPs will not be the primary providers; see Ludlow, chap. 10, this volume), the effectiveness of the "hotter" therapy programs (as measured by frequency of published report, e.g., the Lidcombe Program; see Bernstein Ratner & Guitar, chap. 6, this volume); intensive therapies (Montgomery, chap. 8, this volume), and specific intervention and carry-over techniques; e.g., counseling; see Ambrose, chap. 5, this volume); the role of support groups (Reeves, chap. 11, this volume) can all be linked to a trend that questions the nature of effective treatments and the documentation of efficient, successful outcomes following stuttering therapy (Pietranton, chap. 3, this volume). We additionally ask (as we measure outcomes), whether such outcomes (and even the basic understanding of what stuttering is) can be linked to a single, comprehensive theory that explains this complex disorder (Conture, chap. 2, this volume). These questions are significant challenges for the 21st century. Yet, we are still not even in agreement as to what signifies a valid diagnosis of stuttering (St. Louis, chap. 4, this volume) or what constitutes a successful outcome (Manning, chap. 7, this volume).

How do we get our information today?

Clearly, the answers to such questions will form the basis for evidence-based practice in fluency disorders that achieves its desired ends. However, if researchers converge on diagnostic and therapeutic "best practices," we must still be concerned about how quickly or well this information will reach the practicing clinician. We supposedly live in the "information age," with ever more numerous and enriched sources of data. The average home receives hundreds of television stations, not to mention satellite radio in our cars, cellular and satellite telephones on our person at all times, in addition to that great information source, the Internet. Our access to information is almost limitless, yet how consumers selectively search out and interpret this onslaught of information becomes an important challenge.

Studies in other professions that have recently endorsed "evidence-based practice" have identified some problems inherent in the multiple potential sources of information that are available to clinicians and patients, as well as concerns about both groups' preferred sources of such information. It is not clear that many practicing professionals possess what we might call "information literacy." For example, Nail-Chiwetalu & Bernstein Ratner (in press) note that physicians, nurses, and allied health professionals often obtain information from colleagues, old texts, and the Internet, rather from traditional, peer-reviewed sources, such as the professional journals. In particular, both professionals and their clients/patients often begin a diagnostic or therapeutic inquiry by "Googling."

Does the Internet make life easier for the researcher and for the consumer? Or is it an unsatisfactory replacement for serious library work and review? A number of issues thwart a simple answer to this question. The presence of paid "ads" that surface in prominent fashion after keyword searches may convince both SLPs and potential consumers that certain proprietary treatments represent efficacious and mainstream solutions to the problem of stuttering. The remaining "hits" are no less suspect: they are likely to contain a mix of personal web pages, therapy vendors, and other nonpeer-reviewed subjective reports, interspersed with valid abstracts of peer-reviewed journal articles and other more reliable sources of "evidence" (Nail-Chiwetalu & Bernstein Ratner, in press).

There is no easy solution to the problem of filtering an increasingly large body of information that is increasingly less "labeled" in terms of scientific value. Clinicians will need to become ever more expert in keeping up with evolving evidence of best therapeutic approaches while, at the same time, maintaining a perspective on the types of information that clients are likely to encounter when investigating potential solutions to their symptom complaints. As Bernstein Ratner (2004) noted, the Internet is likely to provide information that is inconsistent with current "best practice" even in the broadest sense for those making inquiries in English. This problem is dramatically exacerbated particularly when clients from non-English speaking backgrounds perform Internet searches using other languages.

How do we best study fluency and fluency disorders?

"I only have faith in those statistics that I have forged myself."
–Sir Winston Churchill

Earlier in this chapter, we discussed what a speech-language pathologist does. Now we may want to discuss how speech-language pathologists come to the conclusions that they hold so close to their hearts. In particular, much has been said recently about the role of carefully controlled randomized clinical trials (RCTs) in determining the best treatment approaches for medical and allied health conditions (Robey, 2004). Although this may represent the "gold standard" for answering certain diagnostic and therapeutic questions, there are many who believe that there are alternative methods to document treatment efficacy, and that, in fact, some disorders or treatments are not ideally suited to the RCT model (Bernstein Ratner, 2005). Some cognitive treatments used in fluency cannot be "washed out" or "blinded," for example. There are additional concerns that the active targets and agents in therapies may not be easily identifiable and manipulable. For fluency, what can be seen and what can be observed is of the utmost importance; however, we may not possess the technology or the desire to measure all that is important, particularly some of the features of stuttering discussed at length by St. Louis (chap. 4, this volume) and Manning (chap. 7, this volume). Starkweather (1999) suggested that we limit our research greatly by only considering those variables that are easily seen or measured (the old "key-hunting drunk under the street light" analogy). One of the great educators and most widely-read scientists of the 20th century, Stephen J. Gould (1995) is quoted (in DiLollo, Manning, & Plaxico, 2004) as saying, "We cannot reject plausible forces because we do not see them directly. Most of science relies on ingenious and rigorous inference, not passive observation alone" (p.167). This is not to belittle or underrate the role of observation in the process of theory generating and application. It is merely one way of studying the complexities of human behaviors.

In a recent article on qualitative methodologies, Tetnowski and Damico (2004) made just this point about the study of fluency and fluency disorders by making an analogy to Procrustes's Bed. For those unfamiliar with this Greek myth, Procrustes lived along a busy route taken by many travelers. Procrustes often offered travelers a place to rest and spend the night. A small limitation to his generosity was the fact that he had only one bed. In an interesting exercise of obsessive-compulsive desire to make the bed appropriate to each visitor, travelers who were too short were "racked" and stretched until they fit into the bed perfectly. If the traveler happened to be too tall, Procrustes simply chopped off appendages that flopped over the edges of the bed. Thus, Procrustes' bed fit everyone, but at substantial cost.[1] It has not been uncommon for theories, models, and practice guidelines in many disciplines to engage in behavior that seems somewhat familiar. In fluency, we hold the wish that many theories, models and treatment approaches will co-exist peaceably to the extent that each finds some evidence-base.

---

[1] We have a friend who notes, "Beware Procrustes carrying Occam's Razor," a sobering thought as well.

The role and emergence of clinical-outcome research and evidence-based practice (EBP)

What might an adequate evidence base look like? Concerns about EBP have begun to pervade speech-language pathology and fluency treatment. Its emergence is often associated with Sackett (1998) in the medical literature; its premises have been highlighted specifically for fluency therapy by Ingham (2003). Perhaps surprisingly, the issues that surround evidence-based practice appear to be among the most heated debates among researchers and clinicians in the area of fluency and fluency disorders. We say "surprisingly" because it would seem as though evidence is a fairly clear-cut concept. But it is not (Bernstein Ratner, 2005).

A major dispute involves the nature of the published evidence that favors particular therapeutic approaches in fluency. It has been common for the research in modeling and treating fluency disorders to follow an experimental paradigm in which a confined set of variables are measured at baseline, manipulated through a finite set of procedures, and measured at study end. Of the research articles published in three major journals (*Journal of Fluency Disorders, Journal of Speech, Language, Hearing Research,* and *Language, Speech and Hearing Services in Schools*) between the years of 1994 and 2003, 254 of the 265 research articles followed this rough experimental format. Only four were qualitative in nature and seven were of a mixed design (Bothe & Andreatta, 2004). This trend may be changing, however. Another survey conducted by Tetnowski and Damico (2004) shows an expansion in published study design, particularly with respect to inclusion of qualitative rather than quantitative methods of inquiry. Thus, although some designs (e.g., RCTs) are probably the gold standard for the testing of certain types of therapeutic intervention, we are optimistic that all carefully planned and executed methods should and will be entered into the stuttering literature. Given a publication proclivity for the new and novel, rather than the *status quo*, we are also hopeful that existing—in addition to evolving—approaches will be researched, and only rejected when the data indicate that they are not valid. History will eventually show which methods and studies are most valid for the study of a human behavior as complex as communication.

The emerging status of evidence-based practice and its ramifications are not new, although the current flurry of attention might make it seem so. Expanding the scope of the query back to the 1990s demonstrates our field's longstanding concern with treatment efficacy. For example, the *Journal of Speech and Hearing Research* ran a series of articles in the 1990s related specifically to this concern. In stuttering, Conture (1996) documented features associated with effective fluency therapy. A few years later, Ingham and Riley (1998) outlined a series of variables that they considered were critical to the documentation of successful outcomes following stuttering therapy. Although there is overlap among features that both articles identify, there is clearly a difference of opinion on how "experts" might view successful treatment. Conture (1996) emphasized the handicapping condition of stuttering and documents the need to examine attitude and other nonspeech symptoms associated with stuttering (e.g., Miller & Watson, 1992). On the other hand, Ingham and Riley place proportionally more emphasis on measurable dependent variables such as stuttering frequency, speech rate, and speech naturalness. For people who stutter and the clinicians who treat them, our models of treatment efficacy should certainly include practices that are measurable and reliable. What matters most in measurement, for efficacy studies and consumer satisfaction, however, is in dispute (see St. Louis, chap. 4, this volume; Manning, chap. 7, this volume; and Montgomery, chap. 8, this volume). We would hope that researchers and clinicians alike will realize the important need to document the impairments, disabilities, and handicaps of the person who stutter. As all three chapters note, important therapeutic variables may include behaviors and attitudes that transcend speech fluency counts.

Defining progress in fluency therapy

What are the primary outcome measures for measuring progress in fluency therapy? Historically, there has been only one type of evidence that qualifies for evidence-based practice and treatment efficacy research (TER), and that is a downward trend in measurable counts of stutter-like dysfluencies (SLDs). However, not everyone agrees that progress in fluency therapy should be limited to this single variable, and thus, there is bountiful discussion about potential outcome measures in the upcoming pages (see Pietranton, chap. 3, this volume; Manning, chap. 7, this volume; and Montgomery, chap. 8, this volume).

Some of the complex features of stuttering motivate this type of discussion. For example, for complicated disorders, there may be several types of research that merit consideration when looking at outcome-based research (Robey & Schultz, 1998). They indicate that efficacy research must address how a treatment works in *real terms*. Unlike medical interventions such as surgery or prescription drug regimens, we need to be concerned that multiple desired outcomes—behavioral, cognitive, and affective (Cooper, 1980)—can be documented in settings that transcend the therapy room, although fluency counts in the therapy room are by far the easiest outcomes to measure. A series of studies by Cream and her collaborators have shown that clients who stutter often talk about the "difficulty of maintaining control" outside of laboratory settings, and the "fear of being different" from others who do not stutter (Cream, Packman, & Llewellyn, 2003; Cream, Onslow, Packman, & Llewellyn, 2003). Concerns such as these in medicine have recently energized a call to involve patients more actively and earlier in the biomedical research process. By doing so, researchers may exploit consulters' "experimental knowledge" (Caron-Flinterman, Broerse, & Bunders, 2005) in setting new research priorities, providing new ideas about etiological or therapeutic concepts that researchers should pursue, and providing feedback about current research priorities and directions.

Years ago, a meta-analysis completed by Andrews and colleagues began compiling relevant outcomes and their associated features (Andrews et al., 1983). Although still widely viewed as a hallmark study for our field, we need to acknowledge that the data on which this meta-analysis is based are more than a quarter of a century old and that we desperately need additional primary research, focusing on potential sources of the underlying deficit in stuttering (e.g., Fox, Ingham, Ingham, Hirsch, Downs, et al., 1996). We should also conduct additional research on the recovery and persistence rates of toddlers who begin to stutter (e.g., Yairi & Ambrose, 1999) because 80% of them will spontaneously remit, and the impact of associated speech characteristics and disorders (Paden, Ambrose, & Yairi, 2002). We also, of course, urgently require updated documentation of therapies that work to alleviate the multiple concerns of stuttering clients; the foci of such studies should encompass both novel and conventional therapies because we will need to validate both emerging and existing approaches to stuttering treatment.

As noted earlier, within the field of evidence-based practice, randomized clinical trials are widely described as the "gold standard" for providing evidence to guide our practice (Bothe, 2004; Ingham, 2003). Therefore, one might ask if randomized clinical trials are indeed the best measure of testing fluency outcomes. The field of speech-language pathology is clearly based on an empirical, quantitative-based history (Tetnowski & Damico,

2001). However, as Walt Manning (2001) observed after broad literature review, humans are "notoriously nonsensical and unfit subjects for scientific scrutiny" (Bannister, 1966, p. 25). That is, it may be argued that human communication is far too complex to control under experimental conditions. How many of us have entered the laboratory with a "perfect client" to gather a particular type of speech sample (usually a severe or unusual type of stuttering), only to have the client speak perfectly fluently? Many of us have lost clients from experimental studies because they stutter extensively in all social contexts, but speak perfectly in the laboratory. Did the evidence show that these clients were actually successful speakers in a functional sense? Do we get to count these individuals as "clinical successes"?

It is indisputable that some conditions affect fluency in the laboratory, just as some interventions markedly change fluency counts within confined experimental parameters. It is the big question that begs someone to "show us the money." We believe that if there is more to success in stuttering therapy than just reducing the observable features of stuttering (i.e. percent of stuttered syllables, etc.), then we need to develop the tools that will document these changes. We are pleased to observe that we are not alone. In recent years we have seen a stream of new assessment tools that range from commercially available tools such as the WAASP (Wright & Ayre, 2000), to clinical research tools such as OASES (Yaruss & Quesal, 2004). However, in order to "practice what we are preaching," we ask that the reader evaluate what they read in this text with the vigor that is recommended to evaluate evidence-based research. These goals (according to Ingham, 2003) include the ability to:

1. Ask a clinically relevant question,
2. Track down the best evidence,
3. Critically evaluate the evidence that we discover, and
4. Integrate the best evidence with clinical judgment and the client's circumstances.

At this point, we would like to suggest that the field might profit from enlarging its reliance on the more traditional measures of success in stuttering therapy. Measures such as percent stuttered words are well-documented outcomes in our literature (e.g. Ingham & Riley, 1998). Among potential adjuncts to such measures, we might consider inclusion of additional documented outcomes, including those that address "social validity" or "social validation" (Lincoln, Onslow, & Reed, 1997).

SOCIAL VALIDITY

Social validity is a means of documenting success through the way that an individual interacts with the environment following some type of intervention. As mentioned earlier, not all levels of success can be measured in a laboratory. This is certainly true with stuttering.

To illustrate this point, we can use a family story. One of our fathers (in his 80s) has, like many of his friends, kept a fine set of hearing aids in his bedroom dresser drawer. He had been tested and expertly fit with a wonderful set of hearing aids many years ago. The hearing aids lowered his hearing thresholds, increased his speech discrimination scores, and gave him what was on paper (in the laboratory) really good hearing. The problem was that, of course, he couldn't communicate well in a noisy environment. Therefore, the hearing aids were retired to the drawer. Recently, he was tested again and fit with some high level digital hearing aids. Now, his wife and entire family are overjoyed with the success that he has shown. He is far more engaged in conversations, is more pleasant to speak with, doesn't say "huh?" nearly as much, and it is a pleasure to be in the house because you can actually hear things other than the television set blaring in the background. Is Dad better? The test data shows that his thresholds are just as good as they were with the other set of hearing aids, and his speech reception and discrimination scores are just as good as they were before, but there is something different in his life. He is different ... better! How do we measure (or validate) that difference? Can his improvement be validated by any type of test score? Or is the real difference in some other factor? Clearly, his wife is happier (she wishes that we would have bought the aids as a Christmas present for HER many years ago). It is more pleasant to visit and indeed many more people seem to be dropping by now "just to say hello!" This is an example of social validation of improvement at its best! We wish to emphasize its qualities: the scores in the limited environment of the "lab" are quite similar, but the functional consequences are quite different.

Can we do the same for stuttering? Can we document positive changes associated with stuttering therapy similar to the changes noted with Dad's hearing aids? Do the current methods of stuttering treatment that we use have some degree of social validity, or are they exercises in academic and statistical rigor? We hope that the following pages will help the reader reflect on these questions as we enter the 21st century and all the challenges that come with it.

What are some of the clinically relevant topics that we must investigate as we enter the 21st century? They may include questions such as: (1) what really constitutes progress in stuttering therapy, (2) what are the new theories and therapies that impact understanding and treating stuttering, (3) what is the impact of allied organizations, such as support groups and self-help groups that are not run by speech-language pathologists in achieving functional progress for those who stutter? Each of these issues is discussed in some detail throughout the following pages.

References

American Speech-Language-Hearing Association (n.d.). *Frequently asked questions about the professions.* Retrieved March 3, 2005, from www.asha.org/about/news/releases/faq_careers.htm

American Speech-Language-Hearing Association (2001a). 2001 *Omnibus survey caseload report: SLP.* Rockville, MD: Author.

American Speech-Language-Hearing Association (2001b). *Scope of practice in speech-language pathology.* Rockville, MD: Author.

Andrews, G., Craig, A., Feyer, A.M., Hoddinott, S., Howie, P., & Nielson, M. (1983). Stuttering: A review of research findings and theories circa 1982. *Journal of Speech and Hearing Disorders, 48,* 226–246.

Bannister, D. (1966). Psychology as an exercise in paradox. *Bulletin of the British Psychological Society, 19,* 21–26.

Bernstein Ratner, N. (2004). Fluency. In B. Goldstein (Ed.), *Bilingual language development and disorders in Spanish-English speakers* (pp. 287–310). Baltimore, MD: Brookes.

Bernstein Ratner, N. (2005). Evidence-based practice in stuttering: some questions to consider. *Journal of Fluency Disorders, 30,* 163–188.

Bloodstein, O. (1995). *A handbook on stuttering.* San Diego, CA: Singular.

Boorstin, D. J. (1983). *The discoverers.* New York: Vintage Books.

Bothe, A. K. (2004). Evidence-based practice in stuttering treatment: An introduction. In A.K. Bothe (Ed.), *Evidence-based treatment of stuttering: Empirical bases and clinical applications.* Mahwah, NJ: Lawrence Erlbaum Associates.

Bothe, A. K. & Andreatta, R. D. (2004). Quantitative and qualitative research paradigms: Thoughts on the quantity and creativity of stuttering research. *Advances in Speech-Language Pathology, 6, (3),* 167–173.

Brisk, D. J., Healey, E. C., & Hux, K. A. (1997). Clinicians' training and confidence associated with treating school-age children who stutter: A national survey. *Language Speech and Hearing Services in Schools, 28,* 164–176.

Caron, A., Jones, P., Neuhauser, D., & Aron, D. (2004). Measuring performance improvement: Total organizational commitment or clinical specialization? *Quality Management in Health Care, 13, (4),* 210–215.

Caron-Flinterman, J., Broerse, J., & Bunders, J. (2005). The experimental knowledge of patients: A new resource for biomedical research? *Social Science and Medicine, 60,* 2575–2584.

Conture, E. (1996). Treatment efficacy: Stuttering. *Journal of Speech and Hearing Research, 39,* S18–36.

Conture, E. G. & Guitar, B. E. (1993). Evaluating efficacy of treatment of stuttering: School-age children. *Journal of Fluency Disorders, 18,* 253–287.

Cooper, E. (1980). Etiology and treatment of stuttering. *Ear Nose and Throat Journal, 59,* 60–81.

Cream, A., Packman, A., & Llewellyn, G. (2003). The playground rocker: A metaphor for communication after treatment for adults who stutter. *Advances in Speech-Language Pathology, 6, (3),* 182–187.

Cream, A., Onslow, M., Packman, A., & Llewellyn, G. (2003). Protection from harm: The experience of adults after therapy with prolonged-speech. *International Journal of Language and Communicative Disorders, 38,* 379–395.

DiLollo, A., Manning, W., & Plaxico, L. (2004). The content analysis of verbal behavior: Applications to stuttering therapy. In A. Packman, A. Meltzer, & H.F.M. Peters (Eds.), *Theory, Research, and Therapy in Fluency Disorders* (Proceedings of the Fourth World Congress on Fluency Disorders; errata supplement, pp. 7–12). Nijmegen, The Netherlands: Nijmegen University Press.

Donahoe, M. (1998). Comparing generalist and specialty care: Discrepancies, deficiencies, and excesses. *Archives of Internal Medicine, 158*, 1596–1608.

Eldridge, K., Kleutz, B., & Donaher, J. (2002). The doctoral student summit: Exploring solutions for the future. *International Stuttering Awareness Day On-Line Conference.* Retrieved March 3, 2005, from www.mnsu.edu/comdis/isad5/papers/donaher5.html

Fox, P. T., Ingham, R. J., Ingham, J. C., Hirsch, T., Downs, J. H., & Martin, C. (1996). A PET study of the neural systems of stuttering. *Nature, 382*, 158–162.

Gould, S. J. (1995). *Dinosaur in a haystack.* New York: Crown Trade Paperbacks.

Illinois Speech-Language-Hearing Association Home Page (1998). Retrieved March 3, 2005, from www.ishail.org.

Ingham, J. C. (2003). Evidence-based treatment of stuttering: I. Definition and application. *Journal of Fluency Disorders, 28*, 197–208.

Ingham, J. & Riley, G. (1998). Guidelines for documentation of treatment efficacy for young children who stutter. *Journal of Speech, Language, and Hearing Research, 41*, 753–770.

Kidsears.com (2003). *Kidspeak.* Retrieved March 3, 2005 from www.kidsears.com/kidspeak.html

Lincoln, M. A., Onslow, M., & Reed, V. (1997). Social validity of the treatment outcomes of an early intervention program for stuttering. *American Journal of Speech-Language Pathology, 6, (2)*, 77–84.

Manning, W. H. (2001). *Clinical decision making in fluency disorders,* 2nd ed. San Diego, CA: Singular.

Miller, S. & Watson, J. (1992). The relationship between communication attitude, anxiety, and depression in stutterers and nonstutterers. *Journal of Speech and Hearing Research, 35*, 789–798.

Nail-Chiwetalu, B. & Bernstein Ratner, N. (in press). Information literacy: a key to evidence-based practice. *Language, Speech and Hearing Services in Schools.*

Paden, E. P., Ambrose, N. G., & Yairi, E. (2002). Phonological progress during the first 2 years of stuttering. *Journal of Speech, Language, and Hearing Research, 45*, 256–267.

Peach, R. K. (2004). From the editor. *American Journal of Speech-Language Pathology, 13*, 2.

Ramig, L. O., Countryman, S., O'Brien, C., Hoehn, M., & Thompson, L. (1995). Intensive speech treatment for patients with Parkinson's disease: Short- and long-term comparison of two techniques. *Neurology, 47*, 1496–1504.

Robey, R. R. (2004, April 13). Levels of evidence. *The ASHA Leader,* p. 5.

Robey, R. R. & Shultz, M. C. (1998). A model for conducting clinical outcome research: an adaptation of the standard protocol for use in aphasiology. *Aphasiology, 12, (9)*, 787–810.

Sackett, D. L. (1998). Evidence-based medicine. *SPINE, 23*, 1085–1086.

Sommers, R. K. & Carusso, A. J. (1995). In-service training in speech-language pathology: Are we meeting the needs for fluency training? *American Journal of Speech-Language Pathology, 4*, 22–28.

Speech Pathology Australia (n.d.). *What is a speech pathologist?* Retrieved March 3, 2005 from www.speechpathologyaustralia.org.au/library/11_FactSheet.pdf

Square-Storer, P. & Hayden, D. (1989). *PROMPT treatment. Acquired apraxia of speech in aphasic adults.* New York: Taylor & Francis.

Starkweather, C. W. (1999). The effectiveness of stuttering therapy. In N.B. Ratner and E.C. Healey (Eds.), *Stuttering research and practice: Bridging the gap* (pp. 231–244). Mahwah, NJ: Lawrence Erlbaum Associates.

Tetnowski, J. A. & Damico, J. S. (2004). Getting out of Procrustes' bed. The needs and benefits of qualitative research in stuttering. *Advances in Speech-Language Pathology, 6, (3)*, 153–158.

Tetnowski, J.A. & Damico, J. S. (2001). A demonstration of the advantages of qualitative methodologies in stuttering research. *Journal of Fluency Disorders, 26*, 17–42.

United States Department of Labor, Department of Statistics (n.d.). *Occupational Outlook Handbook.*

Wright, L. & Ayre, A. (2000). *Wright & Ayre Stuttering Self-Rating Profile.* Bicester, Oxon: Winslow Press.

Yairi, E. & Ambrose, N. G. (1999). Early childhood stuttering I: Persistence and recovery. *Journal of Speech, Language, and Hearing Research, 42*, 1097–1112.

Yaruss, J. S. & Quesal, R. W. (2004). Overall Assessment of the Speaker's Experience of Stuttering (OASES). In A. Packman, A. Meltzer, & H.F.M. Peters (Eds.), *Theory, Research, and Therapy in Fluency Disorders* (Proceedings of the Fourth World Congress on Fluency Disorders; pp. 237–240). Nijmegen, The Netherlands: Nijmegen University Press.

Yaruss, J.S., & Quesal, R.W. (2002). Academic and clinical education in fluency disorders: an update. *Journal of Fluency Disorders, 27*, 43–63.

— 2 —

A Communication-Emotional Model of Stuttering

Edward G. Conture
Tedra A. Walden
Hayley S. Arnold
Corrin G. Graham
Kia N. Hartfield
Jan Karrass
Vanderbilt University

Introduction

The purpose of this chapter is to present a theoretical model of seemingly salient distal, causal, and exacerbating contributors to instances of developmental stuttering in children. Within the conceptual framework provided by this model, the authors describe the possible relation to stuttering of the nontrivial processes of speech, language, experience, and emotions. Distal contributors to stuttering are considered to be antecedent conditions, events, or variables that serve as the foundation for proximal variables that actually trigger particular instances of stuttering. Proximal contributors to stuttering are hypothesized to be those variables that occur somewhere between a person's thoughts and overt behavior, in essence, the domain of speech planning and production. Speech planning and production may be influenced by exacerbating contributors such as emotional reactivity (arousal) and regulation (coping). Emotional reactivity and regulation are considered as contributors to quantitative and qualitative changes in both the processes and the end-products of proximal contributors. Effects of experience are thought to impact the "paths of influence" between emotional and speech-language planning and produc-

tion. In the early stages of stuttering, for most children, proximal contributors are speculated to create instances of stuttering with little or no
emotional exacerbation/regulation; however, with development, emotional processes may exacerbate stuttering, a process strongly influenced by
the effects of experience. Whereas the model attempts to account for central tendencies, it recognizes the presence of individual differences in
speech-language planning/production abilities, emotional reactivity/reg-
ulation, learning histories and environmental expression of these abilities.
In general, however, the model's distinction between variables that cause,
versus variables that exacerbate, stuttering seemingly provides a realistic
conceptualization of the mosaic of factors that initiate stuttering as well
as maintain and aggravate it.

Communication-Emotional Model of Stuttering

The purpose of this chapter is to present a theoretical account of salient
distal and causal contributors to instances of stuttering. This conceptual
framework attempts to provide a means to view empirical studies and
better understand seemingly salient speech, language, learned as well as
emotional processes and their possible relationship to stuttering (see Fig.
2-1). This model attempts to account for developmental, not acquired,
stuttering (e.g., adult onset of stuttering secondary to physiological
and/or psychological trauma), especially stuttering that begins in early
childhood. However, many of the model's basic tenets would seem applicable and/or could be extended to developmental stuttering in older children, teenagers and adults.

We begin with discussing the four interrelated components of the
model, which are (1) distal contributors, (2) proximal contributors, (3)
exacerbation and (4) the resulting overt disruption in speech output (i.e.,
stuttering). Following the above discussion, we present a more detailed
description of each of the four components. Although exemplars of
processes involved within each component are discussed, for this initial
version of the model, we mainly focus on the seemingly essential components of the model and what part they may play in the whole of the variables that contribute to stuttering. We end with a general outline of some
empirical tests of nontrivial hypotheses generated by the model and possible outcomes of such tests.

FIGURE 2-1

The Communication-Emotional (C-E) Model of Stuttering – an overview, as discussed within the text. Within the context of this model, two levels of contributors to the cause of instances of stuttering are posited: (1) distal, interactive contributors of genetics and environment and (2) proximal, interactive contributors of disruptions of speech and language planning and production, with (1) leading to (2) and (2) ultimately leading to instances of stuttering. Through experience, however, emotional reactivity and regulation are thought to exacerbate and maintain instances of stuttering caused by (2).

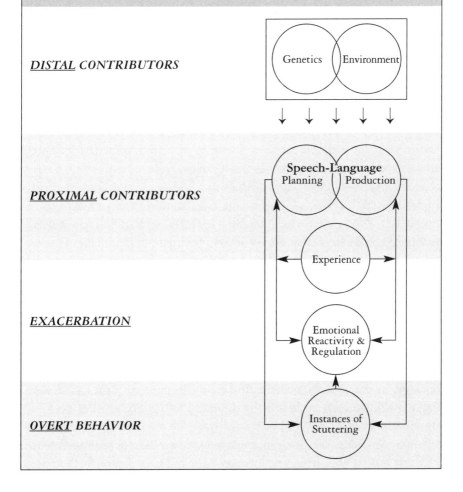

DISTAL, PROXIMAL AND EXACERBATING CONTRIBUTORS

In our opinion, the end-game with any model of stuttering must be stuttering itself. Incumbent on the theoretician, therefore, is the development and explication of some reasoned, motivated account of the events, variables, human characteristics, and so forth that precede, occur during, or follow an instance of stuttering (see Conture, 1990; Yairi, 1997a, for further description of developmental stuttering, particularly in children). We suggest that it is important to keep one's eye on the prize and not overlook the fact that it is stuttering that differentiates people who do stutter from those who don't. Indeed, such oversight typically leads us to lose track of what it is we are trying to address: Why do people stutter? For previous models of stuttering that made very meaningful attempts to account for instances of stuttering, see Brutten and Shoemaker (1967) and Kolk and Postma (1996).

Prior to attempting to address those components that singularly as well as collectively contribute to stuttering, we provide a brief review of current theory of typical speech-language planning and production. Although several models are available for such a review, we will employ that of Levelt and his colleagues (e.g., Indefrey & Levelt, 2000; Levelt, 1989; Levelt, Roelofs, & Meyer, 1999), one of the more widely cited and often experimentally tested models of speech-language planning and production. For example, see Levelt, Roelofs, and Meyer (1999, Fig. 2-1) for a general, graphical depiction of their theory of word production. On average the time course of word production for adult speakers takes about 600 milliseconds (Indefrey & Levelt, 2000), with our findings suggesting that the speech reaction time associated with picture-naming responses of preschool children ranges between 1000–1500 milliseconds (e.g., Melnick, Conture, & Ohde, 2003). Within this broad framework, and for the purposes of our current speculation, we are particularly interested in how children who stutter handle and/or develop lexical concepts, lexical items and retrieval/encoding of the phonological code associated with the lexical item. Table 2-1 (adapted from Indefrey & Levelt, 2000, p. 862) makes clear that these events, collectively and individually, are very rapid for adult speakers.

Here in Table 2-1, we can see some of the possible sites of cerebral localizations and the time windows thought to be associated with various components of word production for adult speakers. Again, one is struck with the rapidity of each of these components of word production as well

TABLE 2-1

Time course of and cortical regions thought to be involved with processes associated with picture naming for adult speakers (adapted from Indefrey & Levelt, 2000, p. 862).		
Event	Critical region involved	
• Stimulus onset • Lexical concept • Selection of lexical item	• Occipital, ventro-medial & arterior frontal; mid-left middle temporal gyrus	275 ms
• Phonological encoding	• Wernicke's • Broca's area	125 ms
• Phonetic encoding	• SMA, cerebellum & other sensorimotor areas	200 ms

as the variety of possible cerebral sites that may be both individually and collectively involved with each component of speech-language production during word production. Of course, these temporal values are averages and the localization sites are generalizations. Obviously, for an individual adult speaker, even a normally fluent adult, the time window for each component as well as sites within the cerebral cortex that may be involved may vary somewhat. In essence, Indefrey and Levelt attempted to relate elements of speech-language planning and processing to the time course and cerebral site associated with each component of word production. By so doing, Indefrey and Levelt help us better appreciate the incredible complexity and rapidity of events associated with word production in adults. Indeed, what should amaze us is not that this incredibly rapid, diverse system sometimes goes awry for adults, but that it so often doesn't!

Adults, one may reasonably assume, are for the most part in the process of skills *maintenance*; that is, their speech-language planning and production is generally established and whatever processes continue are more focused on maintenance than acquisition. In the case of children, particularly young children between 2 and 7 years of age, the time frame that stuttering most generally appears (e.g., Ambrose & Yairi, 1999; Yairi & Ambrose, 1992a, 1992b), we cannot make such an assumption. Rather, these young children are more typically in the process of skills *acquisition* rather than skills maintenance. So the level of development of the essential components and their supposed sites of localization shown in Table 2-1, as well as the various time windows, may be quite different in children than adults. At present, however, we simply don't have the data to meaningfully refute or support specific hypotheses. It is still an open, empirical question whether individuals during skills acquisition (mainly children) differ from individuals during skills maintenance (mainly adults) in terms of the number and nature of components described by Levelt's model as well as the time windows and cerebral sites associated with their operations. Although one can reasonably assume overlap between the two populations of speakers in terms of these components and their processes, the nature and number of such overlaps remain unclear.

What we *do* know about children is that they are generally slower than adults in terms of their speech reaction times or naming responses (e.g., Melnick, Conture, & Ohde, 2003), perhaps requiring twice as much time as adults to name familiar pictures. Further, the speed and accuracy of the children's naming responses are quite variable. Thus, it is reasonable to suggest that slow and variable naming responses are hallmarks of the skills acquisition phase of children's speech-language planning and production. At the least, in children, relatively slow, variable planning and productive abilities may be more easily distressed by internal or external requirements to communicate rapidly, especially about topics that are more referential, abstract and complex. Thus, given this overview of typical speech-language usage, let us consider how such usage may differ between children who do and do not stutter and/or how it may contribute to instances of developmental stuttering, particularly in children.

DISTAL CONTRIBUTORS

For purposes of this discussion, distal contributors to stuttering are conceptualized as antecedent conditions, events or variables that are the foundation for variables that actually trigger instances of stuttering (see Fig. 2-2). Just as a particular genome may make an individual's bronchial system sensitive to airborne allergens, it is the actual inflammation of the internal bronchial tree (along with contraction of smooth musculature surrounding this system) that leads to the wheezing and breathing difficulties that are the primary characteristics of asthma. Relative to stuttering, a particular genome, for example, may set the stage for delays and/or difficulties in a child's ability to combine words with syntax around $2^1/_2$ years of age. These delays/difficulties only become salient for stuttering,

FIGURE 2-2

The C-E model's construct of distal contributors, that is, genetics and the environment. This figure highlights the interactions, within the C-E model, between the distal contributors of "genetics" and the shared as well as unique environmental variables that influence speech-language planning and productions. Graphically shown is the confluence between inherited or dispositional disturbances in speech-language planning and production variables, for example, slow, inefficient lexical retrieval, and situationally/ environmentally "encouraged" behaviors incompatible with underlying, inherent abilities, for example, rapid initiation and production of speech and language.

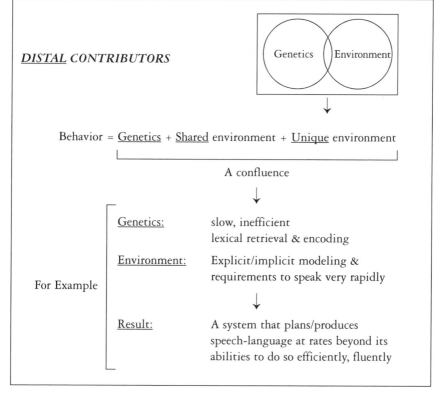

DISTAL CONTRIBUTORS

Genetics   Environment

Behavior = Genetics + Shared environment + Unique environment

A confluence

For Example

Genetics: slow, inefficient
                 lexical retrieval & encoding

Environment: Explicit/implicit modeling &
                 requirements to speak very rapidly

Result: A system that plans/produces
                 speech-language at rates beyond its
                 abilities to do so efficiently, fluently

however, when they "run into" the process of syntactization (e.g., the process by which lexical concepts acquire syntactic categories; Levelt, Roelofs & Meyer, 1999) during the second and third years of life. This may create a "collision" that elicits disruptions, hesitations, and so on, in speech fluency. The confluence of linguistic maturity and increasing complexity of the linguistic components of a child's utterances may create a potent breeding ground for instances of stuttering. By way of analogy, a wobbly three-legged stool may support a 100-lb. individual but completely collapse under the weight of a 200-lb. person. In other words, genes operate in the context of the environment in which they are expressed, not as independent, context-free influences.

Environmental requirements can and do frequently change. Thus, changing environmental requirements may sometimes *adequately* fit underlying abilities and other times *inadequately* fit underlying abilities. Indeed, in terms of distal contributors, genetics may load the gun but the environment seemingly pulls the trigger.

Even given the above caveats, there can be little doubt that genetics play a role in the onset and development of stuttering (e.g., Ambrose, Cox, & Yairi, 1997; Ambrose, Yairi, & Cox, 1993; Cox, Seider, & Kidd, 1984; Curlee & Siegel, 1997; Howie, 1981; Yairi, Ambrose, & Cox, 1996). What is less clear is the nature of genetic transmission, the precise genetic and environmental influences that are involved with stuttering, and whether genetics play a different role for children who recover than for those who persist. Hopefully, research during the present decade will bring us much closer to answering these questions. However, as Yairi and Ambrose (2002) noted, "... that when a gene (or genes) is identified as a factor in a disorder, it may not be known, at least for awhile, what the specific gene actually does: what is it that is inherited via genes or how much of a disorder is governed by them" (p.13). Furthermore, just because a gene is *associated* with stuttering, does not mean that the gene *causes* instances of stuttering. Nor does it address the specific way in which the gene, which directs the synthesis of particular proteins, produces stuttering.

Environmental variables, for example, parents who seem to talk considerably faster than their child (Yaruss & Conture, 1995) or whose duration of "simultalk" maximally overlaps the speech of their child (Kelly & Conture, 1992), may also contribute to a child's stuttering, particularly its quality, severity, or chronicity. However, there is far less evidence that the home and related environments of kids who stutter are significantly different, on a psycho-social level, from those children who do not stutter (e.g., Adams, 1993; Yairi, 1997b). Environmental manipulations, that may range from attempts to get parents to less frequently interrupt and/or telling the child to "smooth out your bumpy speech," are frequent components of stuttering therapy. These oft-observed clinical procedures strongly suggest that clinicians appear to believe in the importance of the environment with regard to stuttering, and that environmental forces can and do change stuttering (for additional discussion, see Ambrose, chap. 5, this volume; Bernstein Ratner & Guitar, chap. 6, this volume). Perhaps the presence of numerous clinical procedures involving environmental manipulations can be taken to suggest that we should not quickly dismiss the environment as a distal contributor. Thus, whereas our further understanding of genetics in general, and genetics in specific, relative to speech and language, will clearly impact our understanding of stuttering, there can be little doubt that the environment influences the expression of genetically-driven behaviors. In other words, there is an inextricable relationship between maturation and experience.

Directly connecting any one genetic and/or environmental contributor to instances of stuttering is, however, a major leap of faith. It is still not understood what speech-language abilities are inherited and/or what environmental (internal or external) factors influence the expression of what is inherited. It is likely, but not a certainty, that all speakers inherit speech-language planning and production abilities that are more or less efficient, rapid, and able to withstand environmental "stressors." Likewise, it is equally possible that each speaker inherits emotional reactivity and regulatory skills that interact with the aforementioned speech-language variables. Taken together, it is our opinion that these two issues can be organized as follows: (1) proximal contributors: speech-language planning and production (see Fig. 2-3) and (2) exacerbating contributors: emotional reactivity and regulation (see Fig. 2-4). Immediately below we discuss both issues.

PROXIMAL CONTRIBUTORS

Between a person's thoughts and his or her overt speech-language behavior lies an often-discussed, still unclearly understood domain: speech planning and production. Specifically, the message of the speaker is transformed into a code that informs/instructs the speech-motor control system that allows the speaker to realize his/her intention in the form of spoken speech and language. The speech-language planning and production "whole" has been parsed into related constituents by those who predominantly examine linguistic variables (e.g., Levelt, Meyer, & Roelofs, 1999) and those who examine motor control variables (e.g., van Lieshout, Hulstijn, & Peters, 2004). At some point, in the future, these parts will have to be brought together to understand the whole (and perhaps by so doing we may find that the whole is greater than the sum of its parts, but

FIGURE 2-3

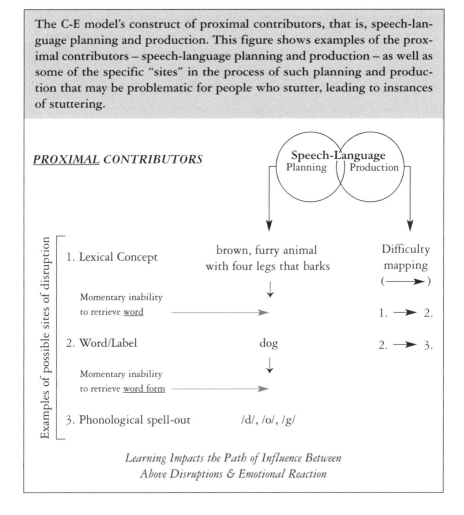

The C-E model's construct of proximal contributors, that is, speech-language planning and production. This figure shows examples of the proximal contributors – speech-language planning and production – as well as some of the specific "sites" in the process of such planning and production that may be problematic for people who stutter, leading to instances of stuttering.

PROXIMAL CONTRIBUTORS

Speech-Language
Planning | Production

Examples of possible sites of disruption

1. Lexical Concept
    brown, furry animal
    with four legs that barks

    Difficulty mapping

Momentary inability to retrieve <u>word</u>

1. ➝ 2.

2. Word/Label   dog   2. ➝ 3.

Momentary inability to retrieve <u>word form</u>

3. Phonological spell-out   /d/, /o/, /g/

*Learning Impacts the Path of Influence Between
Above Disruptions & Emotional Reaction*

that is a matter that must await considerably more empirical study). For the purpose of this review, however, we focus on the former, the planning/linguistic aspects of speech and language and their possible contributions to stuttering, although fully recognizing the possibility that motor speech variables may also contribute (see Caruso, Max, & McClowry, 1999).

FIGURE 2-4

The constructs of emotional reactivity and regulation. This figure shows, within the context of C-E model, how speech-language disruptions may be "filtered" through dispositional as well as situationally emotionally reactions and regulation. Such filtering may aggravate/exacerbate or maintain instances of stuttering, perhaps making them more severe in duration, physical tension and/or changing their type, for example, making reiterative-type (repetitions) speech disfluencies more cessation-like (prolonged) in nature.

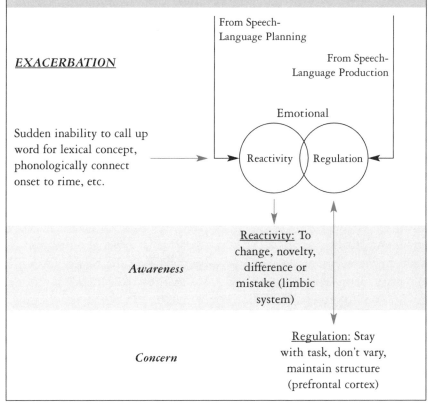

EXACERBATING CONTRIBUTORS

Any and all events resulting from speech planning and production are subject, at least theoretically, to emotional reactivity (arousal) and regulation (coping). These latter events, in our opinion, have potential for both quantitative as well as qualitative changes in the events that result from proximal contributors. For example, these emotional processes could react to a "mistake" of speech-language planning and production by making the mistake more overtly apparent, longer, more physically tense and/or even more frequent. Furthermore, it is theoretically possible for emotional processes to be informed about potential difficulties with speech-language processes before overt speech disfluencies arise (see Levelt's 1996 discussion of internal monitoring). In other words, the speaker's monitoring of internal communicative events that occur *before* overt speech-language makes it possible for the speaker to detect/react or even attempt to correct/regulate his/her communication before it becomes overt. And lest we think that such emotional processes are the sole province of the area of stuttering within the field of speech-language pathology, it should be noted that researchers have empirically assessed the relation of language and emotional regulation in children with specific language impairment (e.g., Fujiki, Brinton, & Clarke, 2002; Fujiki, Spackman, Brinton, & Hall, 2004). Clearly, therefore, researchers are beginning to consider the role that emotions play in speech-language development and disorders in general, something the area of stuttering has long discussed (e.g., Brutten & Shoemaker, 1967) and now is returning to empirically study (e.g., Ezrati-Vinacour & Levin, 2004).

Another process, that of experience, has one foot in the proximal and the other in the exacerbating contributor domains (see Fig. 2-5). It is our position that the effects of experience that are impacted by the person's environment, the person's sensitivity to particular experiences as well as his/her genetic potentials, mainly involve the interaction between speech-language planning/production and emotional reactivity/regulation. One crucial effect of experience, learning, could take the form of, for example, strengthening associations between particular emotional reactions and particular speech-language planning/production "mistakes."

Symptoms resulting from proximal and exacerbating reactions. For the purposes of this chapter, the foregoing discussion, although interesting, is little more than that unless it is tied specifically to stuttering. Such discussion should not only consider the most common types of stuttering—sound/syllable repetition, sound prolongations, whole-word repetitions, and so forth—but changes in the topology of stuttering, for example, duration, type, associated physical tension, and the like. Although no one model can adequately account for all such symptomology, the present model attempts to account for the more defining elements of stuttering itself, that is, reiterations and cessations in the forward flow of speaking (see Fig. 2-6).

Symptoms resulting from proximal contributions. Given a moment's reflection, there are nearly an infinite number of permutations of events that could go awry in speech-language planning and production to disrupt

FIGURE 2-5

The construct of experience. The C-E model posits that through experience, a connection is established between disruptions of speech-language planning and production and emotional reactivity and regulation, with the latter exacerbating the former. The rate of development and nature of this connection is undoubtedly individualistic, but experiential connection between speech-language and emotional variables, as posited by the model, should be experienced by most if not all people who stutter, particularly for those whose stuttering become chronic (i.e., lasts for 18 months or longer after onset of stuttering).

PROXIMAL CONTRIBUTORS,
EXACERBATION

Experience

Reac**t** to and then through experience retain reaction to disruption (awareness): Change quality of stutterings, for example, decrease length.

Regul**ate** reaction and then through experience develop regulation (concern): Doing things to cope with reactions to disruption, refocus attention to minimize need to deal with change/variance, for example, change word choice, diminimsh amount of talking, etc.

FIGURE 2-6

> The overt behavior(s) that represent the sine qua non of stuttering. As mentioned within the text, a theoretical account of stuttering, that is, reiterations and cessations of production that typically occur at the level of the word or below, should, ideally, tie its hypothetical constructs as well paths of influence to stuttering. According to the C-E model, disruptions within the process of speech-language planning/production may lead to those types of speech disfluency typically judged to be stuttering.

<u>*OVERT* BEHAIVOR</u>

Instances of Stuttering

Typical instances of stuttering/some possible sources of disruption:

1. Word onset disconnected from word rime   *m-m-mommy*
   (difficulty with phonological spell-out)   *mmmommy*

2. Lexical concept not mapping onto label, or

3. Syntax not mapping on label   *mommy-mommy-mommy*

speech fluency; however, similar reflection suggests that some events seem a bit more likely than others to play a role. Although the following focuses on disturbances in speech-language planning that may contribute to stuttering, that is not to say that speech, motor control and/or execution might not also play a role (e.g., Caruso, Max, & McClowry, 1999; van Lieshout, Hulstijn, & Peters, 2004). So, although some (e.g., Conture, 2001) have strongly suggested the need to explore linguistic aspects of speech-language planning and production, one should not overlook the fact that linguistic and speech motor processes operate as a whole, with manifold interactions and reactions to one another, dynamically changing through the course of conversational discourse.

Returning to speech-language planning, there would appear to be two "sites" of disruption that bear strong consideration relative to disruptions in speech fluency: (1) mapping the lexical concept onto a word, and/or (2) mapping the word onto the phonological word form. In terms of site (1), the speaker may find it momentarily difficult to map a known lexical concept, "brown, furry animal with four legs that barks" onto its associated word, "dog." Relative to site (2), the speaker may find it momentarily difficult to map a known label, like "dog," onto its associated, phonological word frame, "/d/, /o/, /g/." Difficulty at the former site (1), we predict, would result in whole-word repetitions, perhaps associated with interjections, as the speaker attempts to "come up with" the label connected to the known lexical concept. Difficulty at the latter site (2), we predict, would result in sound/syllable repetitions, as the speaker finds it momentarily difficult to map the known word with its associated word form; in other words, the speaker has slow and/or inefficient phonological spell-out of the word (reasoning similar to that of Kolk & Postma, 1996). Again, there are clearly other "sites" within formulation that could contribute to instances of stuttering. However, it is our contention that the seeds of stuttering could just as well be sown during the planning as the production of stuttering. Once this chain of events begins, it is quite possible, with experience and time, that the speaker could come to react to these events, especially if that individual is quick to react to change, differences, novelty, and mistakes.

Exacerbation. As our model suggests (see Fig. 2-1), the mistake, disturbance, or error in speech-language planning and production, and the communicative repair of the same may "bypass" emotional reactivity, and directly lead to speech disfluencies/stutterings (particularly in the very early stages of childhood stuttering, especially close to the onset of stuttering). Such stutterings should be, on the whole, fairly physically relaxed, short in duration, and most apt to be observed in children at or near the onset of the problem (i.e., 18 months or less, postonset). In essence, emotional reactions to and regulations of stuttering should be minimal due to minimal experience with such disruptions. However, the model also allows for these disruptions to interact with emotional reactivity and regulation, with the latter "hot cognitive" processes changing the quality, if not quantity, of the resulting disfluency. The model further suggests that the path of influence—from emotional processes to disfluencies/stuttering—is mediated by speech planning and production, that is, emotional processes impact speech-language planning and production which, in turn, impacts the quantity and quality of speech disfluencies. Such interactions, we predict, would become more apparent and/or obvious as the frequency of the child's stutterings continues to be outside of normal limits and/or as the time since onset of the child's stuttering grows longer.

The presence and/or onset of emotional reactivity and regulation, we speculate, is quite individualized among children who stutter. Thus, some children, perhaps as many as 25% of those who begin to stutter between 30 to 36 months, may quickly and strongly react to disruptions in speech-language planning/production and/or the instances of stuttering they produce. Whether the early, strong reactions of some children have prognostic value, for example, as to whether such children are more likely to persist with stuttering, is presently unclear. We think that for most children the "layering on" of emotional reactivity and regulation onto their stuttering is a more gradual process, evolving over time and experience with stuttering.

Awareness (Reactivity) Vs. Concern (Regulation). We expect, for example, that the sudden inability to retrieve and encode a word for a lexical concept could produce an emotional reaction in the child, especially if the child quickly and strongly responds to novelty, change, difference, or mistakes. This reactivity, we believe, is the basis for the child's "awareness" or "cold cognition" of a disruption in his or her speech fluency. Over time, however, and with increased experience with stuttering, the child may try to cope with or "regulate" his or her feelings. In attempts to cope with his or her feelings, the child may try to stay with the task to maintain structure or to minimize variability in output, in attempts to "calm down." Such emotional regulation, in turn, although not causing stuttering, may contribute to changes in its typology and duration, among other things.

EFFECTS OF EXPERIENCE

The effects of experience on child's speech-language and emotional learning are as varied as experience itself. Within these effects would be such variables as learning, prenatal exposure to hormones, postnatal exposure to environmental variables, and so forth. Related to these issues is the child's sensitivity to experience, that is, how readily and strongly particular experiences effect the child. We use the term *experience* rather than *learning* because the former captures a larger segment of the child's daily or routine encounters. Of course, experimental as well as clinical applications of learning theory and processes have a long history in the field of stuttering (e.g., Ingham, 1984; Onslow & Packman, 1996; Starkweather, 1996). However, it is not the purpose of this chapter to review all such work. Rather, it is our intention to suggest that experience is an important component, that it most likely plays a role as both a proximal as well as exacerbating contributor to instances of stuttering. In the present version of our model, we have not specified the exact nature of the learning model, for example, instrumental versus classical conditioning (e.g., see Hill, 2001, for reviews of these models) that contributes to "the effects of experience."

With regard to the effects of experience and developmental stuttering, we are inclined to agree with Guitar (1998; pp. 95–96) that the effects of experience relative to stuttering relate to "connections." Guitar's speculation is somewhat similar to Gutherie's (1960, p. 23) contiguity theory of learning which suggests that, A combination of stimuli which has accompanied a movement will on its recurrence tend to be followed by that movement." In this case, the connections are between specific disruptions in speech-language planning and production and specific emotional reactions and regulations. Or, as Figure 2-3 suggests, experience impacts the "path of influence" (i.e., connection) between proximal and exacerbating contributors. As mentioned earlier, the speed of development and strength of these connections will vary among children who stutter, given different learning histories, experiences, and other variables. Importantly related to this is the child's sensitivity to a particular kind of experience. That is, it is not merely the strength of the emotion itself which leads to the bond or connection to the experience itself, but the child's sensitivity to the experience (see Anderson, Pellowski, Conture, & Kelly, 2003, for empirical evidence regarding relatively heightened sensitivity to change of children who stutter). It may only take one time for Child A to develop a strong connection between behavior and emotional reactivity to an experience, whereas another child may require 15 or more repetitions of an experience before the connection is as strong.

Although we further agree with Guitar (1998) that such connectivity is quite strong for those events that are "… experienced again and again with similar stimuli" (p. 95) we are not as clear, in terms of speech-language production, that "utterances are learned and stored in patterns that reflect all of their past uses in all their emotional and cognitive contexts" (p. 95). The latter position, although interesting and plausible, seems a bit less than an efficient way of learning, storing, retrieving, and encoding syntactic, semantic, and phonological units. Furthermore, our model suggests, at least in the beginning, that emotional stimuli do not trigger stuttering, for most children who stutter, but by mediation through speech-language planning and production may come to exacerbate instances of stuttering.

Rather, we believe that emotional reactivity and regulation can be one means by which the child responds to proximal disruption, and that only with time, for most children, are the emotions connected to these proximal disruptions and hence to the overt stuttering itself. We would "broaden" Guitar's suggestions about connection and suggest that disruptions of a general type/class may become connected, by learning and experience, to a general type/class of emotional reactivity and regulation. For example, a generalized inability to quickly and efficiently map lexical concepts onto words might, with experience, come to be connected to a generalized emotional reaction to both the causal disruption and associated disfluency. In essence, for emotional processes to "trigger" overt instances of stuttering, we believe that most children must have, over time, continued experience of difficulties quickly and efficiently retrieving and/or encoding words, accompanied by a finite number of emotional reactive and regulatory processes. Again, some children, because of their sensitivity to experience and/or strong emotional reactivity to differences, mistakes, and change, may "fast forward" through this process and develop these connections very rapidly.

Be that as it may, it is very hard to conceive of the fact that so many different children under so many different circumstances, with so many different abilities and backgrounds, could *all* have the same emotional "triggers" of their stuttering around 2½ to 3 years of age, when most begin to stutter (e.g., Yairi & Ambrose, 1992a, 1992b). Rather, we believe it is much more plausible that these children are *all* progressing through some challenges to/difficulties with speech-language planning and production milestones that occur between 2½ to 3 years of age. Furthermore, we believe that these challenges and difficulties are most likely the proximal source of initial, overt instances of stuttering. Certainly, it is quite possible as well as plausible that some of these children very close to the onset of stuttering come to quickly and strongly react to these difficulties and try to regulate both disruption and disfluency; however, presently there is little empirical evidence that most children known to be or at risk for stuttering initially exhibit strong and persistent emotional reactivity and/or regulatory attempts to "cope" with their disruptions and disfluencies. With repeated experiences and learning, of course, it is possible as well as plausible, as our model suggests, that many of these children develop an emotional response to both disruptions in speech-language planning and productions as well as attendant stutterings. However, the consistent loci (e.g., beginning of utterance, pronouns vs. verbs, etc.; Bernstein, 1981) as well as surrounds of instances of stutterings (e.g., Zackheim & Conture's, 2003, finding that approximately 70% of stuttering is contained in utterances above a child's MLU), both within and between children, strongly suggest that emotions more likely exacerbate rather than cause instances of stuttering. That is, for most children who stutter, there are consistent speech-language planning and production variables that trigger instances of stuttering that inconsistently collide with greater or less emotional reactivity on the part these children. In other words, we believe that experience influences the strength of connection between emotion and disruptions in speech-language behavior rather than initially causing the disruption of fluency.

EMPIRICAL ASSESSMENT OF THE MODEL

Some models are designed to provide an overarching conceptual framework within which to view a particular phenomenon and/or its consequences (e.g., Yaruss & Quesal, 2004). These models are generally not developed to be empirically tested but more to serve as guides for users in terms of how to think about, conceptualize, and/or organize existing and/or future facts about the phenomenon of interest. Our model does that as well, but it also permits the empirical testing of hypotheses derived from it. Below, we provide some empirical support for the above speculation regarding the speech-language planning and production elements of the model as well as the emotional reactivity/regulation component.

Empirical evidence for our speculation: Speech-language planning and production

The first author has speculated about (e.g., Conture, Zackheim, Anderson, & Pellowski, 2004), as well as reviewed, literature concerning (e.g., Conture, 2001; Louko, Conture, & Edwards, 1999) the relation between phonology, semantic and syntactic variables, and developmental stuttering. We have also empirically studied how childhood stuttering may relate to (1) articulation/phonology (e.g., Louko, Edwards, & Conture, 1993; Melnick, Conture, & Ohde, 2003; Melnick, Conture, & Ohde, 2005; Pellowski, Conture, Anderson, & Ohde, 2001; Wolk, Edwards, & Conture, 1993), (2) semantics (Pellowski & Conture, 2004), and (3) grammatical/syntactic variables (e.g., Anderson & Conture, 2004; Graham, Conture, & Camarata, 2004; Zackheim & Conture, 2003).

Phonology. To date, most of our empirical studies of speech-language planning and production have focused on the relation of articulation/ phonology to childhood stuttering. Although we still lack adequate understanding of this relation, early work appeared to suggest that the prevalence of articulation/phonological delays and/or difficulties is somewhat higher in children who do versus do not stutter (see Louko et al., 1999, for review; cf., Nippold, 2002). For example, a clinical study of one hundred 2- to 6-year-old children (Yaruss, LaSalle, & Conture, 1998) found that 37% of this sample exhibited disordered phonology, a frequency of occurrence of disordered articulation/phonology that far exceeds that reported in the typical population (e.g., Beitchman, Nair, Clegg, & Patel, 1986). It should be noted, however, that this "disorder A (e.g., stuttering) co-occurring with disorder B (e.g., disordered phonology)" or "co-morbidity" approach characterized much of our early work in this area (e.g., Wolk, Edwards, & Conture, 1993). For example, Wolk, Edwards, & Conture (1993) reported that preschoolers who stuttered and exhibited disordered phonology exhibited significantly more sound prolongations and significantly fewer iterations per whole-word repetitions when compared to preschool children who stuttered without exhibiting disordered phonology.

Our more recent empirical findings, for example, those of Pellowski, Anderson, and Conture (2001), have lead us to temper our earlier "co-morbid" approach to the relation between stuttering and disordered phonology. That is, findings of Pellowski et al. (2001) suggest that children who stutter, as a group, are roughly within normal limits based on standardized tests of articulation/phonology (see also Bernstein Ratner & Silverman, 2000); however, Pellowski et al. also reported that children who stutter scored significantly lower than their normally fluent peers on standardized tests of articulation and phonology. Similarly, even more recent work (Melnick et al., 2003, p. 1440) further suggests "... no significant mean differences between [preschool children who do and do not stutter] in terms of the overall mastery of their speech sound articulation … [but] significantly differed in terms of their relationship between mastery and speed of articulatory performance." Similarly, findings of Byrd, Conture, & Ohde (2004) further suggests that the relative lack of organization in terms of the articulatory/phonological systems of young children who stutter may also be reflected in their tendency to continue to process speech and language at a word rather than sound level, long after their normally fluent peers are exhibiting a more sound-based processing mechanism. Interestingly, phonological neighborhood density (e.g., words that share many versus few phonological characteristics) seem to have about the same influence on preschoolers who do versus those who do not stutter (Arnold, Conture, & Ohde, 2004).

Taken as a whole, empirical studies of the relation of phonology to stuttering suggests that although disordered phonology may be somewhat more likely to occur with children who stutter than children who do not stutter, the overall mastery of articulation/phonology of children who stutter is roughly within normal limits, albeit in the lower ends of normal limits. "Looking below the surface" of standardized test results, however, has uncovered findings that have lead us to conjecture that the speed/accuracy relation is not as well developed for children who stutter as that of their normally fluent peers. Further, we have reason to believe that our initial work (Byrd et al., 2004) will replicate, indicating that the seemingly less organized systems of children who stutter results in these children continuing to process speech and language at a word level long after most of their fluent counterparts have begun processing at a sound level.

Syntax. Of course, phonology is but one part of the triology—phonology, semantics, and syntax—of processes that make up speech-language planning. Our study of the other two processes—semantics and syntax—has not been as extensive to date. From a descriptive perspective, we have shown that approximately 70% of the stutterings of children who stutter occur in utterances above their MLU (Zackheim & Conture, 2003). This, of course, does not prove that morpho-syntactical construction variables "cause" stuttering, but neither does it disprove the possibility that morpho-syntactic construction may contribute to instances of stuttering. Likewise, we (Graham, Conture, & Camarata, 2004) have recently found that preschoolers who stutter exhibit significantly more stutterings on

function than content words, regardless of utterance syntactic characteristics, a finding contrary to that based on adults (e.g., Brown, 1943) but
consistent with that of Bernstein (1981), Bloodstein & Grossman (1981),
and later replications by Howell and colleagues (e.g., Howell, Au-Yeung,
& Sackin, 1999). Most recently, Anderson and Conture (2004) reported
that preschool children who stutter exhibited slower speech reaction
times, when initiating sentence-level utterances, in the absence of audi-
torily-presented priming sentences and greater syntactic priming effects
than their peers who do not stutter. Taken together, these findings, particularly those of Anderson and Conture, suggest that grammatical processing may contribute to childhood stuttering, that is, children who
stutter may have difficulties rapidly, efficiently planning and/or retrieving sentence-structure units.

Semantics. To date, we have completed only one empirical study of the
relation between semantic processing and childhood stuttering
(Pellowski & Conture, 2004) although at least one more is in process
(Hartfield, 2004). Our findings to date indicate that when compared to a
no-prime condition, presentation of semantically-related words prior to a
picture-naming response (e.g., child hears "cat" before seeing picture of
"dog" to name) led to shorter or faster speech reaction times for children
who do not stutter, but for children who stutter, led to longer or slower
reaction times. Further, similar to our findings regarding the relationship
of overall articulatory mastery to speed of picture-naming (Melnick et al.,
2003), Pellowski and Conture (2004) found that children who do not
stutter with the highest receptive vocabulary were the most influenced by
semantic priming but no such relation was found for children who stutter. Although our findings that CWS may have difficulties with lexical
encoding are preliminary, taken together with our findings regarding
phonological and syntactic processing of children who stutter, they seem
to suggest that speed, efficiency and effectiveness of speech-language
planning may contribute to childhood stuttering. Such speculation is
consistent with findings of others, for example, Cuadrado and Weber-Fox
(2003), who report differences between adults who do and do not stutter
in cortical activities associated with syntactic processing.

Again, although none of the above arguments, discussion or findings
"proves" that subtle to nonsubtle disruptions, delays, disturbances, and so
on in rapid, efficient speech-language planning "causes" stuttering nei-

ther does it disprove that such difficulties are unrelated to stuttering. What is needed, at present, are testable models, such as that presented in this space, that lead to hypotheses permitting the empirical testing of nontrivial aspects of the model. With a testable model, focused in on a probable variable(s) that contribute to stuttering, advances in our understanding of developmental stuttering are likely as well as needed. As a result of such descriptive as well as experimental empirical studies, we believe that more than one, but a relatively finite number of, variables will be shown to "cause" stuttering, with some more salient than others, but with all interacting with one another and stuttering in a myriad of complex but understandable ways.

Futher empirical studies: Dissociations among subcomponents of speech-language planning

Anderson and Conture (2000) reported that differences between two standardized measures—one of receptive/expressive language and the other of receptive vocabulary—were significantly greater for preschool children who stutter than their normally fluent peers. Bernstein Ratner & Silverman (2000) also found evidence of depressed expressive vocabulary in preschool children who stutter. Whether Anderson and Conture's approach—comparing two talker groups in terms of differences in standardized tests—constitutes the best approach to "double dissociations" (Bates, Appelbaum, Salcedo, Saygin, & Pizzamiglio, 2003) is of debate. Such dissociation might be seen, for example, when two talker groups (A and B) exhibit differential impairment on two different tasks or tests (1 and 2). For example, talker group A would be impaired on Task 1 but spared on Task 2 while talker group B is impaired on Task 2 but spared in Task 1. In brief, whether double dissociations in speech-language planning are related to childhood stuttering is presently an open empirical question; however, such imbalances or dissociations have been studied with regard to developmentally language-disordered children who are highly disfluent (Hall, Yamashita, & Aram, 1993) as well as adults with aphasia (e.g., Saygin, Dick, Wilson, Dronkers, & Bates, 2003).

Thus, it is intriguing to consider the possibility that at least some children who stutter may exhibit such dissociations. Again, whether children who stutter do exhibit such dissociations is an empirical question, but one of seeming relevance to a comprehensive empirical assessment of the relation between speech-language planning and childhood stuttering.

Relation of emotional reactivity and regulation to stuttering

Besides difficulties with speech-language planning and production, our model also predicts that there is a connection between emotional reactivity/regulation and exacerbation/maintenance of childhood stuttering. Of course, the quantity and quality of such connections and/or their mere existence is unknown. In general, we predict that children who stutter will be more highly reactive than children who do not stutter, particularly to moderate and high levels of stimulation. We further predict that children who stutter who exhibit high levels of reactivity will differ from other children who stutter in terms of various aspects of stuttering, such as frequency and type of stuttering (e.g., sound/syllable repetitions vs. sound prolongations). What follows provides some empirical evidence with which to assess our speculations regarding emotional reactivity/regulation and childhood stuttering.

Empirical evidence for our speculation: Emotional reactivity and regulation

Those familiar with stuttering, whether from a clinical or research perspective, will recognize the fact that emotions are often discussed in relation to developmental stuttering (e.g., Alm, 2004). Indeed, in recent years several empirical studies of the temperamental characteristics of children who stutter have been published (e.g., Anderson, Pellowski, Conture, & Kelly, 2003; Embrechts, Ebben, Franke, & van de Poel, 2000; Oyler, 1996; Wakaba, 1997; Wakaba, Iizawa, Gondo, Inque, & Fujino, 2003). In general, these findings indicate that children who stutter differ from those who do not stutter in specific aspects of their emotional characteristics. In specific, children who stutter, when compared to children who do not, are less adaptive/more reactive to their environments and/or environmental change, exhibit higher levels of sensitivity, and seem more likely to persist with tasks once the task has begun. Somewhat similar results have been reported with adults, that is, adults who stutter, when compared to adults who do not stutter, have been shown to score significantly higher on the temperamental trait labeled "nervous" (Guitar, 2003) and have significantly higher trait anxiety (e.g., Craig, Hancock, Tran, Craig, & Peters, 2002).

With the possible exception of Guitar (2003), most of the studies just mentioned have looked at the stable or *dispositional* aspects of temperament, that is, those temperamental characteristics present in the early years of life that are minimally variable. What these studies of emotions and stuttering have not typically addressed is *situationally* driven emotional behaviors, that is, behaviors that are less than stable, seemingly waxing and waning in relation to situational changes and/or demands. In specific, how does the child who stutters react to situations and what does he or she do to regulate or cope with his or her reactions? The present writers would like to suggest that these two variables—and their joint effect—have significant potential for exacerbating and/or maintaining childhood stuttering. So, although dispositional aspects of emotion may set the overall stage for reactivity towards stuttering, we believe that situationally-related reactivity and regulation are most likely to be associated, dependent on the arousability of a situation and how easily one can cope within the situation. Although the present writers have just begun to assess the relation between emotional reactivity, regulation, and childhood stuttering, early work (Karrass, Walden, Conture, Graham, Arnold, Hartfield, & Schwenk, 2004) based on relatively large sample of preschool children who stutter (n = 74) and their normally fluent peers (n = 63), indicates that preschoolers who stutter, when compared to those who do not stutter, are significantly more reactive, significantly less able to regulate their emotions, and exhibit significantly poorer attention regulation. These findings suggest that preschool children who stutter are more emotionally reactive to situational requirements, less able to regulate any emotions they do experience, and less able to flexibly control their attention, for example, shifting their attention from a challenging stimuli to another in the environment that is less challenging.

Taken together, findings suggest that children who stutter exhibit both dispositional as well as situationally-related aspects of emotion that may contribute to the problems these children have establishing reasonably fluent speech and language. What is not known, but is the focus of our current work, is how the two talker groups—children who do versus do not stutter—respond to experimental manipulations of emotional reaction and regulation and whether these responses can be related to their instances of stuttering. Again, it is our contention that the essential cause of instances of stuttering relates to problems with speech-language planning and/or production, with emotional reactivity and regulation occurring in response to these problems, leading to exacerbation and/or maintenance of stuttering. Although addressing such speculation will involve a series of motivated, inter-related studies, the review just discussed suggests that both areas—speech/language planning and emotional reaction and regulation—warrant further study, with findings having broad implications for our understanding and eventual assessment and treatment of stuttering.

Likened to a mosaic, a model of stuttering is not about one variable, but about the confluence, melding, and interaction of several, albeit finite number of, co-occurring processes. Although experimental study requires us to investigate each of these processes separately, it is up to the theoretician to pull these disparate lines of evidence into one framework. The model just discussed is our attempt to weave together empirical evidence with a theoretical construct.

Summary

An overview as well as components of a model of developmental stuttering are presented in this chapter. This model suggests that genetic potential interacts with environmental factors to cause difficulties in speech-language planning and production and that these difficulties are the direct contributors to instances of stuttering. The model suggests, at least at the onset of stuttering, that internal and external disruptions do not impact emotional reactivity and regulation to a large degree for most children. With experience, however, more and more of a connection between communicative and emotional behavior occurs resulting in changes in the quality if not quantity of stuttering. Although the precise processes involved with each of these various components are purposely left under-specified, it is hypothesized that selective aspects of speech-language formulation, such as mapping lexical concepts onto words and/or words onto phonological word forms, are likely "sites" of disturbance relative to disruptions in speech fluency. The model implies that a confluence of innate abilities, at all levels, with communicative requirements is very importantly related to whether a particular utterance will be more or less fluent. Above all, the speed and diversity of the processes involved and the seemingly manifold areas of neurocortical tissue involved lead one to wonder not that the system goes awry on occasion but that it doesn't do so much more often!

Acknowledgments

This chapter was supported in part by NIH (DC000523-09A) and NICHD (P30HD15052) grants to Vanderbilt University.

References

Adams, M. (1993). The home environment of children who stutter. *Seminars in Speech and Language, 14,* 185–192.

Alm, P. (2004). Stuttering, emotion and reduction of heart rate during anticipatory anxiety. *Journal of Fluency Disorders, 29,* 123–134.

Ambrose, N. & Yairi, E. (1999). Normative disfluency data for early childhood stuttering. *Journal of Speech, Language, & Hearing Research, 42,* 895–909.

Ambrose, N., Cox, N., & Yairi, E. (1997). The genetic basis of persistence and recovery in stuttering. *Journal of Speech & Hearing Research, 40*(3), 567–580.

Ambrose, N., Yairi, E., & Cox, N. (1993). Genetic aspects of early childhood stuttering. *Journal of Speech, Language, & Hearing Research, 36,* 701–706.

Anderson, J. & Conture, E. (2000). Language abilities of children who stutter: A preliminary study. *Journal of Fluency Disorders, 25,* 283–304.

Anderson, J. & Conture, E. (2004). Sentence-structure priming in young children who do and do not stutter. *Journal of Speech Language and Hearing Research, 47,* 552–571.

Anderson, J. D., Pellowski, M. W., Conture, E. G., & Kelly, E. M. (2003). Temperamental characteristics of young children who stutter. *Journal of Speech Language & Hearing Research, 46,* 1221–1233.

Arnold, H., Conture, E., & Ohde, R. (2004). *Phonological neighborhood density influence on the picture naming of children.* Manuscript submitted for publication.

Bates, E., Appelbaum, M., Salcedo, J., Saygin, A., & Pizzamiglio, L. (2003). Quantifying dissociations in neuropsychological research. *Journal of Clinical and Experimental Neuropsychology, 25,* 112–1153.

Beitchman, J., Nair, R., Clegg, M., & Patel, P. (1986). Prevalence of speech and language disorders in 5-year-old kindergarten children in the Ottawa-Carleton region. *Journal of Speech and Language Disorders, 51,* 98–110.

Bernstein, N. (1981). Are there constraints on childhood dysfluency? *Journal of Fluency Disorders, 6,* 341–350.

Bernstein Ratner, N. & Silverman, S. (2000). Parental perceptions of children's communicative development at stuttering onset. *Journal of Speech Language and Hearing Research, 43,* 1252–1263.

Bloodstein, O. & Grossman, M. (1981). Early stutterings: some aspects of their form and distribution. *Journal of Speech and Hearing Research, 24,* 298–302.

Brown, S.F. (1943). *An analysis of certain data concerning loci of "stutterings" from the viewpoint of general semantics.* Paper from the second American congress on general semantics, University of Denver, August, 1941, pp. 194–199.

Brutten, E. & Shoemaker, D. (1967). *The modification of stuttering.* Englewood Cliffs, NJ: Prentice Hall.

Byrd, C., Conture, E., & Ohde, R. (2004). *Word begin- and end-related phonological priming in picture naming of young children who stutter.* Manuscript submitted for publication.

Caruso, A., Max, L., & McClowry, M. (1999). Perspectives on stuttering as a motor speech disorder. In A. Caruso & E. Strand (Eds.) *Clinical management of motor speech disorders in children* (pp. 319–344). New York: Thieme.

Conture, E. (2001). Dreams of our theoretical nights meet the realities of our empirical days: Stuttering theory and research. In H-G. Bosshardt, J.S. Yaruss & H.F.M. Peters (Ed.). *Fluency disorders: Theory, research, treatment and self-help* (pp. 3–29). Nijmegen, The Netherlands: University of Nijmegen Press.

Conture, E. (1990). Childhood stuttering: What is it and who does it? *ASHA Reports, 18,* 2–14.

Conture, E., Zackheim, C., Anderson, J., & Pellowski, M. (2004). Childhood stuttering: Many's a slip between intention and lip. In B. Maassen, R. Kent, H. Peters, P. van Lieshout, & W. Hulstijn (Eds), *Speech motor control in normal and disordered speech* (pp. 253–282). Oxford, United Kingdom: Oxford University Press.

Craig, A., Hancock, K., Tran, Y., Craig, M., & Peters, K. (2002). Epidemiology of stuttering in the community across the life span. *Journal of Speech, Language and Hearing Research, 45,* 1097–1105.

Cox, N. J., Seider, R. A., & Kidd, K. K. (1984). Some environmental factors and hypotheses for stuttering in families with several stutterers. *Journal of Speech & Hearing Research, 27,* 543–548.

Cuadrado, E. M. & Weber-Fox, C. M. (2003). Atypical syntactic processing in individuals who stutter: Evidence from event-related brain potentials and behavioral measures. *Journal of Speech, Language, and Hearing Research, 46,* 960–976.

Curlee, R. F. & Siegel, G. M. (1996). *Nature and treatment of stuttering: New directions* (2nd ed.). Needham Heights, MA: Allyn & Bacon.

Embrechts, M., Ebben, H., Franke, P., & van de Poel, C. (2000). Temperament: A comparison between children who stutter and children who do not stutter. In H. G. Bosshardt, J. S. Yaruss & H. F. M. Peters (Eds), *Proceedings of the Third World Congress on Fluency Disorders: Theory, research, treatment and self-help* (pp. 557–562). Nijmegen, The Netherlands: University of Nijmegen Press.

Ezrati-Vinacour, R. & Levin, I. (2004). The relationship between anxiety and stuttering: a multidimensional approach *Journal of Fluency Disorders, 29,* 135–148.

Fujiki, M., Brinton, B., & Clarke, D. (2002). Emotion regulation in children with specific language impairment. *Language, Speech and Hearing Services in Schools, 33,* 102–111.

Fujiki., M., Spackman, M., Brinton, B., & Hall, A. (2004). The relationship of language and emotion regulation skills to reticence in children with specific language impairment. *Journal of Speech, Language and Hearing Research, 47,* 637–646.

Graham, C., Conture, E., & Camarata, S. (2004). *Influence of function and content words on the stutterings of young children who stutter.* Manuscript in preparation.

Guitar, B. (2003). Acoustic startle responses and temperament in individuals who stutter. *Journal of Speech, Language and Hearing Research, 46,* 233–240.

Guitar, B. (1998). *Stuttering: An integrated approach to its nature and treatment.* Baltimore, MD: Williams & Wilkins.

Guthrie, E. (1960). *The psychology of learning* (Rev. ed.). Gloucester, MA: Smith.

Hall, N., Yamashita, T., & Aram, D. (1993). Relationship between language and fluency in children with developmental language disorders. *Journal of Speech and Hearing Research, 36,* 568–579.

Hartfield, K. (2004). *Semantic processing of children who stutter.* Work in progress.

Hill, W. (2001). *Learning: A survey of psychological interpretations* (7th ed.). Needham Heights, MA: Allyn & Bacon.

Howell, P., Au-Yeung, J., & Sackin, S. (1999). Exchange of stuttering from function words to content words with age. *Journal of Speech, Language and Hearing Research, 42,* 345–354.

Howie, P. M. (1981). Intrapair similarity in frequency of disfluency in monozygotic and dizygotic twin pairs containing stutterers. *Behavior Genetics, 11,* 227–238.

Ingham, R. (1984). *Stuttering and behavior therapy: Current status and experimental foundations.* San Diego, CA: College-Hill, Press.

Indefrey, P. & Levelt, W. (2000). The neural correlates of language production. In M. Gazzaniga (Ed.). *The new cognitive neurosciences* (2nd ed; pp. 845–865). Cambridge, MA: MIT Press.

Karrass, J., Walden, T., Conture, E., Graham, C., Arnold, H., Hartfield, K., & Schwenk, K. (2004). *Relation of emotional reactivity and regulation to childhood stuttering.* Manuscript submitted for publication.

Kelly, E. & Conture, E. (1992). Speaking rates, response time latencies, and interrupting behaviors of young stutterers, nonstutterers and their mothers. *Journal of Speech and Hearing Research, 35,* 1256–1267.

Kolk, H. & Postma, A. (1996). Stuttering as a covert repair phenomenon. In R. Curlee & G. Siegel (Eds.), *Nature and treatment of stuttering: New directions* (2nd ed.; pp. 182–203). Boston, MA: Allyn & Bacon.

Levelt, W. (1996). Perspective taking and ellipsis in spatial descriptions. In P. Bloom & M.A. Peterson (Eds.), *Language and space: Language, speech, and communication* (pp. 77–107). Cambridge, MA: The MIT Press.

Levelt, W. (1989). *Speaking: From intention to articulation*. Cambridge, MA: Bradford Books/The MIT Press.

Levelt, W. J. M., Roelofs, A., & Meyer, A. S. (1999). A theory of lexical access in speech production. *Behavioral and Brain Sciences, 22*, 1–75.

Louko, L., Conture, E., & Edwards, M. (1999). Treating children who exhibit co-occurring stuttering and disordered phonology. In R. Curlee (Ed.), *Stuttering and related disorders of fluency* (2nd ed.; pp. 124–138). New York: Thieme Medical Publishers, Inc.

Louko, L., Edwards, M., & Conture, E. (1993). Phonological characteristics of young stutterers and their normally fluent peers: Preliminary observation. *Journal of Fluency Disorders, 15*(4), 191–210.

Melnick, K., Conture, E., & Ohde, R. (2003). Phonological priming in picture naming of young children who stutter. *Journal of Speech, Language and Hearing Research, 46*, 1428–1443.

Melnick, K., Conture, E., & Ohde, R. (2004). Phonological encoding in young children who stutter. In R. Hartsuiker, Y. Bastiaanse, A. Postma, & F. Wijnen. *Phonological encoding and monitoring in normal and pathological speech* (pp. 102-118). East Sussex, England: Psychology Press Ltd.

Nippold, M. (2002). Stuttering and phonology: Is there an interaction? *American Journal of Speech-Language Pathology, 11*, 99–110.

Onslow, M. & Packman, A. (1996). Designing and implementing a strategy to control stuttered speech in adults. In R. F. Curlee & G. M. Siegel (Eds.), *The nature and treatment of stuttering: New directions* (2nd ed.). Boston: Allyn & Bacon

Oyler, M. (1996). Vulnerability in stuttering children. *Dissertation Abstracts International, 56*, 3374 (UMI No. 9602431).

Pellowski, M., Conture, E., Anderson, J., & Ohde, R. (2001). Phonological/articulatory abilities of children who stutter. In H-G. Bosshardt, J. Yaruss, & H. Peters (Eds.), *Stuttering: Research, therapy and self-help* (pp. 248–252). *Proceedings of 3rd World Congress on Fluency Disorders (Nyborg, Denmark)*. Nijmegen, The Netherlands: University of Nijmegen Press.

Pellowski, M. & Conture, E. (2005). Lexical priming in picture naming of young children who do and do not stutter. *Journal of Speech Language Hearing Research, 48*, 278–294.

Saygin, A., Dick, F., Wilson, S., Dronkers, N., & Bates, E. (2003). Neural resources for processing language and environmental sounds: Evidence from aphasia. *Brain, 126*, 928–945.

Starkweather, C. (1996). Learning and its role in stuttering development. In R. F. Curlee & G. M. Siegel (Eds.), *The nature and treatment of stuttering: New directions* (2nd ed.; pp. 79–95). Needham Heights, MA: Allyn & Bacon.

van Lieshout, P., Hulstijn, W., & Peters, H. (2004). Searching for the weak link in the speech production chain of people who stutter: a motor skill approach. In B. Maassen, R. Kent, H. Peters, P. van Lieshout, & W. Hulstijn (Eds.), *Speech motor control in normal and disordered speech* (pp. 313–356). Oxford, England: Oxford University Press.

Wakaba, Y. (1997). Research on temperament of stuttering children with early onset. In E. C. Healey & H. F. M. Peters (Eds.), *Stuttering: Proceedings of the Second World Congress on Fluency Disorders* (Vol. 2, pp. 84–87). Nijmegen, The Netherlands: University Press Nijmegen.

Wakaba, Y., Iizawa, M., Gondo, K., Inque, S., & Fujino, H. (2003, August). *Preliminary study of effects of temperament characteristics on early development of stuttering children*. Fifth Annual International Fluency Conference, Montreal, Canada.

Wolk, L., Edwards, M.L., & Conture, E. (1993). Coexistence of stuttering and disordered phonology in young children. *Journal of Speech and Hearing Research, 36*, 906–917.

Yairi, E. (1997a). Disfluency characteristics of childhood stuttering. In R. Curlee & G. Siegel (Eds.), *Nature and treatment of stuttering* (2nd ed.; pp. 49–78). Needham Heights, MA: Allyn & Bacon.

Yairi, E. (1997b). Home environment and parent-child interaction in childhood stuttering. In R. Curlee & G. Siegel (Eds.), *Nature and treatment of stuttering* (2nd ed.; pp. 24–48). Needham Heights, MA: Allyn & Bacon.

Yairi, E. & Ambrose, N. (2002). Evidence for genetic etiology in stuttering. *Perspectives on fluency and fluency disorders, 12*(2), 10–14.

Yairi, E. & Ambrose, N. (1992a). A longitudinal study of stuttering in children: A preliminary report. *Journal of Speech and Hearing Research, 35,* 755–760.

Yairi, E. & Ambrose, N. (1992b). Onset of stuttering in preschool children: Selected factors. *Journal of Speech and Hearing Research, 35,* 782–788.

Yairi, E., Ambrose, N., & Cox, N. (1996). Genetics of stuttering: A critical review. *Journal of Speech and Hearing Research, 39*(4), 771–784.

Yaruss, J. S. & Conture, E. (1995). Mother and child speaking rates and utterance lengths in adjacent fluent utterances: Preliminary observations. *Journal of Fluency Disorders, 20,* 257–278.

Yaruss, J. S., LaSalle, L., & Conture, E. (1998). Evaluating stuttering in young children: Diagnostic data. *American Journal of Speech-Language Pathology, 7,* 62–76.

Yaruss, J. S. & Quesal, R. (2004). Stuttering and the International Classification of Functioning, Disability, and Health (ICF): An update. *Journal of Communication Disorders, 37,* 35–52.

Zackheim, C. & Conture, E. (2003). Childhood stuttering and speech disfluencies in relation to children's mean length of utterance. *Journal of Fluency Disorders, 28,* 115–142.

— 3 —

An Evidence-Based Practice Primer: Implications and Challenges for the Treatment of Fluency Disorders

Arlene A. Pietranton

American Speech-Language-Hearing Association

Introduction

This chapter provides an overview of evidence-based practice (EBP; sometimes referred to as evidence-based treatment (EBT)) as it relates to the delivery of clinical services, specifically speech-language pathology treatment services. EBP topics covered in this chapter include a historical perspective on its development, related terms and concepts, levels of evidence and classification of recommendations, how evidence is applied to clinical decision making, and examples of related evidence resources and processes.

History and definition

The philosophical origins of evidence-based practice, sometimes referred to by the more narrowly defined term of evidence-based medicine, can be traced to mid-19th century Paris (Sackett, Rosenberg, & Richardson, 1996) and perhaps even earlier. It has been defined in somewhat varied but conceptually compatible terms such as:

> *The explicit and unbiased use of current best research results in making clinical (individual) and health policy (population) decisions.* (Sacket et al., 1996, p. 71)

> *... an approach to decision making in which the clinician uses the best evidence available, in consultation with the patient, to decide upon the option which suits that patient best.* (Gray, 1997, p. 8)

At the turn of the 21st century, EBP indeed has become a clinical "hot topic" as evidenced by the fact that an online search for the term *evi-*

dence-based practice can yield well over 1,000,000 possible websites. A search of scholarly published articles using a database such as PubMed will bring up over 18,000 citations of journal articles using the term *evidence-based,* most going back only a few years, because EBP has only recently become such a widespread concept. Many of the most popular and well-developed online EBP sites are based in the United Kingdom. In recent years, EBP has experienced a growing momentum in the United States, due in large part to the growth of managed care and its consequences, such as shifting the locus of clinical decision making from providers to payers and changing the medical–legal mindset from a defensive to offensive clinical practice perspective. To preview the discussion that follows, however, EBP is not a move to cookbook clinical practice, or to cost-cutting clinical practice, or an in-vogue management approach. Rather, it is desirable, necessary—and possible—to integrate EBP into clinical decision-making in speech-language pathology.

Getting started: Steps in the EBP process

Although there are a variety of ways to use an EBP approach, the classic steps are to:

- Identify a clinical problem/question;
- Construct a well-built clinical question;
- Select the appropriate resource(s) and conduct a literature search;
- Critically appraise the evidence for its validity and applicability; and
- Integrate that evidence with clinical expertise and patient preferences, and apply it to your patient.

Each of the steps involves probing deeper by constructing a well-built question to research. In order to do this one must:

- Consider the patient: who is the patient? What are the patient's most important characteristics and needs?
- Determine the goals for diagnosis/intervention/prognosis: what do you want to do for the patient?
- Make a comparison to other options: what are the main alternatives to compare with the interventions you have identified?
- Specify the desired outcomes: what are you trying to measure in terms of changes in the patient?

After obtaining evidence, critically appraise its value by asking:

- Are the results of the studies that you have consulted valid? Did the methodology involve factors such as control groups, randomization, follow-up, blinding of the researchers, and comparison of treatment to baseline characteristics?

- What are the results, specifically? Are they relevant to my specific case? Will the results help in caring for my patient(s)?

Evidence-based practice applications

EBP can be applied in a variety of ways and at a variety of levels in clinical decision making:

At the individual/patient level: Evidence may be used by a patient and/or provider to weigh the pros and cons of different intervention options. For example, a surgical intervention may produce better functional outcomes but carry a higher morbidity rate than a long-term pharmacological management for certain clinical conditions.

At the level of the health care system: Health plans may evaluate the evidence to determine typical outcomes—or the anticipated "return on investment" to be derived from particular kinds of treatment. For example, it can lead to the common practice of establishing a smaller copay for a generic versus a "brand name" drug.

In the public policy arena: Evidence may be considered prospectively, as in the case of the Centers for Medicare and Medicaid Services when they state that they intend to base coverage decisions on the strength of the available evidence, or retrospectively, as when used in a court case to determine a prevailing legal standard of care. At this level, larger policy may emerge, such as that mandating universal newborn hearing screening, because the benefits have been found to outweigh its costs.

There are a variety of applications of an EBP approach, including:

- *Assisting clinical decision-making:* by helping the patient and/or provider identify the most effective intervention option(s);

- *Improving the quality of care:* by reducing the amount of variability from provider to provider, program to program, or region to region;

- *Educating patients:* by providing objective data/information about typical outcomes associated with different clinical options;

- *Reducing costs:* by eliminating trial and error approaches to care or the use of less effective approaches;
- *Guiding resource allocation:* by helping to objectively determine how much and/or how often services are most effective;
- *Reducing legal liability risks:* by using a more objective and defensible approach to clinical decision making.

Core terms and concepts

In order to understand and effectively employ an EBP approach, there are a number of core concepts and terms that should be understood:

Outcomes. Outcomes represent the change, or the lack of it, that may occur as a result of time, treatment, or both. Outcomes typically involve a comparison or measurement of an observation made at one point in time (e.g., admission, or start of therapy) to that made at another point in time (e.g., discharge).

Efficacy. Efficacy is the probability of benefit to individuals in a defined population from a technology or procedure applied for a given condition under ideal conditions of use (AHRQ, www.AHRQ.gov). In other words, efficacy documents whether or not a treatment can work.

Effectiveness. Effectiveness measures the probability of benefit to individuals in a defined population from a technology or procedure applied for a given condition under average conditions of use (AHRQ). In other words, treatment effectiveness documents whether or not a treatment does work as typically implemented.

Efficiency. Efficiency of a treatment assesses the amount of waste, expense, or unnecessary effort involved in its application; typically, treatment efficiency involves comparisons between therapeutic approaches to determine which yields a better outcome, or the same outcomes at a lower level of intensity, duration, or cost.

Cost-Effectiveness/Cost-Benefit. Cost-effectiveness measures the outcome attained in relationship to the expense of providing the treatment; in the business world, this concept can be compared to the "return on investment."

Meta-analysis. It should be apparent that measures such as the ones outlined above cannot be obtained from single studies or even a small series of studies. It may require a meta-analysis, which is a mathematical process for combining statistics from many primary studies that can extract an objectively determined, single, and coherent conclusion. Meta-analysis is essentially an analysis of analyses that can provide the "big picture," and smooth out differences in study design, sample size, and results that are inevitable in testing treatment approaches.

Levels of evidence

In evaluating evidence to determine best practice, there are several schemes or hierarchies that rank the relative strength of the evidence under consideration. Although some of the intermediate steps vary, in medicine the highest level of evidence is consistently considered to be that derived from randomized clinical trials (RCT), although other approaches may be more appropriate to some questions in speech-language pathology. Typically, the lowest level of evidence is that based on expert opinion (what a writer, teacher or speaker asserts without specific evidence) or case studies (observations of single individuals). A scheme developed by the AHRQ depicts the levels of evidence as:

- Level 1: *Randomized controlled trials*. Includes quasi-randomized processes such as alternate allocation.

- Level 2: *Nonrandomized controlled trial*. A prospective (pre-planned) study with predetermined eligibility criteria and outcome measures.

- Level 3: *Observational studies with controls*. Includes retrospective, interrupted time series (a change in trend attributable to the intervention), case-control studies, cohort studies with controls, and health services research that includes adjustment for likely confounding variables.

- Level 4: *Observational studies without controls* (e.g., cohort studies without controls and case series).

EBP reports are usually of an advisory nature (e.g., "we have found that a particular option is/is not effective or efficacious") versus prescriptive (i.e., "you should/should not use certain options"), such as the following Classification of Recommendations from the United States Preventive Services Task Force:

Classification of Recommendations:

    A—Good evidence to consider

    B—Fair evidence to consider

C—Poor evidence to consider or not to consider
D—Fair evidence not to consider
E—Good evidence not to consider
I—Insufficient evidence from which to make a recommendation

Why should speech-language pathologists embrace an EBP approach to clinical practice?

The EBP approach to clinical practice is both responsible and pragmatic. It's responsible because it helps to assure that the approach(es) clinical practitioners employ are those that have been objectively proven to be most effective. It's pragmatic because an increasing number of payers, public policy entities, and administrative decision-makers are requiring evidence to support clinical decision making. Some examples of key EBP decision-makers related to the delivery of speech-language pathology services include the Agency for Healthcare Research and Quality.

Agency for Healthcare Research and Quality's (AHRQ; previously the Agency for Health Care Policy and Research). AHRQ's mission is to support research designed to improve the outcomes and quality of health care, reduce its costs, address patient safety and medical errors, and broaden access to effective services. Research that is sponsored, conducted, and disseminated by AHRQ is intended to provide information that will help in making better decisions about health care. The agency was created in December 1989 as a Public Health Care Service agency in the federal government Department of Health and Human Services (HHS). Sister agencies within HHS include the National Institutes of Health (NIH), the Centers for Disease Control (CDC), the Food and Drug Administration (FDA), the Centers for Medicare and Medicaid Services (CMS), and the Health Research Services Administration (HRSA). Its annual budget is approximately $270 million (a relatively small budget by federal government standards), most of which is awarded as grants and contracts to researchers at universities or evidence-based practice centers. It has a staff of about 300.

AHRQ has three primary components that are particularly relevant to EBP:

Evidence-based Practice Centers (EPC). These are actually contractual arrangements with 13 institutions throughout the United States and

Canada to: produce "evidence reports" on specified topics that are based on a thorough review and analysis of all scientific literature on the topic; conduct research on particular clinical methodologies and their effectiveness; and participate in various technical assessment activities. Most of their evidence reports and technology assessments address clinical topics that are common, expensive, and/or significant for the Medicare and Medicaid populations. AHRQ encourages public and private sector organizations to use the evidence reports and technology assessments as the basis for their own clinical guidelines and other quality improvement activities. Several EPC reports deal with issues related to audiology or SLP (e.g., acute otitis media [AHRQ Publication No. 01-E010, May 2001], dysphagia {AHRQ Publication No. 99-E024, July 1999], traumatic brain injury {AHRQ Publication No. 00-E001, October 2000]).

National Guidelines Clearinghouse (NGC). The mission of the NGC is to provide physicians, nurses, other health care professionals, providers, health plans, delivery systems, purchasers, and others with an accessible mechanism for obtaining objective, detailed information on clinical guidelines and to further their dissemination, implementation, and use. The criteria regarding which guidelines may be included in the NGC include: (1) systematically developed statements with strategies, recommendations, and so on, to assist health care practitioners' and patients' health care decisions; (2) guidelines produced under the auspices of medical specialty associations or "relevant" professional societies; (3) guidelines based on a systematic literature search and review of existing scientific evidence published in peer reviewed journals; and (4) guidelines that are developed and reviewed/revised within the last 5 years to maintain currency of the recommendations. To date, the last two criteria have proven challenging to existing speech-language pathology practice policy guidelines being included in the NGC. As speech-language pathology further matures within the EBP framework, we should expect to see reports of treatment guidelines from the NGC that are relevant to speech and language therapy.

U.S. Preventive Services Task Force (USPSTF) is an independent panel of experts in primary care and prevention charged with systematically reviewing evidence and developing recommendations for clinical preventive services. Recent audiology/SLP topics addressed by the USPSTF include developmental delay and newborn hearing that can be accessed via an online topic index on the USPSTF website: www.ahrq.gov/clinic/prevenix.htm.

Centers for Medicare and Medicaid Services (CMS; formerly the Health Care Finance Administration or HCFA). The CMS has stated that national coverage policies are now "evidence-based"; however, CMS does not appear to be taking specific steps to implement processes to support this stance.

Education policy makers. Although EBP may have its origins in health care, it also applies to clinical and policy decision making in education, as evidenced by references to "scientifically proven techniques" found in language related to accountability and outcomes in education in the President's Commission on Excellence in Special Education and the Early Reading First and Reading First Grant bills. Recent literature in education, such as that regarding recommended approaches to reading instruction, makes reference to an evidence-based practice framework.

EBP—friend or foe?

As noted, there are many benefits to patients, providers, and payers from an EBP approach. However, there are also certain realities that must be kept in mind, such as the currently limited availability of higher levels of evidence across numerous clinical disciplines (such as our own) and the potential for overly zealous application of EBP to limit or deny coverage for clinical options.

For example, there are estimates that as much as 80% of health care practice has yet to be validated by randomized controlled clinical trials (DeJong, 1999). In fluency, similarly cautionary notes regarding availability of validated treatments have been voiced (Ingham, 2003). The good news is that across many disciplines, there is a clear proliferation of practice guidelines as tracked by the Institute of Medicine. The bad news is that some EBP reports require careful analysis and insight when considering their validity and relevance. For example, speech-language pathology, not unlike quite a few other clinical professions, has identified a number of concerns related to both process and content related to several AHRQ's EPCs' reports, such as:

- The composition of the "expert" panels issuing the guidelines, which have tended to be physician-dominated, even when dealing with topics for which the primary subject matter experts are clearly speech-language pathologists (e.g., dysphagia);

- Inconsistency in how levels of evidence are applied to reach the report's recommendations; for example, in less broadly researched areas of practice, including recommendations based on "expert opinion," while discarding recommendations supported by published research studies that involve small numbers of subjects;

- Methodological concerns, such as including findings from studies with subjects who were more heterogeneous than the population addressed in the evidence report (e.g., ECRI, 1999).

Where does a clinician start?

Having made the commitment to seek and use the best available evidence to guide your clinical decisions, how does one do that in day-to-day clinical practice? Fortunately, the power of the Internet as well as expanded journal benefits to ASHA members have made this important, but somewhat daunting task, much more manageable.

Broad-based EBP resources

A number of resources to examine evidence-based practice concepts or findings relevant to a wide variety of medical conditions or interventions are available on the Internet:[1]

- Agency for Healthcare Research and Quality (AHRQ) Evidence-Based Practice Program: www.ahrq.gov/clinic

- Bandolier: www.jr2.ox.ac.uk/Bandolier

- Clinical Evidence, BMJ Publishing Group: www.clinicalevidence.com

- Cochrane Collaboration: www.cochrane.org

- Evidence-Based Practice Newsletter: www.ebponline.net

Let's take a closer look at a couple of these websites:

AHRQ (www.ahrq.gov). After logging onto AHRQ's home page at www.ahrq.gov, one can select from a number of options, including AHRQ's Evidence-Based Practice Centers (EPCs) and their reports, several of which are either specific or relevant to speech-language pathology,

---

[1] Internet addresses age quickly. If you have difficulty connecting to a resource via the web link provided, please do a web search by the name of the resource.

including Evidence Report/Technology Assessment: Number 52—
Criteria for Determining Disability in Speech-Language Disorders.

The Cochrane Collaboration (www.cochrane.org). This is an international-
al "virtual organization" developed in 1992 by Oxford University in
response to Cochrane's call for the systematic, up-to-date review of all relevant randomized clinical trials of health care. The Cochrane Library is a
subscription service, which is available at some University and medical
school libraries for interested users. Cochrane also operates a consumer
network (www.cochraneconsumer.com) at no fee that provides synopses of
Cochrane Reviews, which can then be retrieved in full by accessing the
subscription service.

But, it's not all on the "information superhighway"

Not all information relevant to decision-making in EBP will be available
on open Internet sites or searchable by "Googling." Given the increased
reliance that many students and professionals place on such sources, it is
critically important to emphasize the role of primary research articles and
texts in determining best practice (Nail-Chiwetalu & Bernstein Ratner,
2003). Growing numbers of web surfers are finding it difficult to evaluate information on websites (a good resource for considering the value of
a website can be found at www.lib.umd.edu/UES/webcheck.html), or distinguish web-posted materials from peer-reviewed scientific research findings. Until a problem area in practice has been studied to the point where
recommendations are posted to sites such as those sponsored by AHRQ,
BMJ, or Cochrane, for example, speech-language pathologists must con-
sult the latest and highest quality professional published literature in the
topic area. The text of most published articles cannot be located or
retrieved by open Internet searches. First, the existence of relevant articles
must be compiled by using free-access utilities such as PubMed
(www.ncbi.nlm.nih.gov/entrez/query.fcgi), or library-sponsored vendors
such as Medline, PsychInfo, CINHL, and so on. Once references to relevant studies are located, the articles themselves must be retrieved either
through libraries or subscription services. Increasingly, university, school
system, and hospital-based professionals can download full article text
directly to their computers, making this process easier and more
affordable.

This is an area in which ASHA has taken an important lead in making the scientific literature accessible to its members. All ASHA and NSSLHA members can search and download full-text articles from all of its scholarly journals (*Journal of Speech, Language and Hearing Research; American Journal of Speech-Language Pathology; American Journal of Audiology; Speech, Language and Hearing Services in Schools;* and *Contemporary Issues in Communication Sciences and Disorders*), by accessing them at ASHA journals online: (www.asha.org/members/deskref-journals). In order to implement EBP, it is important for practicing professionals to keep current with the published literature in their areas of practice on a regular basis.

SLP-related EBP resources on the Web

In addition to the availability of full-text ASHA publications that address treatment issues for specific conditions, there are also a number of EBP online resources that include SLP-specific information:

- ASHA's National Center for Treatment Effectiveness in Communication Disorders Treatment Efficacy Bibliographies: www.asha.org/members/research/NOMS/efficacy

- Combined Health Information Database (CHID) online: www.chid.nih.gov

- The Dome: www.asha.org/members/services/affinity/contentscan.htm

- ERIC: www.eric.ed.gov

- Ingenta: www.ingenta.com

- Health Sciences Library at UNC: www.hsl.unc.edu/visitors.cfm

- PubMed: www.ncbi.nlm.nih.gov/PubMed

- National Institute on Deafness and Other Communication Disorders (NIDCD): www.nidcd.nih.gov

- Research Navigator: www.ablongman.com/researchnavigator

Let's take a closer look at one of these resources—ASHA's National Center for Treatment Effectiveness in Communication Disorders (NCTECD). The NCTECD's mission is to develop and manage a valid and reliable source of data, the NOMS: the National Outcome Measurement System, that:

- Is meaningful to clinical and nonclinical audiences;

- Can be used for: quality assurance, patient education, and reimbursement guidelines;
- Generates research questions.

The NCTECD provides education and consultation to ASHA members in collecting, interpreting, and using outcomes data. The NCTECD's resources include Treatment Efficacy Bibliographies, which can be found at www.asha.org/members/research/NOMS/efficacy.

Giving EBP a try

Let's visit and use an EBP site such as the health sciences learning center at the University of North Carolina (www.hsl.unc.edu/visitors.cfm). First, go to Learning Modules, then click on "Evidence Based Medicine." Let's begin by performing a (too) general search. Using "child stuttering" as a search term, typed with quotation marks to indicate a phrase rather than individual words, retrieves about 1001 references ("hits"), clearly too many to be helpful. Refining the clinical question to be: "What is the optimal therapy schedule for children who stutter?" yields a more manageable 54 references, most of which are good, all of which relate to stuttering therapy and many of which provide recommendations regarding the schedule of treatment (example: "Conture, E.G., Treatment efficacy: Stuttering. *J Speech Hear Res.* 1996 Oct; 39(5):S18–26"). We can then obtain copies of these references and evaluate them to adjust our therapy procedures.

ASHA's EBP activities to date

As a professional association, ASHA has been involved in a number of EBP activities and initiatives to date, including:

- The development and support of a National Outcomes Measurement System (NOMS) and the National Center for Treatment Effectiveness in Communication Disorders (NCTECD).
- ASHA Special Interest Division 2: Neurologic Communication and Communication Disorders produced a 2001 Newsletter Series on EBP.
- EBP home page on the ASHA Web site www.asha.org/members/slp/topics/ebp/
- Publication of the *JSLHR* Treatment Efficacy Series (1996 & 1998) and the development and recent updating of accompanying Fact

Sheets, which addressed the following areas of clinical practice:

- ◆ Cognitive-Communicative Disorders Resulting from TBI (*JSHR*, Vol. 39, S5–17, October 1996)
- ◆ Stuttering (*JSHR*, Vol. 39, S18–26, October 1996)
- ◆ Aphasia (*JSHR*, Vol. 39, S27–36, October 1996)
- ◆ Hearing Aids in the Management of Hearing Loss in Adults (*JSHR*, Vol. 39, S37–45, October 1996)
- ◆ Dysarthria (*JSHR*, Vol. 39, S46 - 57, October 1996)
- ◆ Hearing Loss in Children (*JSHR*, Vol. 41, S61–84, February 1998)
- ◆ Functional Phonological Disorders in Children (*JSHR*, Vol. 41, S85–100, February 1998)
- ◆ Voice Disorders (*JSHR*, Vol. 41, S101–116, February 1998)

- Evaluating the effectiveness of programs, products, procedures. In 1998, the ASHA Executive Board determined that ASHA has neither the resources or infrastructure to legitimately evaluate the effectiveness of programs, products, or procedures. As an alternative, it develops resources to help professionals and consumers such as sample questions to help guide professionals and consumers, which are posted on the ASHA Web site www.asha.org/members/evaluate.htm

- A financial contribution to help support the Academy of Neurologic Communication Disorders and Sciences (ANCDS)'s EBP Guidelines Project. Other co-sponsors are ASHA Special Interest Division 2: Neurophysiology and Neurogenic Speech and Language Disorders and the U.S. Dept. of Veterans Affairs. Documents are under development in the following areas: dysarthria, acquired apraxia of speech, aphasia, dementia, and cognitive-communication disorders after TBI. The unabridged reports with data tables are posted on the ANCDS Web site (www.ancds.dqu.edu) and published in the *Journal of Medical Speech-Language Pathology*.

Readers are encouraged to look to *The ASHA Leader* or ASHA's Web site for further information and updates regarding ASHA's continued EBP activities, including a 2004 Joint Coordinating Committee of several ASHA Vice Presidents that will review our professions' EBP needs, the Association's EBP activities to date, and develop a plan for ASHA's future EBP resources, activities, and initiatives.

Conclusion

Evidence-based practice is a reality and a responsibility for clinical professionals. Our clients and those who pay for or fund our services are entitled
to know that the services have been shown to be effective. As clinicians,
we must use evidence to guide and justify our decisions. While the broad
concepts of EBP are indisputably valuable, successful infusion in clinical
practice, including in the field of speech-language pathology, will require
time and may necessitate adjustments to the medical and surgical models
that are currently considered the "gold standards." This is an important
commitment we all must make to assure the well-being of our clients,
recognition of the value of our services, and the integrity of our profession.

References

Agency for Healthcare Research and Quality (AHRQ) (www.ahrq.gov)

Centers for Medicare and Medicaid Services (www.hhs.cms.gov)

Conture, E.G. (1996). Treatment efficacy: Stuttering. *Journal of Speech and Hearing Research, 39,* S18–26.

DeJong, G. (1999). Toward an evidence-based rehabilitation culture: The role of values, outcomes, disclosure, and stakeholder groups. *Rehabilitation Outlook, 4,* 9–11.

ECRI. (1999, July). *Diagnosis and treatment of swallowing disorders (dysphagia) in acute-care stroke patients.*
Evidence Report/Technology Assessment No. 8. AHCPR Publication No. 99-E024. Rockville,
MD: Agency for Health Care Policy and Research.

Gray, J. A. Muir. (1997). *Evidence based healthcare: How to make health policy and management decisions.*
London: Churchill-Livingstone.

Ingham, J.C. (2003) Evidence-based treatment of stuttering: I. Definition and application. *Journal of
Fluency Disorders, 28*(3), 197–206.

Institute of Medicine www.iom.edu

The John Hopkins University Bloomberg School of Public Health Summer Institute of Epidemiology and
Biostatistics. (2001). *Making health care safer: A critical analysis of patient safety practices.* Evidence
Report/Technology Assessment: Number 43. AHRQ Publication No. 01-E058, July 2001. Agency
for Healthcare Research and Quality, Rockville, MD. www.ahrq.gov/clinic/ptsafety/

Nail-Chiwetalu, B. & Bernstein Ratner, N. (2003, April). *Fostering information literacy competency in communication sciences and disorders.* Paper presented at the annual Council of Academic Programs in
Communication Sciences and Disorders, Albuquerque, NM. Retrieved from www.capcsd.org/
proceedings/2003/talks/chiwetalu2003.pdf

Sackett, D. L., Richardson, W. S., Rosenberg, W. M., & Haynes, R. B. (1996). *Evidence-based medicial: How
to practice and teach EBM.* London: Churchill-Livingstone.

Sackett, D. L., Rosenberg, W. M. C., & Richardson, W. S. (1996). Evidence based medicine: What it is
and what it isn't. *British Medical Journal, 312,* 71–72.

U.S. Preventive Services Task Force Ratings: Strength of Recommendations and Quality of Evidence.
Guide to clinical preventive services, third edition: Periodic updates, 2000–2003. Agency for Healthcare
Research and Quality, Rockville, MD. Retrieved from www.ahrq.gov/clinic/3rduspstf/ratings.htm

—4—

Measurement Issues in Fluency Disorders

Kenneth O. St. Louis
West Virginia University

Structuring evaluations and monitoring therapy: What should be measured?

TAKING THE PULSE OF PROFESSIONALS

As a participatory activity at the 10th Annual Leadership Conference for the Special Interest Division 4 on Fluency and Fluency Disorders, a brief questionnaire was distributed. It included a list of most of the obvious things a clinician might measure in a stuttering evaluation or in ongoing stuttering therapy (see Table 4-1). Importantly, the list was not—nor was meant to be—exhaustive. The purpose of the exercise was to provide a quick snapshot of the opinions of current Board Recognized Specialists in Fluency Disorders and others interested in stuttering.

Participants were asked to check one of three categories for each of the 12 items according to whether they considered measuring that item as "essential," "helpful but not necessary," or "not really necessary" in a typical evaluation for a stuttering client. They were asked to mark their first reactions and to work quickly. They also were asked to indicate whether they were: consumers or advocates for people who stutter, clinicians who treat people who stutter, clinical researchers who are developing or documenting treatment for people who stutter, experimental researchers who are trying to better understand the nature of stuttering, or others. They were asked to mark all that applied to them. After marking questionnaires, participants placed colored Post-it® notes on 12 posters, one for each question. They placed green notes for "essential" categories, yellow notes for "helpful but not necessary," and red notes for "not really necessary." These posters were then displayed so all participants could visually compare their own responses to those of others. The number of Post-it® notes pasted onto the various 12 posters ranged from 52 to 59, with a mean of 56.6.

At the end of the session, 37 participants chose to turn in their questionnaires. From the actual questionnaires, although more limited than the results from the posters, two characteristics of the respondents were

TABLE 4-1

Percentages of participants at the Special Interest Division 4 Conference who believed that measuring various aspects of stuttering during a clinical evaluation is: (1) "essential," (2) "helpful but not necessary," or (3) "not really necessary."			
To Be Measured	"Essential"	"Helpful But Not Necessary"	"Not Really Necessary"
Observed stuttering frequency, duration, and/or severity	73%	21%	6%
Client/parent self-assessment measures of stuttering variability in reactions to–and/or attitudes toward–speaking in different situations (at work, school, home, other)	90%	7%	3%
Degree of disability, handicap, disorder, and suffering	77%	16%	7%
Anxiety, personality, psychological adjustment, and/or mental health	50%	43%	7%
Personal experience with stuttering	60%	39%	2%
Physiological aspects of respiration, phonation, and/or (co)articulation	28%	58%	14%
Pragmatics, semantics, syntax, morphology, and/or phonology/articulation	30%	64%	5%
General health, medical history, and/or developmental history	48%	47%	5%
Non-speech motor and/or sensory skills	16%	57%	27%
Genetic evidence of stuttering	41%	54%	5%
Cognitive, academic, and/or intellectual abilities	33%	60%	7%
Cultural and/or family attitudes, beliefs, and reactions	82%	16%	2%

revealed. First, it was clear that far more items on the questionnaire were considered "essential" than "helpful but not necessary." Specifically, for these respondents, the mean number of responses (out of 12) for each of the three choices were as follows: 7.2 for "essential", 4.2 for "helpful but not necessary," and 0.4 for "not really necessary." Second, these questionnaires provided information on areas of specialization. Sixteen percent regarded themselves as consumers or advocates, 76% as clinicians, 24% as clinical researchers, 16% as experimental researchers, and 16% as other (primarily professors or doctoral students).

Table 4-1 shows the percentage of participants who indicated each of the three choices for the 12 items on the posters. None of the items were considered "essential" by all participants. The highest percentage of "essential" ratings, selected by 90% of respondents, were client or parent self-assessment measures of reactions and attitudes. Next in order were cultural and/or family attitudes, beliefs, and reactions, which were selected by about 82% of respondents. The third-highest ranked component of an evaluation at 77% was for degree of disability, handicap, disorder, or suffering, and the fourth most often selected at 73% was for observed stuttering frequency, duration, and/or severity. This was surprising because conventional wisdom would have suggested that frequency or severity of stuttering would be considered the primary index of the degree of stuttering (Cordes & Ingham, 1994; Ingham, 1984). The item least frequently considered "essential," and most frequently considered "not really necessary" for measurement was appraisal of nonspeech motor and/or sensory skills.

Although these data cannot be considered to be a representative sample, or even a completely accurate reflection of the opinions of the participants at the conference, they do nevertheless provide a snapshot of current thinking of clinicians about priorities for measurement in stuttering clients. Most significant perhaps is that most session participants believed that many of the "intangible," or less observable, aspects of stuttering must be included in customary clinical measures.

Factors affecting choices of measures

It is clear that the measures we use to assess stuttering are affected by a number of factors. Tradition is important. Clinicians and researchers typically use those measures they (1) learned about in graduate school and/or

(2) have used repeatedly through the years. Choices are affected also by the evidence that exists to support—or not support—the utility and value of certain potential measures. Certainly, one's frame of reference is important. It is reasonable to assume that clinicians (the large majority of respondents to this questionnaire) seek to provide the best possible treatment for each individual person who stutters. Clinicians, therefore, are likely to view the preceding exercise differently than those who are researchers. For example, measures that capture individual differences will be valued if those differences seem to affect the treatment of some clients, even if these measures might not be useful with all stutterers. Furthermore, there are differences among researchers: clinical researchers often aspire to develop measures that can be utilized by other clinicians for a particular treatment, while experimental researchers typically choose measures that best provide data for the aspect of stuttering they hope to better understand, whether or not it has obvious clinical relevance at the time.

A SNAPSHOT FROM CURRENT CLINICAL TEXTBOOKS

Appendix A (at the end of this chapter) provides a different type of snapshot of current thinking about what clinicians should measure. I perused 12 clinically oriented stuttering textbooks published between 1995 and 2003 (Bloom & Cooperman, 1999; Conture, 2001; Gregory, 2003; Guitar, 1998; Ham, 1999; Manning, 2001; Onslow, Packman, & Harrison, 2003; Rustin, Cook, & Spence, 1995; Ryan, 2001; Shapiro, 1999; Silverman, 2004; Wall & Myers, 1995) and generated a list of fluency or stuttering measures recommended by the authors for clinical use. I also added a few measures that are not yet in the textbooks (e.g., St. Louis, 2001; Vanryckeghem & Brutten, 2002; Yaruss & Quesal, in press). Undoubtedly, the Appendix does not list all the measures mentioned in the various textbooks and other sources. If all possible measures were included, for example, those used strictly in research studies, the list would be very long indeed.

The listing of measures in Appendix A is classified according to whether it is best described as: quantitative, but where normative comparisons are usually not necessary to use the measures effectively; quantitative, where normative comparisons are necessary for meaningful use of the measures; and qualitative (or non-numeric) measures. This chapter will not describe and evaluate the measures because (1) they are typically described in the sources cited and (2) the primary purpose of the list is to show that clinical experts recommend measuring multiple aspects of the stuttering problem in a variety of manners.

What does the list illustrate? Most of the measures were designed for stuttering, although at least one was developed specifically for cluttering. They cover the common measures of frequency, severity, and speech rate, but also include such traditional measures as anticipation, adaptation, and consistency of stuttering. A few measures of other aspects of articulation, voice, language, breathing, nonspeech oral motor skills, hearing, and other speech-related processes are recommended by at least some current clinical authors as well. A number of norm-referenced speech reaction and attitude scales are recommended, as well as several related instruments, for example, for state or trait anxiety, temperament, and neurological integrity. Qualitative or inferential assessments are also widely recommended, most following traditional speech-language diagnostic traditions. These include, but are not limited to: case history questionnaires and interviews, teacher interviews, listings of accessory (secondary) behaviors or emotional reactions to stuttering, awareness of stuttering difficulties, family interaction, judgments of client interest and motivation, and psychosocial adjustment. A few authors emphasize the value of measuring cultural factors.

A SNAPSHOT FROM A HYPOTHETICAL COURT CASE

An exercise designed to challenge speech-language pathologists (SLPs) to select measures of stuttering that are credible and defensible was also used for discussion among the conference participants. It is provided in Appendix B. The exercise involves consideration of a hypothetical court case in which Board-Recognized Fluency Specialists are asked to choose measures of stuttering that could prove or disprove in court that an adult stuttering client was "damaged" by ineffective speech therapy. One specialist is retained by the client's attorney and alleges that the client was made worse. Another specialist is retained by the SLP who treated the client and who alleges that the client actually improved. Both specialists must agree on a set of measures to be administered by a "neutral" specialist acceptable to both of them.

Obviously, selecting "no more than five widely-accepted measures of stuttering that will prove that therapy made—or did not make—the client worse" would be a difficult task. Moreover, it is likely that most specialists would not agree entirely on (1) the measures to be chosen, (2) the anticipated challenges from the opposition, or (3) the likely decision of the jury. Nevertheless, this exercise, if considered seriously, brings into focus many of the issues, covered in the next section, regarding measurement that must be considered.

Issues in measurement

Measurement is a complex process. Most of the important issues related to measurement are covered in classes in research methods, but perhaps not in the context of stuttering evaluations. I am indebted to Babbie (2001) for his clear exposition of many of these issues.

CONCEPT VERSUS INDICATORS

First, we consider the difference between a concept (such as "stuttering") and indicators or certain aspects that we can measure about it. It is important to realize that we cannot measure a concept; we can only measure its various indicators. What this means is that it is a logical impossibility to ever capture what stuttering "really is." We must be careful not to confuse the indicators with the concept, but that is something that we do all the time (Bloodstein, 1990).

Babbie (2001) described how this confusion can occur. First, we notice a group of observations that all seem to point to some common phenomenon or concept. In speaking, these might include: difficulty in getting words out, repeating syllables, executing unusual movements like blinking the eyes while speaking, avoiding specific situations that involve talking to people in authority, or experiencing difficulty with talking, but being able to sing with ease. We then give this concept a name, for example, "stuttering." Next and often without realizing it, we begin to consider this conceptual category as an unambiguous entity that exists in a tangible form. Of course, at this point, we no longer need a collection of observations to point to the entity. Finally, as we become accustomed to measuring the concept, we can easily fall into a logical trap of debating which indicator is "really" the best measure of the concept when, in fact, none of them completely describes or characterizes it.

LEVEL OF MEASUREMENT

The level of measurement affects the conclusions we can draw from whatever measures are involved (Babbie, 2001; Siegel, 1956). Data can be categorical, such as male versus female. Typically, there are no assumptions regarding the degree of maleness or femaleness with such categorical measures. The next level is ordinal measures. In this case, there is a sense of more versus less, but the differences between categories are not even. For example, from interviews, we might determine the extent to which stuttering is mild, moderate, or severe. With this ordinal measure, we could rank-order the results from a number of people who stutter, but we cannot assume that the differences between adjacent categories are equal. The next level of measurement involves interval data. In this case, data can be rank-ordered but also have equal differences between adjacent categories. An example would be 5- or 7-point Likert scale ratings on attitudes toward stuttering, assuming that intervals are shown as equal. The last level is ratio measurement, which can be rank-ordered, have equal differences between adjacent categories, but additionally, start with a baseline of zero. Frequency of stuttering in percent syllables stuttered (%SS) or stuttered syllables per minute (SS/M) are examples of ratio data.

After taking measures, researchers usually need to determine the likelihood their results are due to chance or to the independent influences or variables they have identified. Inferential statistics are used to accomplish this. Ordinarily, different types of nonparametric statistical procedures are used to generalize from data characterized by categorical or ordinal levels of measurement (Siegel, 1956). Parametric statistics can be used to test the significance of the results of ratio level data and most interval data (Schiavetti & Metz, 1997).

PRECISION OF MEASURES

Precision refers to the exactness with which something can be measured. Measures should not be reported any more precisely than we can measure them. Can a wristwatch be set to measure milliseconds precisely? Very likely, it cannot. Can a clinician measure the duration of speech segments or pauses precisely with a digital stopwatch that records time in hundredths of seconds? Again, the answer is "no," because normal human reaction time precludes starting and stopping a stopwatch to measure intervals of time that small. Therefore, it is important that duration measures not be reported in fractions of seconds that represent greater precision than was actually the case. For example, if a clinician measured the duration of a stutter as 5.29 sec with a digital stopwatch, the result should probably be rounded to the nearest half-second, or 5.5 sec.

ACCURACY OF MEASURES

A related concept is accuracy, certainly more familiar than precision. Accuracy deals with questions such as, "What kinds of errors are likely with this measure?" Consider again a clock or watch. Suppose a person could view a reference clock and then record the exact time from a number of watches, large wall clocks, and other devices. Some time pieces would allow the person to set the time with smaller errors than others. Those would provide more accurate times. Furthermore, clocks that do not add or subtract seconds or minutes over a period of time, say a week, are more accurate than those that do. If a clinician plans to measure syllables per minute as an indicator of speaking rate, can he or she start and stop a stopwatch without introducing errors? Consider responses on an attitude questionnaire that asks for the respondent to circle a number from 1 to 5 to indicate "Strongly Disagree" to "Strongly Agree." If a stutterer's circled response was on the wrong line, or missed the number entirely, the measurement is degraded due to problems of accuracy.

RELIABILITY OF MEASURES

Following are some of the more serious issues that affect the day-to-day use of measurements by clinicians and scientists. Two of them are reliability and validity, and we consider them in that order.

There are several different ways to think about reliability, but two types are used commonly: interjudge reliability and intrajudge reliability (sometimes referred to as *agreement*[1]). Interjudge reliability refers to the degree to which two different observers will get the same results when they measure the same phenomenon. Intrajudge reliability refers to the extent to which the same observer will get the same results of the same phenomenon over repeated re-measurements. In other words, with interjudge reliability, the concern is how closely observers or judges agree with one another, and with intrajudge reliability, it is how closely they agree with themselves.

Consider the various ways frequency of stuttering and speech output can be measured. Typically, a clinician or a researcher listens to an audiotape—or views a videotape—of a person who stutters and counts

---

[1]See Cordes (1994) for an in-depth review of reliability and its many meanings.

instances of stuttering by pressing a button for each occurrence. Those instances may be every word stuttered; every syllable stuttered; every part-word repetition, prolongation, or block; every time segment of speech that contains an instance of stuttering; or several other possibilities. The frequency of stuttering is seen as a good indicator of the amount of stuttering the speaker manifests and is typically expressed as a percentage of total words or syllables stuttered or as the number of words, syllables, or instances of stuttering in a given period of time.

When evaluating any measure of stuttering frequency, a number of questions might be asked about any of these procedures: Can we agree on what does and does not constitute stuttering? For example, are whole word and phrase repetitions to be considered stuttering or normal disfluency? Can we agree on which words or syllables are stuttered? To what extent do accessory behaviors constitute stuttering, especially such strategies as substituting synonyms for words on which stuttering is anticipated? There is a great deal of compelling evidence that we must be concerned about the reliability of stuttering measures in the laboratory as well as the clinic (Cordes, 1994). A number of our most productive scientists have spent years struggling to improve reliability of common stuttering measures (Curlee, 1981; Ham, 1989; Ingham & Cordes, 1992; Kully & Boberg, 1988; MacDonald & Martin, 1973). Moreover, as difficult as it is to train judges to get satisfactory intrajudge reliability, it is often quite another matter to obtain satisfactory interjudge reliability. Depending on instructions to judges, their clinical orientation, their experience, and a host of other confounding factors, perfect agreement among different judges is impossible, and even satisfactory agreement is difficult (e.g., Gregory, 2003; Ryan, 2001).

As difficult as it is to obtain satisfactory reliability in research studies, the problem is also relevant to clinical care of people who stutter. It is common for stuttering clients to change clinicians for numerous reasons, as when either clients or clinicians move to new locations. Therefore different clinicians end up judging or counting stuttering or categories of disfluency in the same client, and it is here that reliability problems may be most acute. I provide two related examples. Nan Bernstein Ratner (personal communication) reports that she has had speech-language pathology students identify stuttering in a 125-word passage for many years. The students are allowed as many viewings of the video sample as they desire. A subgroup of the student judges reportedly consistently miss many stutterings, identifying less than one third of the mean number identified. Similarly, another subgroup identifies more than three times the mean number. In a similar clinical exercise that I have assigned in classes for many years, students listen to audiotapes of five stutterers speaking for five minutes each. Mean stuttered syllables per minute counts in the lowest and highest deciles (i.e., 0–10th percentile and 90–100th percentile) have differed from the median ratings by as little as 15% for a severe stutterer with laryngeal blocks to 74% for a mild stutterer with rapid speech and short repetitions.

Such examples imply that much of the concern about reliability has dealt with stuttering frequency measures over the years, but reliability is important for qualitative measures as well. For example, if a person who stutters is judged to have "low self-esteem" because of a history of being penalized for stuttering or judged to be "motivated to improve" from an interview, we need to be concerned that the person who reached the conclusion would reach the same conclusion at a different time after watching a videotape of the interview or that others watching the tape would reach the same conclusion.

VALIDITY OF MEASURES

Face validity

If the issues surrounding reliability are confusing, those surrounding validity are even more difficult. At the risk of oversimplification, we can discuss them in the context of *face validity*, *construct validity*, and *predictive validity* (Schiavetti & Metz, 1997). Face validity, sometimes known as content validity, is the easiest to explain and can be illustrated by the following question. Would a reasonably informed and intelligent person conclude that the measure chosen is an obvious indicator of the concept in question? In other words, does the measure seem like it would accurately reflect the concept? Consider the following: Does electrical skin conductance seem like an obvious measure of the moment-to-moment occurrence of stuttering? Does the ratio of more typical versus less typical disfluency types provide an accurate differentiation of stuttering from normal disfluency? Does a speaker's own appraisal of the amount of penalty or suffering she experiences on a scale of 1 to 5 reflect that actual penalty? Skin conductance would have low face validity because electrical resistance and conductance of the skin seems quite different from the repetitions, prolongations, and blocks that characterize stuttering. By contrast, the ratio of disfluency types and self-appraisals would have higher face validity, since they use the same language and pertain to the obvious behaviors that are allegedly being measured. That, of course, does not mean they are better measures, or that they are reliable, but face validity will figure into the decision of what measures to use.

Construct validity

Construct validity is a bit more complex. It refers to the extent to which previous research indicates that the measured indicator truly reflects the concept. The term *construct* is used to highlight that various *concepts* or *constructs* can be measured by different indicators. If different measures of the same general phenomenon yield similar results, it can be argued that the measures are indicators of the same concept. To illustrate, consider attitudes of people who stutter toward speaking. It is well established that a big part of the problem of stuttering relates to a host of fears and avoidances pertaining to various speaking situations (e.g., Starkweather & Givens-Ackerman, 1997; Van Riper, 1981). Moreover, numerous questionnaires have been used to measure these attitudes, such as the Andrews and Cutler (1974) *S-24 Scale,* the Woolf (1967) *Perceptions of Stuttering Inventory,* or Brutten's *Communication Attitude Test* (Brutten, 1985; Brutten & Dunham, 1989). If all three were given to the same group of stutterers and they yielded similar profiles across all the people tested (e.g., higher and lower scores for the same stutterers), we could say that they all have relatively high construct validity.

There are other ways of establishing construct validity as well. Sometimes published research from the literature will document or strongly indicate that a given measure has considerable support. If a clinician wanted to measure the language dominance (lateralization of the language centers in the cerebral cortex) of his stuttering clients, existing research would suggest that dichotic listening would have higher construct validity than a questionnaire about handedness or simply observing which hand is used to do a variety of tasks. (Neither dichotic listening nor handedness, of course, would have high face validity.)

The usefulness of construct validity is especially relevant when a new measure is presented. I recently developed a questionnaire called the *St.*

Louis Inventory of Life Perspectives and Stuttering (SLP♦ILP-S) as a self-study instrument to be used by people who stutter (St. Louis, 2001). It is a 13-item instrument that asks stutterers to rate themselves on 9-point scales. It cannot be considered an instrument with normative comparisons, and it is not for several reasons. The most important of these is that its construct validity has not been established. The argument could be made that its face validity is high—and that may be sufficient reason for stutterers and clinicians to use it, but we cannot know if it really measures what I think it does until I can compare it with other measures whose validity has already been established.

Predictive (criterion) validity

Predictive validity, sometimes called criterion validity, is probably the "gold standard" for validity because it refers to the ability of an indicator to predict future measures or behavior. Assuming that treatments which can foster less or no stuttering, more positive attitudes, and/or fewer stuttering-related life difficulties are available, it is highly desirable to have indicators that could predict whether or not these are likely to happen to our clients. If we had such measures, we would be much better at making accurate prognoses both about the outcome of therapy and its probable duration. For example, Andrews and Craig (1988) published a study in which the combined measures of the frequency of stuttering in %SS, the score on the *Locus of Control of Behavior Scale* (Craig, Franklin, & Andrews, 1984), and the score on the *S-24 Scale* (Andrews & Cutler, 1974) at the end of intensive therapy could predict with some accuracy that clients would maintain their gains and which ones would not.

But this issue is fraught with controversy. Most measures of intangible or nonobservable aspects of stuttering, such as attitudes toward speaking, are based on self-reports. We know that sometimes people do not report on surveys what they would actually do. An unusual study reported in *Psychology Today* 30 years ago provides an excellent illustration (Bickman, 1974). In one part of the study, experimenters stopped people on the street and asked them how much a person's dress affected them. Most of the respondents insisted that the way a person dresses would have no effect on their behavior. After being interviewed, these respondents turned a corner and were confronted with a person standing next to a parking meter looking for change in his pocket. The person asked each respondent for money for the meter. One third of the time, he was dressed casually like most everyone else, one third of the time, he was dressed in a milkman uniform, and one third of the time he was dressed as a security or police officer in uniform. The results were not surprising. He received the most dimes when dressed as a security officer, followed by the job-related uniform, and finally by casual clothes. Many have argued that similar disconnects occur between what stutterers say they do or feel and how they actually behave (Ingham, 1981). Careful research is really the only way to resolve these arguments, but in the day-to-day use of questionnaires and surveys, we need to remain alert to this potential problem.

RELIABILITY VERSUS VALIDITY

The following example from Babbie (1995) illustrates some of the ways that reliability and validity are related. Consider bullet holes in a paper target in a shooting gallery. We must assume that hitting the bull's eye reflects measuring what we intend to measure or validity. (In this example, it does not reflect the more obvious case of accuracy.) If there is a compact cluster of shots anywhere on the target, we can assume that they indicate reliable measures. Imagine such a target with a compact cluster of holes that are far from the bull's eye. In this case, they symbolize measuring something but not what is intended, that is, a reliable but invalid measure. Consider another target in which the holes comprise a wide scatter, the center of which is over the bull's eye, even though many of them missed it. On the average in this case, the shots measured what is intended or reflect valid measurement. Yet, selecting any one or two of them at random, it is likely that one would reach an erroneous conclusion because the measures are highly scattered, or are not reliable. Finally, consider a compact cluster of results, all within the bull's eye. This scenario would reflect both a reliable and a valid measure.

PRACTICAL ISSUES

Is it possible?

In selecting measures of fluency disorders, practitioners and researchers face a number of practical issues. They would certainly ask, "Is it possible?" A clinician might be convinced that a complete DNA workup is necessary for all her stuttering clients and their relatives to determine whether or not stuttering runs in that family. Unfortunately, no one has yet identified the specific gene or set of genes that are responsible for stuttering, even though some say we are getting close (Drayna, 1997; Drayna,

Kilshaw, & Kelly, 1999; Felsenfeld, 1997; Yairi & Ambrose, 2002; Yairi, Ambrose, & Cox, 1996). A researcher may wish to know what happens differently to the brain of someone who learns to approach speech as a struggle event versus someone who has always viewed speech as an easy, natural behavior. Although this might be a ripe area for experimental research, currently we do not know with any certainty what neural indicators would measure those potential anatomical or physiological changes or how we would best measure them, if we did know (e.g., see Ingham, 2003). A clinical researcher may wish to build a computer hardware and software system that could recognize and classify stutterings and then generate automatic %SS and S/M data from monologues initiated by clients over the telephone. Again, we may be close to being able to make such measures, but there are still numerous problems that need to be overcome in order to be sure that the counts of stuttered and nonstuttered syllables would be accurate, reliable, and valid. For a discussion of some of the difficult issues involved, see Howell, Sackin, and Glenn (1997a, 1997b).

Cost versus benefit?

A second practical issue relates to whether or not measures would be worth the time, effort, or money involved. Would the time involved in doing a complete battery of norm-referenced language and articulation tests with all stutterers be too great for the potential useful information to be obtained? With adults who stutter, most clinicians would answer, "yes." The answer is likely to be different when evaluating children because the population of children who stutter is at risk statistically to have a coexisting communication disorder requiring treatment or affecting the child's ability to successfully complete certain therapy tasks (see Arndt & Healey, 2001; Blood, Ridenour, Qualls, & Hammer, 2003; St. Louis, Ruscello, & Lundeen, 1992). Would it be worth our client's time and effort—or our own—to have every adult stutterer being evaluated tell his entire story of stuttering in order to discover the kind of role stuttering has played in his life? Possibly "yes"; possibly "no." If so, would it be worth the additional money to hire a trained interviewer to carry out the interviews and transcribe tapes of the interview into written protocols? Is it time-, effort-, and cost-effective to do a complete phonetic transcription and detailed disfluency analysis of a relatively few hundred syllables for every client? Some believe so (e.g., Gregory, 2003). (For another perspective, see Yaruss, 1998.) Would the cost of purchasing a system to do a complete aerodynamic workup on every client be justified, even if the testing could be done quickly and easily?

Cost, in terms of time, effort, money, and potential risks, is typically considered in juxtaposition to benefit. For example, would the benefit of including brain blood-flow or functional magnetic resonant imaging studies on subjects in a research study on linguistic loci of stuttering outweigh the risk, a question the human subjects ethics committee would surely ask to be addressed? Most ethics committees currently would disallow brain studies of children because it would be difficult to make the case that the young subjects could potentially benefit from the research. Does the potential benefit to be derived from a complete audiological evaluation for every stuttering client outweigh the time and money involved?

Evidence-based practice

Sometimes other issues that would not obviously enter into a decision of whether or not to use a certain measure become important. Recently, the concept "evidence-based practice" has become popular. Of course, good clinical practice should and must be based on evidence. Yet the issue of evidence-based practice has become somewhat of a mine field in fluency disorders with arguments about how stringently "evidence" must be defined. First, the current climate of litigation for malpractice damage has partly motivated the emphasis on evidence-based practice, particularly in medicine. Fortunately, that state of affairs has not yet reached the field of speech-language pathology, but I have submitted before that the treatment of stuttering might be an area of clinical speech-language pathology where something like this could get started (De Nil, Healey, Smith, & St. Louis, 2000). The reason is that we have such capable and informed clients, a fair number of whom are as informed—or more informed—as the clinicians who treat them. One occasionally sees references to "the incompetent speech pathologist who treated [someone]..." on self-help listservs. It is not far-fetched to assume that one reason for advocating evidence-based practice is that SLPs need to be able to justify their therapy if it ever is challenged in court. (See Appendix B.)

Another important issue is that evidence-based practice is strongly advocated by clinical researchers. After all, that is what they try to achieve. Yet, we face the situation that the weight of existing evidence has been generated by research in quite selected areas. The argument can be made that existing empirical results for using certain approaches to treatment—

or arguments that certain approaches to treatment do not have empirical bases—are based as much on the *zeitgeist* (or what is important in any point in time) as a commitment to science. Clinical research has been in vogue in the past three or four decades. Within that time frame, most of the treatments investigated have been based on operant or fluency shaping procedures that were popular during this period. To date, a critical mass of good empirical studies is not available, for example, to adequately compare stuttering modification with fluency shaping or contingent management approaches. Whereas it is difficult to argue that practitioners should not base their practice on existing efficacy data, if published evidence must be used to recommend one approach over another—even if both might be equally effective—the choice will always be to choose an approach that has a longer tradition of empirical research. The irony is that some of the most "tried and true" methods of treatment, such as a combination of desensitization and stuttering modification, are deficient in terms of the weight of the evidence supporting them, simply because efficacy research was not in vogue when they were being widely applied.[2]

Nevertheless, one very good reason for advocating evidence-based practice relates to third-party (e.g., insurance) reimbursement. Without discussing the dismal track record of obtaining such reimbursement for stuttering therapy, measurement will no doubt play a key role in any positive changes that may be forthcoming. Insurance companies require objective results, and—aside from doing the best job possible for our clients—that is a very good reason to do evidence-based practice (see Watson, 2003).

Finally and obviously, evidence-based practice is dependent on measures clinicians and researchers select for use. These, of course, will determine what will be regarded as "evidence." They will also strongly influence what is to be construed as "good evidence" or "better evidence."

TROUBLING ISSUES

In addition to these practical issues, it is worth mentioning several highly neglected issues in measurement of fluency disorders. Can current measures of stuttering discriminate or identify "covert" stutterers from typical stutterers? Similarly, can they discriminate or diagnose occasional covert stuttering? If such a measure is developed, it is likely that some-

---

[2]For a point–counterpoint discussion of this issue, see Ryan, 2003; Yaruss and Quesal, 2002b.

thing akin to Perkins' notion of a "feeling of being out of control" will play a role (Perkins, 1990). Raising an old disagreement, can existing measures for stuttering discriminate between nonstuttered excessive disfluency and stuttering? This is a particularly relevant question in studies that have shown relationships between language impairments and higher-than-normal levels of disfluency, for instance, Hall, Yamashita, and Aram (1993) and Boscolo, Bernstein Ratner, and Rescorla (2002).

Can existing measures of stuttering detect a malingerer or someone who fakes stuttering, for example, to gain disability payments (Silverman, 2004)? In a suspected case of malingering in which I had been contacted, I had to confess to the private investigator hired by an insurance company that I did not believe there was any way I could prove the person in question was malingering. This is related to the question of whether or not existing measures can discriminate between real and voluntary stuttering. At the moment, about all we can do is to rely on self-reports, which, obviously, invite real problems with malingerers.

Finally, a number of researchers have begun to explore the problem of cluttering. We face a real challenge developing indicators and measures for that illusive disorder (e.g., Daly & Burnett, 1999; St. Louis, Raphael, Myers, & Bakker, 2003). Some believe it cannot be reliably differentiated from stuttering or does not exist at all (Ryan, 2001).

A "magic battery"

For a long time, we have searched for a "magic battery" of measures for stuttering. A strong case could be made that the status and resources accorded to fluency disorders, once in the forefront of speech-language pathology (Bloodstein, 1995), have fallen behind numerous other speech, language, hearing, and swallowing disorders (e.g., Quesal, 2001) because we have not developed a standard battery of measures that work for everyone involved. I submit that such a "magic battery" would have the following characteristics: It would be relatively easy to use and cost-effective in terms of time, resources, and effort for both the person measuring and the person being measured. Administration of the battery would provide necessary and sufficient evidence of stuttering. That is, the battery would identify all the indicators that are necessary for a diagnosis of stuttering and exclude all those that either are not stuttering or are not sufficient to warrant a diagnosis of stuttering.

It is worth speculating about some of characteristics of this elusive "magic battery." All the measures in the battery would be simple and elegant but contain quantitative and qualitative information that are accurate, precise, valid, and reliable. It would be practical and comprehensible for consumers, clinicians, and researchers. Moreover, and perhaps most important, the magic battery would be equally acceptable to all stakeholders: clinicians wishing to provide excellent treatment, consumers who receive the treatment, third-party reimbursement agencies who pay for the treatment, researchers who seek to better understand stuttering or its treatment, and funding agencies who would potentially pay for the research.

At the risk of oversimplification, measurement of hearing disorders provides an excellent illustration of the sort of "magic battery" suggested here. Those in the enterprise of dealing with hearing loss have done a masterful job of deciding how to measure hearing losses. The same or very similar audiograms are used routinely by clinical audiologists, research audiologists, deaf educators, hearing aid dealers, insurance companies, federal granting agencies, consumers, and the general public. Certainly hearing loss appears to be more amenable to elegant quantification than stuttering, but the success of this approach clearly points to potential benefits of developing an analogous "audiogram" for fluency disorders.

Are we close to developing and agreeing on a "magic battery" for fluency disorders? Not at all! Measuring the essence of stuttering has been a challenge since the field of speech-language pathology began. The frequency of abnormal disfluency types or global measures of severity were popularized in the 1930s to quantify stuttering (e.g., Johnson & Knott, 1936), and these measures have been the most widely used up to and including the present in clinical reports and research investigations. Many would claim that the frequency of stuttering (notwithstanding differences of opinion of how it should be achieved) would provide the agreement needed in a major aspect of a "magic battery." Nevertheless, in light of recent debates that have been growing about the need—or lack thereof—to reclaim emotion in the diagnosis and treatment of stuttering (Manning, 2001), the field is no doubt further from agreeing on what to measure than was the case even a decade ago.

What, specifically, will be included in the battery? I do not presume to know but can advance some guesses. Certainly, it will capture the observable symptoms of stuttering. In addition to behavioral and self-report information, biochemical data will likely be included. It will also be equally relevant to all natural languages. For example, there are languages such as Turkish where "words" are highly variable in length, depending on a long series of suffixes that are applied to denote possessive, person, negation, location, certainty regarding the verb action, and so on. In such languages, there is insufficient available data to determine the extent to which the loci of stuttering is similar to English. Given these and other differences in natural languages, using stuttered syllable frequency measures would probably be more prudent than using stuttered word frequency measures, especially for clinicians who work in bilingual or multilingual settings. The battery will account for non-observable aspects of stuttering and will measure the degree of psychological and physiological "control"—or lack of "control"—experienced by the speaker. The battery will provide meaningful measurements for such intangibles as suffering, disability, or handicap as well as the need or desire for therapy and/or self-help. It will also assess the impact of stuttering on life activities and life satisfaction.

As we wait, there is fortunately much that we can and should do. First and foremost, we need to continue to plan, carry out, and publish good research on all the measures that are being used or contemplated. This is especially true of qualitative measures that deal with life experiences that make a difference to those who stutter. Another potentially fruitful enterprise would be to come up with better measures of fluency. What is fluency? What goes wrong with it in stuttering, cluttering, foreign language learning, and reading? An effort was made for several years to develop a test for fluency by the International Fluency Association (Starkweather, 1998), but the enterprise did not succeed. Finally, we most certainly will continue to better utilize the technology that changes before our eyes every day. Klaas Bakker discusses many of these promising possibilities in Chapter 9 of this volume.

The search for the "magic battery" will no doubt continue in the disjointed, erratic way that such processes unfold (Kuhn, 1962). In the meantime until we achieve an elegant "audiogram for fluency," we'll continue to discover, discard, rediscover, and advocate as best we can.

References

Andrews, G. & Craig, A. (1988). Prediction of outcome after treatment for stuttering. *British Journal of Psychiatry, 153,* 236–240.

Andrews, G. & Cutler, J. (1974). Stuttering therapy: The relation between changes in symptom level and attitudes. *Journal of Speech and Hearing Research, 25,* 208–216.

Arndt, J. & Healey, E. C. (2001). Concomitant disorders in school-aged children who stutter. *Language, Speech and Hearing Services in Schools, 32,* 68–78.

Babbie, E. (1995). *The practice of social research* (7th ed.). Belmont, CA: Wadsworth Publishing.

Babbie, E. (2001). *The practice of social research* (9th ed.). Belmont, CA: Wadsworth Publishing.

Bellak, L. (1954). *The Thematic Apperception Test and the Children's Apperception Test in clinical use.* New York: Grune & Stratton.

Bickman, L. (1974, April). Clothes make the person. *Psychology Today, 7,* 48–51.

Blood, G., Ridenour, V., Qualls, C., & Hammer, C. (2003). Co-occurring disorders in children who stutter. *Journal of Communication Disorders, 36,* 427–448.

Bloodstein, O. (1995). *A handbook on stuttering* (5th ed.). San Diego, CA: Singular.

Bloodstein, O. (1990). On pluttering, skivering and floggering: A commentary. *Journal of Speech and Hearing Disorders, 55,* 392–393.

Bloom, C. & Cooperman, D. K. (1999). *Synergistic stuttering therapy: A holistic approach.* Boston: Butterworth Heinemann.

Boscolo, B., Bernstein Ratner, N., & Rescorla, L. (2002). Fluency of school-aged children with a history of specific expressive language impairment: An exploratory study. *American Journal of Speech-Language Pathology, 11,* 41–49.

Brutten, E. G. (1985). *Communication Attitude Test,* Author.

Brutten, G. J. & Dunham, S. (1989). The Communication Attitude Test: A normative study of grade school children. *Journal of Fluency Disorders, 14,* 371–377.

Butler, P. E. (1982). Checklist for assertiveness with different people. *Self-assertion for women.* San Francisco: Harper.

Campbell, J. G. & Hill, D. G. (1994). *Systematic disfluency analysis.* Evanston, IL: Northwestern University.

Conture, E. G. (2001). *Stuttering: Its nature, diagnosis, and treatment.* Boston: Allyn & Bacon.

Cooper, E. B. & Cooper, C. S. (1985). *Cooper Personalized Fluency Control Therapy Handbook.* Allen, TX: DLM Teaching Resources.

Cordes, A. K. (1994). The reliability of observational data: I. Theories and methods for speech-language pathology. *Journal of Speech and Hearing Research, 37,* 264–278.

Cordes, A. K. & Ingham, R. J. (1994). The reliability of observational data: II. Issues in the identification and measurement of stuttering events. *Journal of Speech and Hearing Research, 37,* 279–294.

Craig, A. R., Franklin, J. A., & Andrews, G. (1984). A scale to measure locus of control behavior. *British Journal of Medical Psychology, 57,* 173–180.

Crowe, T. A., DiLollo, A. P., & Crowe, B. T. (2000). *Crowe's protocols: A comprehensive guide to stuttering intervention.* San Antonio, TX: The Psychological Corporation.

Curlee, R. F. (1981). Observer agreement on disfluency and stuttering. *Journal of Speech and Hearing Research, 24,* 595–600.

Daly, D. A. & Burnett, M. (1999). Cluttering: Traditional views and new perspectives. In R.F. Curlee (Ed.). *Stuttering and related disorders of fluency* (2nd ed.; pp. 222–254). New York: Thieme Medical Publishers.

Darley, F. L. & Spriesterbach, D. C. (1978). *Diagnostic methods in speech pathology* (2nd ed.). New York: Harper & Row.

De Nil, L. F. & Brutten, G. J. (1991). Speech-associated attitudes of stuttering and nonstuttering children. *Journal of Speech and Hearing Research, 34,* 60–66.

De Nil, L. F., Healey, C., Smith, A., & St. Louis, K. O. (2000, November). *Understanding & treating stuttering: Forecasting the future.* Seminar presented at the American Speech-Language-Hearing Association Convention, Washington, DC.

Drayna, D. T. (1997). Genetic linkage studies of stuttering: Ready for prime time. *Journal of Fluency Disorders, 22,* 237–241.

Drayna, D., Kilshaw, J., & Kelly, J. (1999). The sex ratio in familial persistent stuttering. *American Journal of Human Genetics, 65,* 1473–1475.

Erickson, R. L. (1969). Assessing communication attitudes among stutterers. *Journal of Speech and Hearing Research, 12,* 711–24.

Felsenfeld, S. (1997). Epidemiology and genetics of stuttering. In R. F. Curlee & G. M. Siegal (Eds.), *Nature and treatment of stuttering: New directions* (2nd ed.; pp. 3–23). Needham Heights, MA: Allyn & Bacon.

Gregory, H. H. (Ed). (2003). *Stuttering therapy: Rationale and procedures.* New York: Allyn & Bacon.

Guitar, B. (1998). *Stuttering: An integrated approach to its nature and treatment.* Philadelphia, PA: Lippincott Williams & Wilkins.

Guitar, B. & Grimes, C. (1977, November). *Developing a scale to assess communication attitudes in children who stutter.* Poster session presented at the American Speech-Language-Hearing Association Convention, Atlanta, GA.

Hall, N. E., Yamashita, T S., & Aram, D. M. (1993). Relationship between language and fluency in children with language disorders. *Journal of Speech and Hearing Research, 36,* 568–579.

Ham, R. E. (1999). *Clinical management of stuttering in older children and adults.* Gaithersburg, MD: Aspen.

Ham, R. E. (1989). What are we measuring? *Journal of Fluency Disorders, 14,* 231–243.

Hanson, B. R., Gronhovd, K. D., & Rice, P. L. (1981). A shortened version of the Southern Illinois University Speech Situation Checklist for the identification of speech-related anxiety. *Journal of Fluency Disorders, 6,* 351–360.

Howell, P., Sackin, S., & Glenn, K. (1997a). Development of a two-stage procedure for the automatic recognition of dysfluencies in the speech of children who stutter: II. ANN recognition of repetitions and prolongations with supplied word segment markers. *Journal of Speech, Language, and Hearing Research, 40,* 1073–1084.

Howell, P., Sackin, S., & Glenn, K. (1997b). Development of a two-stage procedure for the automatic recognition of dysfluencies in the speech of children who stutter: I. Psychometric procedures appropriate for selection of training material for lexical disfluency classifiers. *Journal of Speech, Language, and Hearing Research, 40,* 1085–1096.

Ingham, R. J. (1981). Evaluation and maintenance in stuttering treatment: A search for ecstacy with nothing but agony. In E. Boberg (Ed.), *Maintenance of fluency* (pp. 179–218). New York: Elsevier.

Ingham, R. J. (1984). *Stuttering and behavior therapy: Current status and experimental foundations.* San Diego, CA: College Hill Press.

Ingham, R. J. (2003). Brain imaging and stuttering: Some reflections on current and future developments. *Journal of Fluency Disorders, 28,* 411–420.

Ingham, R. J. & Cordes, A. K. (1992). Interclinic differences in stuttering event counts. *Journal of Fluency Disorders, 17,* 171–176.

Johnson, W. (1961). Measurement of oral reading and speaking rate and disfluency of adult male and female stutterers and nonstutterers. *Journal of Speech and Hearing Disorders Monograph Supplement No. 7,* 1–20.

Johnson, W., Darley, F. L., & Spriesterbach, D. C. (1952). *Diagnostic manual in speech correction: A professional training workbook.* New York: Harper & Brothers.

Johnson, W. & Knott, J. R. (1936). The moment of stuttering. *Journal of Genetic Psychology, 48,* 475–479.

Kalinowski, L. S., Lerman, J. W., & Watt, J. (1987). A preliminary examination of perception of self and others in stutterers and nonstutterers. *Journal of Fluency Disorders, 12,* 317–331.

Kully, D. & Boberg, E. (1988). An investigation of inter-clinic agreement in the identification of fluent and stuttered syllables. *Journal of Fluency Disorders, 13,* 309–318.

Kuhn, T. S. (1962). *The structure of scientific revolutions.* Chicago: University of Chicago Press.

MacDonald, J. & Martin, R. R. (1973). Stuttering and disfluency as two reliable and unambiguous response classes. *Journal of Speech and Hearing Research, 16,* 691–699.

Manning, W. H. (2001). *Clinical decision making in fluency disorders* (2nd ed.). Vancouver, Canada: Singular Thomas Learning.

Manning, W. H. (1994, November). *The SEA-Scale: Self-efficacy scaling for adolescents who stutter.* Paper presented at the American Speech-Language-Hearing Association convention, New Orleans, LA.

Mutti, M., Sterling, H., & Spaulding, N. (1978). *Quick Neurological Screening Test* (Rev. ed.). Novato, CA: Academic Therapy Publications.

Onslow, M., Packman, A., & Harrison, E. (Eds.) (2003). *The Lidcombe program of early stuttering intervention: A clinician's guide.* Austin, TX: Pro-Ed.

Ornstein, A. & Manning, W. H. (1985). The self-efficacy scale for adults who stutter. *Journal of Communication Disorders, 18,* 313–320.

Oyler, M. E. (1996). *Vulnerability in stuttering children* (No. 9602431). Ann Arbor, MI: UMI Dissertation Services.

Perkins, W. H. (1990). What is stuttering? *Journal of Speech and Hearing Disorders, 55,* 370–382.

Quesal, R. W. (2001, October). *The death of fluency disorders.* Paper presented at the International Stuttering Awareness Day On-Line Conference. Retrieved January 25, 2004, from www.mankato.msus.edu/dept/comdis/isad4/papers/quesal3.html

Riley, G. D. (1972). A stuttering severity instrument for children and adults. *Journal of Speech and Hearing Disorders, 37,* 314–320.

Riley, G. D. (1981). *Stuttering Prediction Instrument for Young Children* (Rev. ed.). Austin, TX: Pro-Ed.

Riley, G. D. (1994). *Stuttering Severity Instrument for Children and Adults* (3rd ed.). Austin, TX: Pro-Ed.

Riley, G. D. & Riley, J. (1989). Physician's screening procedure for children who may stutter. *Journal of Fluency Disorders, 14,* 57–67.

Rosenburg, M. (1979). *Rosenburg Self-Esteem Scale: From conceiving the self.* New York: Basic Books.

Rustin, L., Cook, F., & Spence, R. (1995). *The management of stuttering in adolescence.* San Diego, CA: Singular.

Ryan, B. P. (1974). *Programmed stuttering therapy for children and adults.* Springfield, IL: Charles C Thomas.

Ryan, B. P. (2001). *Programmed therapy for stuttering in children and adults* (2nd ed.). Springfield, IL: Charles C. Thomas.

Ryan, B. P. (2003). Treatment efficacy research and clinical treatment. *Perspectives on Fluency and Fluency Disorders, 13*(1), 31–33.

Schiavetti, N. & Metz, D. E. (1997). *Evaluating research in communicative disorders* (3rd ed.). Needham Heights, MA: Allyn & Bacon.

Shapiro, D. A. (1999). *Stuttering intervention: A collaborative journey to fluency freedom.* Austin, TX: Pro-Ed.

Sherman, D. (1952). Clinical and experimental use of the Iowa Scale of Severity of Stuttering. *Journal of Speech and Hearing Disorders, 17,* 316–320.

Siegel, S. (1956). *Nonparametric statistics for the behavioral sciences.* New York: McGraw-Hill.

Silverman, F. H. (1970). Concern of elementary school stutterers about their stuttering. *Journal of Speech and Hearing Disorders, 35,* 361–363.

Silverman, F. H. (1974). Disfluency behavior of elementary-school stutterers and nonstutterers. *Language, Speech and Hearing Services in Schools, 5,* 32–37.

Silverman, F. H. (1980). The Stuttering Problem Profile: A task that assists both client and clinician in defining therapy goals. *Journal of Speech and Hearing Disorders, 45,* 119–123.

Silverman, F. H. (2004). *Stuttering and other fluency disorders* (3rd ed.). Long Grove, IL: Waveland Press.

Spielberger, C. D., Edwards, C. D., Luschene, R. E., Montuori, J., & Platzek, D. (1972). *STAI preliminary manual.* New York: Consulting Psychologists Press.

St. Louis, K. O. (Ed.) (2001). *Living with stuttering: Stories, basics, resources, and hope.* Morgantown, WV: Populore.

St. Louis, K. O., Raphael, L. J., Myers, F. L., & Bakker, K. (2003). Cluttering updated. *ASHA Leader, 8*(21), 4–5; 20–22.

St. Louis, K. O., Ruscello, D. M., & Lundeen, C. (1992). Coexistence of communication disorders in schoolchildren. *ASHA Monographs, 27.*

Starkweather, C. W. (1998). Purposes and concepts related to the development of a test of fluency. In E. C. Healey & H. F. M. Peters (Eds.), *2nd World Congress on Fluency Disorders proceedings* (pp. 442–445). Nijmegen, The Netherlands: University Press.

Starkweather, C. W. & Givens-Ackerman, J. (1997). *Stuttering*. Austin, TX: Pro-Ed.

Stocker, B. (1980). *The Stocker Probe*. Tulsa, OK: Modern Education Corporation.

Thompson, J. (1983). *Assessment of fluency in school-age children*. Danville, IL: Interstate.

Van Riper, C. (1981). *The nature of stuttering* (2nd ed.). Englewood Cliffs, NJ: Prentice-Hall.

Vanryckegham, M. & Brutten, G. J. (2002). *KiddyCAT: Communication Attitude Test: Preschool–Kindergarten*. Orlando, FL: Authors.

Wall, M. J. & Myers, F. L. (1995). *Clinical management of childhood stuttering*. Austin, TX: Pro-Ed.

Watson, J. B. (2003). Reimbursement for stuttering treatment: Are we getting it? *Perspectives on Fluency and Fluency Disorders, 13*(1), 8–9.

Watson, J. B. (1987). Profiles of stutterers' and nonstutterers' affective, cognitive, and behavioral communication attitudes. *Journal of Fluency Disorders, 12,* 389–405.

Williams, D. E. (1978). The stuttering problem. In F. L. Darley & D. C. Spriestersbach (Eds.), *Diagnostic methods in speech pathology* (pp. 65–72). New York: Harper & Row.

Woolf, G. (1967). The assessment of stuttering as struggle, avoidance, and expectancy. *British Journal of Disorders of Communication, 2,* 158–171.

Yairi, E. & Ambrose, N. (2002). Evidence for genetic etiology in stuttering. *Perspectives on Fluency and Fluency Disorders, 12*(2), 10–14.

Yairi, E., Ambrose, N., & Cox, N. (1996). Genetics of stuttering: A critical review. *Journal of Speech and Hearing Research, 39,* 771–784.

Yaruss, J. S. (1998) Real-time analysis of speech fluency: Procedures and reliability training. *American Journal of Speech-Language Pathology, 7,* 25–37.

Yaruss, J. S. & Quesal, R. W. (in press). *Overall Assessment of the Speaker's Experience of Stuttering (OASES)*. *Journal of Fluency Disorders*.

Yaruss, J. S., & Quesal, R. W. (2002b). Research-based stuttering therapy revisited. *Perspectives on Fluency and Fluency Disorders, 12*(2), 22–24.

Appendix A

Sampling of measures from recent treatment-oriented textbooks in stuttering and a few other sources (The list is not exhaustive.)

Quantitative measures not necessarily requiring normative comparisons or for which meaningful normative comparisons are not possible

Frequency of stutterings (percentages of words or syllable stuttered or stutterings per minute of talking time)

Severity scale of stuttering

Frequency of disfluency types

Duration in number of iterations and/or seconds per moment of stuttering

Rate of speech in words or syllables per minute

Adaptation

Consistency

Anticipation (prediction) of stuttering

Self-rating of range of severity

Stutterer's Self-Rating of Reactions to Speech Situations (Johnson, Darley, & Spriesterbach, 1952)

Checklist of Stuttering Behaviors (Darley & Spriesterbach, 1978)

Iowa Scale of Severity of Stuttering (Sherman, 1952)

Stuttering Problem Profile (Silverman, 1980)

Speech Situation Checklist (Hanson, Gronhovd, & Rice, 1981)

Perceptions of Self Semantic Differential Task (Kalinowski, Lerman, & Watt, 1987)

Crowe's Protocols (Crowe, DiLollo, & Crowe, 2000)

St. Louis Inventory of Life Perspectives and Stuttering (St. Louis, 2001)

Overall Assessment of the Speaker's Experience of Stuttering (Yaruss & Quesal, 2002a)
Assessment Digest and Treatment Plan—Adolescent and Adult Verson (Cooper & Cooper, 1985)
Assessment Digest and Treatment Plan—Children's Verson (Cooper & Cooper, 1985)
Stocker Probe (Stocker, 1980)
KiddyCAT Communication Attitude Test Preschool—Kindergarten (Vanryckeghem & Brutten, 2002)
Assessment of Fluency in the School-Aged Child (Thompson, 1983)
Problem Profile for Elementary-School-Age Children Who Stutter About Talking (Williams, 1978)
Physician's Screening Procedure for Children Who May Stutter (Riley & Riley, 1989)
Checklist for Identification of Cluttering (Daly & Burnett, 1999)
Naturalness ratings of speech
Tests of articulation
Measures of coarticulation
Tests of language (vocabulary/morphology, syntax, semantics, pragmatics)
Test and measures of reading
Diadochokinesis
Rhythmokinesis
Measures of respiration
Measures of voice
Measures of hearing
Measures of laterality
Measures of motor oral motor, gross motor, visual motor skills
Measures of muscle tension
Measures of auditory sensation, memory, discrimination
Measures of neuromotor skills or integrity

Quantitative measures that have been published that permit meaningful normative comparisons or comparison to published data

Stuttering Severity Instrument (Riley, 1972, 1994)
Systematic Disfluency Analysis (Campbell & Hill, 1994)
The S-Scale (Erickson, 1969)
Modified Erickson Scale of Communication Attitudes (S-24) (Andrews & Cutler, 1974)
Perceptions of Stuttering Inventory (Woolf, 1967)
Inventory of Communication Attitudes (Watson, 1987)
Fluency Interview (Ryan, 1974)
Criterion Test (Ryan, 1974)
A-19 Scale for Children Who Stutter (Guitar & Grimes, 1977)
Children's Attitudes About Talking (CAT-R) (De Nil & Brutten, 1991)
Communication Attitude Test (Brutten, 1985; Brutten & Dunham, 1989)
Self-Efficacy Scaling for Adult Stutterers (Ornstein & Manning, 1985)
Self-Efficacy Scaling for Adolescents Who Stutter (Manning, 1994)
Stuttering Prediction Instrument (Riley, 1981)
Locus of Control of Behavior Scale (Craig, Franklin, & Andrews, 1984)
Temperament Characteristics Scale (Oyler, 1996)
State-Trait Anxiety Measure for Children (Spielberger, Edwards, Luschene, Montuori, & Plazek, 1972)
Rosenberg Self-Esteem Scale (Rosenberg, 1979)
Assertiveness Scale (Butler, 1982)
Quick Neurological Screening Test (Mutti, Sterling, & Spaulding, 1978)

Qualitative measures, judgements, or impressions
"Three Wishes" Task (Silverman, 1970)
Job Task (Johnson, 1961)
TAT Task (Bellak, 1954; Johnson, 1961)

CAT Task (Bellak, 1954; Silverman, 1974)
Case history
Client or parent interview
Dialogue/conversation with client
Unstructured play with children
Teacher interview
Audible and visible struggle or tension
Location of fragmentation during stuttering
Accessory (secondary) behaviors
Influence of DAF, metronome, masking, slowed speech, singing
Avoidance
Fear hierarchy
Family interaction
Classroom observation
Client's desire for change
Degree to which stuttering affects life choices
Degree to which person reacts with struggle
Number of stuttering relatives
Awareness and knowledge of stuttering
Psychosocial adjustment
Self-concept
Cultural factors
Eye contact
Listening
Assertiveness
Empathy
Temperament

Appendix B

*Hypothetical malpractice court case involving
selection of measures of stuttering.*

The reader is invited to consider that he or she is involved in the following scenario.

You have been called by an attorney to become an expert witness in a malpractice case. A 25-year-old adult stuttering client has alleged the following. He claims to be a "bad stutterer" who was made worse by an "incompetent speech-language pathologist." He reportedly underwent speech therapy once a week for six months with a private practitioner. He "understood" that the therapy was supposed to "reduce his stuttering." He claims his stuttering was "worse at home and at work" after the six-month period and that he lost a promotion because of it. The SLP claims he was making satisfactory progress. The client has filed a lawsuit against the SLP to recoup the $2,500 he spent on therapy plus a six-figure amount for negligent damages.

The SLP did an initial evaluation, but the very brief report stated little more than the client was a moderate-severe stutterer with 17.6%SS who had stuttered since the age of 3 years and who reported never receiving any prior therapy. Therapy, obviously, was recommended. Apparently a videotape of the client was made during the initial evaluation as he carried out a series of speaking situations ranging from rote tasks, such as counting and saying the days of the week, to oral reading, to conversations with the clinician, another listener, and several people over the telephone. He had also read a short passage aloud five times in succession with no feedback. The client had filled out a standard case history questionnaire, the *Perceptions of Stuttering Inventory* (Woolf, 1967), and had written a four-page "autobiography" of his stuttering. A daily therapy log only shows a stuttering frequency figure, and the last three session logs showed 12.1%SS, 10.5%SS, and 15.9%SS. Copies of the videotape and all the evaluation and daily log documents were subpoenaed by the defense.

Both the plaintiff attorney (for the client) and the defense attorney (for the SLP) have contacted Board Recognized Specialists in Fluency Disorders (BRSFD). The client has agreed to undergo an additional "routine" evaluation by a third ("neutral") BRSFD acceptable to both of the other specialists. The neutral specialist will carry out the measures that were agreed on and jointly recommended by both of the specialists. Each of these specialists will then seek to prove that the man did—or did not—get worse as a result of therapy. Some of these measures could be "routine" analyses of the original evaluation tape or written documents. Of course each specialist will no doubt interpret different parts of the results of both the original evaluation data and the follow-up evaluation differently. Each specialist will also advise the attorney who hired him or her about cross-examining the other specialist.

First, assume that you are the BRSFD expert witness for the plaintiff (the client who claims he was made worse). You have been advised by the attorney to make clear, simple recommendations for evaluation measures that can be defended on the witness stand. What are no more than five widely accepted measures of stuttering that you will use to prove that therapy made the client worse? For those measures, what arguments do you believe the defense will use to discredit your claim that the client is worse as a result of therapy?

Second, assume you are the BRSFD expert witness for the defense (the SLP who claims he did not make the client worse). You have been advised by the attorney to make clear, simple recommendations for evaluation measures that can be defended on the witness stand. What are no more than five widely accepted measures of stuttering that will you use to prove that therapy did not make the client worse? For those measures, what arguments do you believe the plaintiff will use to discredit your claim that the client is not really worse as a result of therapy?

In both cases, you must select a few of the very best measures that will prove that the client either did or did not get worse as a result of poor therapy. In addition, you must also try to anticipate how the opposition will try to discredit your results.

— 5 —

Early Stuttering:
Parent Counseling

Nicoline G. Ambrose
University of Illinois at Urbana-Champaign

Incorporating recent research findings on early stuttering into parent counseling

There are many shades of meaning for the word "counseling." It involves direct advice, listening, training, and most of all, a certain type of relationship between the counselor and the counselee(s). The speech-language pathologist working with stuttering children should be trained in, and feel comfortable with, providing basic counseling to parents. Regardless of the general counseling approach taken by the clinician, and regardless of the specific techniques employed, the art of counseling should draw heavily on scientific-based knowledge. Inasmuch as scientific information concerning stuttering is continually expanding, and new knowledge replaces old notions, counseling in clinical settings should reflect such developments.

Why is this important? Not only does knowledge provide power, but it also creates a context for understanding current findings and recommendations. When parents have a solid grasp of what stuttering is, their fears for their child often abate as they discover that their child's symptoms are probably quite typical of early stuttering. As with any disorder or difference, well-meaning people may have offered advice or even cast blame. Parents can better understand how and why people may have different views, and more importantly, can respond to comments, when they themselves are well informed.

In regard to early childhood stuttering, this chapter will not review the literature on parent counseling, but covers specific changes in several areas of knowledge that should impact parent counseling. These are briefly summarized below. The primary focus lies on data generated by the Illinois Stuttering Research Program.

ETIOLOGY OF STUTTERING

Over the years, three major possible ideas about causes of stuttering provided the backdrop for clinicians' interpretations and explanations to parents:

Psychogenic

In this view, some kind of emotional interference, disturbance, or maladjustment causes stuttering. In the early 1900s and into the 1950s, elements of Freud's psychoanalytic theory were applied to speech pathology, and in particular, to stuttering (e.g., Brill, 1923; Coriat, 1928; Travis, 1957). It was thought that stuttering represented a deep psychological disturbance, and that problems in family relationships, especially parent–child relationships, lay at the root of the problem. We now know that people who stutter, and parents of children who stutter, are no more apt to have psychological or psychiatric disorders than the population in general, or do not exhibit them in ways that can be suspected as the cause of stuttering (Bloodstein, 1995; Yairi, 1997). Still, the child's personality or temperament cannot be ruled out as factors that influence the disorder after it has appeared. There is active exploration of psychological factors that may impact stuttering development at the current time in children and adolescents (Anderson, Pellowski, Conture, & Kelly, 2003; Craig, Hancock, Tran, & Craig, 2003).

Learning

In this view, stuttering is an acquired behavior. It is clear that stuttering is a complex behavior, and people who stutter and clinicians alike know that certain coping and avoidance behaviors, ranging from head movement to circumlocution to complete avoidance of certain words or situations, are learned. For quite a period in time, the popular view was that stuttering originated as a behavioral response to environmental cues (Bloodstein, 1958; Shames & Sherrick, 1963; Sheehan, 1953; Wischner, 1950). The extreme of this is represented in Wendell Johnson's (Johnson & Associates, 1959) idea that normal disfluencies were behaviorally shaped into stuttering mainly through interaction between parents' negative reaction and the child's responses to them (the so-called "Diagnosogenic" theory). This would imply that because stuttering is a learned behavior, it could be unlearned. Most current scientists have largely abandoned theories of learning as the direct cause of stuttering, although it is an important factor in the development of the disorder.

Biological or organic

Such theories view stuttering as the result of structural or physiologic abnormalities. Early ideas of organic causes of stuttering are extremely numerous and have included having too large a tongue, or being left-handed and forced to write with the right hand, to mention only a few hypotheses (e.g. Bryngelson & Rutherford, 1937; Travis, 1931; see Van Riper, 1982, for a summary). Although these ideas too have fallen by the wayside, others have emerged, and it is now widely accepted that the ultimate roots of stuttering are in fact physiological in nature (Buchel & Sommer, 2004).

The current state of affairs in terms of the etiology of stuttering has evolved over many years. Clinicians must be aware of these slowly developing changes and discriminate between theories supported by scientific research and lingering traditional or common ideas that are not well supported. For example, more recently, it has become increasingly clear that there is a strong genetic component underlying childhood stuttering (Ambrose, Yairi, & Cox, 1993; Howie, 1981; Kidd, 1984), although no specific genes have been identified to date (Ambrose, Cox, & Yairi, 1997). Clinicians, then, should be able to convey to parents the information that, in order for a child to stutter, a certain genotype is necessary, but that is only part of the picture. Stuttering is a complex disorder and as such requires environmental components in addition to genes in order for stuttering to be expressed. It is not yet clear what exactly the environmental factors are (see Felsenfeld, Kirk, Zhu, Statham, Neale, et al., 2000), nor do we yet understand what precisely a gene might be doing that could result in disfluent speech. What current information seems to suggest is that a susceptibility to stuttering is transmitted genetically through one or both parents (Andrews & Harris, 1964; Kidd, 1984), and this results in some very subtle differences in how the brain develops and functions in areas that are involved in auditory perception, language formulation, and speech planning and function (Braun, Varga, Stager, Schulz, Selbie, et al., 1997; Fox, Ingham, Ingham, Hirsch, Downs, et al., 1996; Salmelin, Schnitzler, Schmitz, Jancke, Witte, et al., 1998; Sommer, Koch, Paulus, Weiller, & Bechel, 2001; Wu, Maguire, Riley, Fallon, LaCasse, et al., 1995). These areas of the brain are still maturing as a child's language skills rapidly grow. It may be only as language becomes more and more complex that the fluency generating system may break down, which is precisely the time when stuttering typically first appears. Thus, it may be that the internal development of the child can trigger the onset of noticeable stuttering. People have also reported the onset of childhood stuttering following physical or emotional stress. These environmental factors thus are not the physiologic cause of stuttering, but prompt its symptoms, just as allergies can be caused by malfunction of the immune system and triggered by presence of pollen, dust, mold, pet dander, and many other substances. Although a particular difficult time in their child's life may have triggered the onset of, or an episode of, stuttering, if that event had not occurred, something else would likely have happened resulting in the same outcome.

The impact of this information on parent counseling is great. It means that a parent can not have been too lax nor too strict, too mean, or too nice to have caused the stuttering. Most importantly, it is highly unlikely that the parent inadvertently "trained" their child to stutter, despite very old research that suggested this potential (Ambrose & Yairi, 2002). Similarly, it is most unlikely that many other hunches about the cause of stuttering harbored by parents, for example, various accidents, frights, or imitation, were sufficient to create stuttering. Generally, then, the new information about the cause of stuttering can provide an enormous relief for parents. To the best of our current knowledge, there is no good evidence of anything the parents could have done differently to avoid the onset of the stuttering. Still, once the child stutters, the immediate environment can have significant influence on its further development.

Although it is clear that genetics plays a significant role in stuttering, there are a considerable number of families of stuttering children without any known history of stuttering. There may be two reasons for this curious observation. First, there may be cases of stuttering in past generations that no one recalls. This can happen easily when stuttering lasts only a short time in childhood, but it can also occur if an individual who stuttered was not in close contact with very many other family members. Second, most current American families are small in size. When families have zero to two or three children, there is not much opportunity for stuttering to occur. For example, if genetic susceptibility to stuttering exists in a family where two only children marry and have only one child, it would not be surprising if none of them stuttered. Indeed when an individual who stutters comes from a large family, there is a much higher likelihood of finding relatives who have ever stuttered.

EPIDEMIOLOGY

Incidence and prevalence data as well as gender and age distribution are basic information about a disorder that can be used effectively in counseling. Bloodstein (1995) summarized studies that show a prevalence of about 1% for the general population, and looking at the more reliable studies (e.g., Andrews & Harris, 1964), an incidence of about 5%. Recently, the incidence figure received additional support (Mansson, 2000). More detailed evidence has been accumulating. For example, it is important for parents to know that the incidence figure means that as many as 5% of preschool children may experience stuttering for at least some period. Furthermore, new data show that at any point in time about 2.5% of this age group may stutter (Proctor, Duff, & Yairi, 2002). This, together with recent data that the prevalence of stuttering in African-American preschoolers is very similar to that of their European American counterparts (2.5%), is also revealing. It reinforces the idea that stuttering is universal, regardless of race and culture—an idea that should further reduce parents' guilt feelings about causing stuttering.

Much more important are recent data that strongly confirm a high rate (75%) of natural recovery from stuttering (Yairi & Ambrose, 1999). It is important to note that although the stuttering may have not continued over a long period of time, it is clearly stuttering rather than "developmental disfluency." Our research shows that children who eventually recovered showed clear signs of stuttering, sometimes severe, when first seen in the clinic, and should not be thought of as children who went through a phase of an extreme form of normal developmental disfluency that they somehow grew out of. Whereas in the past, prevailing learning theories influenced clinicians to tell parents that stuttering tends to increase in severity and complexity with time (Johnson & Associates, 1959), the new information radically changes the general direction of the overall prognosis. It allows clinicians to provide parents with a reasonable general probability estimate over the course of early childhood. The newest data (Yairi & Ambrose, 2004) not only provide information about the changing risk estimates with the passage of time from onset, but also provide some differentiation of risk by gender, in that more females than males recover. When stuttering begins, there are about two males for every female, but in adulthood, the male-to-female ratio rises to four or five to one, because more females than males recover.

SYMPTOMATOLOGY

Traditional counseling for parents of preschool age children who began stuttering included a significant attempt to teach parents that disfluency is normal and that all children are normally disfluent quite frequently. Such counseling included the idea that stuttering begins with normal disfluency that is erroneously perceived by parents as a problem. Data obtained during the past 25 years for normally fluent children as well as for children who stutter near the time of the disorder's onset, however, should convince clinicians to modify this information. Although the majority of normally speaking children do produce disfluencies, most of them produce few disfluencies (e.g., Yairi, 1981), and, when the disfluencies most typical of stuttering are examined, there is very little overlap between the speech behaviors of children regarded by their parents as stuttering and those children perceived to be normally fluent (Ambrose & Yairi, 1995; Ambrose & Yairi, 1999). Part-word repetitions, prolongations, blocks, and to some extent single syllable word repetition (these three types we call stuttering-like disfluencies or SLDs), constitute the majority of disfluencies in children judged to stutter. In addition, acoustic data have shown substantial differences in the temporal characteristics or timing of syllable repetitions of disfluencies of the two groups (Throneburg & Yairi, 1994), in that the repetitions of the stuttering children occur at a faster rate than those of normally fluent children. Thus, for the most part, the clinician can state that stuttering is not a normal part of development. Yairi and Ambrose (2004) described stuttering onset as occurring in a previously fluent child, typically between the ages of $2^{1}/_{2}$ to $3^{1}/_{2}$ years of age, and although stuttering is distinct from normal disfluency, there is great variability in its early expression. The onset may be gradual, or it may be as sudden as over a period of hours. It may be mild, moderate, or even severe; it may consist of primarily repetitions, primarily prolongations, or a combination. Repetitions may contain one or many extra units; secondary characteristics may or may not be present; and children may either indicate awareness of the problem very early on or appear oblivious (Ambrose & Yairi, 1994; Van Riper, 1982).

Instead of doubting the parents' initial recognition of stuttering, the counselor can probably confirm their diagnosis of stuttering. Perhaps most importantly, the new information should convince the clinician that, in most cases, parents' reports are quite reliable. The stuttering did not begin in their ears or in their supposedly negative attitudes. In fact, research by Zebrowski and Conture (1989) shows that parents of fluent and stuttering children are in very good agreement when they are asked to distinguish between normal and stuttered disfluencies in children's speech.

PROGNOSIS

The new data we have reported provide clinicians with the ability to give parents some estimation of the presence of possible risk factors for chronic stuttering for their child, taking into account several factors. If, looking at the entire group of children who stutter from onset forward, about 75% of this group experiences natural recovery within one to four years following onset (Yairi & Ambrose, 1999, 2004), then the compelling question becomes how to determine who falls into this group and who will continue to stutter. As in some other childhood communication disorders, such as late talking, the bulk of recovery occurs during the first three years of the disorder: Yairi and Ambrose (2004) reported that once a child has been stuttering for 2 years, the remaining chance of recovery is 47%; by 3 years postonset, it is 16%; and by 4 years following onset, only 5% are still statistically likely to recover naturally (without treatment). One factor in predicting possible recovery is gender. Looking at boys who ever stutter as a group, right from onset, about 25% will recover by 2 years following the onset of their disorder, about 50% will still recover, and about 25% will continue to stutter; but for girls, 45% will recover by this time, an additional 40% will still recover, and about 15% will continue (Yairi & Ambrose, 2004). Girls, then, have a somewhat better chance of recovery than do boys. The clearest prognostic indicator, however, is family history. A child from a family with a history of several individuals who stuttered into adulthood has a greater statistical likelihood of persistent stuttering, while a family history of early recovery from stuttering, or no family history of stuttering, may indicate that a child may also recover early (Ambrose et al., 1997).

In addition to family history and gender, disfluency characteristics bear some relation to fluency outcome after the first few months of stuttering. Looking back at a large cohort of children who eventually persisted or recovered from stuttering, those whose stuttering had not sharply decreased by a year or so after onset, or who continued to experience significant prolongations or blocks, were those whose stuttering continued (Throneburg & Yairi, 2001; Yairi & Ambrose, 1999, 2004). Certainly, early childhood stuttering may be quite variable in its level of severity over time. There may be minor changes, or children may stutter severely for a few weeks and then improve dramatically, only to return to more severe stuttering. Those who recover, however, have a distinct overall downward trend and any previous spikes of more severe stuttering are absent. It is also the case that children who continue to stutter do not necessarily ever have periods of severe stuttering, but at whatever level, they do not show a sharp drop in frequency of stuttering that continues to remain at a low level.

There are other differences between children who have just begun to stutter and their peers who are normally fluent, but these are of little help in predicting the future course of stuttering. The phonological development of children whose stuttering continues into school age and beyond may lag behind slightly, but soon catches up (Paden, Yairi, & Ambrose, 1999). Language skills may be precocious near the time of stuttering onset, and it appears that as these skills normalize, children may recover from stuttering (Watkins, Yairi, & Ambrose, 1999; Yairi & Ambrose, 2004). The contribution of these factors to eventual fluency status is quite small, however, and there is not yet sufficient evidence to justify use of these criteria as prognostic indicators (Yairi, Ambrose, Paden, & Throneburg, 1996).

One of the most fascinating facts is that very early severity bears no relation to eventual outcome, nor does manner of onset (Yairi & Ambrose, 1999, 2004). Characteristics of onset do not provide information, at the current stage of research, that can be helpful in planning. It is true, though, that severe stuttering is much more likely to cause reaction in the children who stutter themselves as well as in those around them and this can be of immediate concern.

Because our current appreciation of prognostic indicators does not currently enable us to know for sure which children will recover early and which will persist, it is always important that parents seek professional evaluation and that close monitoring is continued until either the child is receiving therapy or has recovered. There have been forward strides in attempts to differentiate children who are likely to spontaneously recover from those who will not when their stuttering is first noted, but the combination of factors contributing to stuttering is not yet well understood, and so it is difficult to give a meaningful percent chance for any given child to recover or persist. In this sense, what clinicians can discuss with parents are statistical probabilities, in much the same way that parents weigh other decisions in their child's educational and medical care. We can say that there are certain indicators which point to higher risk or lesser risk and that these may be considered in regard to treatment decision, waiting period, or timing of intervention. Nevertheless, so far we are talking about estimated chances, not definite prognoses; as Bernstein Ratner (1997) stated, "knowing the odds does not predict the future" (p. 31). Clinicians should make it clear that we cannot be sure what the outcome will be, with or without treatment.

TREATMENT

A critical aspect of counseling parents of preschool children who stutter is the recommendation(s) given concerning treatment. Progress in research has changed the picture in several ways in this regard.

For a long period of time, there was a strong tendency to recommend indirect treatment, that is, intervention limited to parent counseling (see Bernstein Ratner & Guitar, chap. 6, this volume). This was the case primarily for two reasons: (1) the belief that parents' attitudes and behaviors might have caused the stuttering and thus, may perpetuate it, and (2), the belief that preschool age children are mostly unaware of their stuttering, and that bringing stuttering to the child's attention in direct therapy would cause further damage. New information about causes of stuttering discussed earlier, and some data indicating that a good number of children already have some awareness of their stuttering shortly after symptoms appear must now be taken into consideration. Although indirect treatment can be warranted because parents' behavior is relevant once the child starts stuttering, there are many reasons to consider direct therapy with the preschool child once stuttering has been diagnosed. Indications that therapy should be considered, even if prognostic indicators are relatively positive for natural recovery, might include extreme distress on the part of the child.

Beyond providing valid information to parents about the nature of stuttering, counselors are expected to give specific advice about the best way to proceed in dealing with their own child's specific symptoms and needs. Although the literature is replete with advice to parents, very little of it has been subjected to rigorous scientific evaluation. The reader is referred to Bothe (2003) and Ingham (2003) for discussion of the issue of evidence-based treatment. The relatively low level of published empirical support for a variety of popular treatment programs underscores the vital role of clinicians in presenting parents with what is known, what is not known, and what is the clinician's opinion, if scientific support is lacking. Curlee and Yairi (1997), Bernstein Ratner (1997), and Zebrowski (1997) discussed this very difficult issue of weighing factors of natural recovery, treatment efficacy, and risks of unnecessary treatment versus waiting. There is no easy answer.

Over the past few years, more treatment options have become available as result of the development of several therapeutic methods that have enjoyed some experimental support for their effectiveness (see Bernstein Ratner & Guitar, chap. 6, this volume). In considering treatment, the two obvious preliminary issues are (1) is therapy indicated? and (2) if yes, when? It is not enough to point out whether or not stuttering is present—what must be determined is if a problem with stuttering is present. This hinges on several factors. First, how long has the stuttering continued? In making recommendations for very early stuttering (a few weeks to a few months in a preschool child), if the child's communication is not inhibited, that is they talk freely and volubly in spite of stuttering, and they do not show signs of distress, there is no evidence to show that waiting a few more months will exacerbate the problem as long as there is close monitoring (Curlee & Yairi, 1997; Jones, Onslow, Harrison, & Packman, 2000). A good rule of thumb is to have contact with parents within 3 months. Parents can be asked to keep a stuttering diary and to call at any time if they have questions or if the stuttering increases in severity. If, by 6 to 9 months or so past onset, stuttering has not shown a very significant drop in frequency, especially reduction or elimination of blocks and prolongations, concern rises and the issue of treatment is raised. Thus, even when therapy is not initiated after diagnosis, a plan for ongoing monitoring and reevaluation should be established and followed.

A note of caution must be made. Many clinicians never, or rarely, see the stuttering population who recovers very early. Many children do not come to the attention of an SLP until they have been stuttering for 2 or 3 years or more, well after the statistical window for natural recovery has narrowed significantly. Once stuttering has continued for a period of years, regardless of its unknown future course, the considerations for counseling are quite different from what I have discussed earlier. The diagnostic process would be much more concerned with assessing affective and cognitive components to the stuttering profile in addition to speech fluency ratings (see Montgomery, chap. 8, this volume). There would then be much more emphasis on treatment choices, including those that address the child's emotional reactions, peer reactions, and so forth (see Manning, chap. 1, this volume; Montgomery, chap. 8, this volume). Although recent advances in knowledge concerning etiology and epidemiology are exciting and hopeful, we have not yet found a crystal ball to predict a particular child's persistence or recovery patterns, the exact cause of the original stuttering symptoms, or a single therapy for stuttering that "cures" it or addresses each person's specific profile or needs. This is why clinicians have an obligation to keep up with emerging research data on each of these important issues, to most effectively counsel concerned parents and families of stuttering children.

Acknowledgment

Research Supported by: National Institutes of Health, National Institute of Deafness and Other Communication Disorders, Grant #R01-05210, PI Ehud Yairi.

References

Ambrose, N., Cox, N., & Yairi, E. (1997). The genetic basis of persistence and recovery in stuttering. *Journal of Speech, Language, and Hearing Research, 40,* 567–580.

Ambrose, N. G. & Yairi, E. (1994). The development of awareness of stuttering in preschool children. *Journal of Fluency Disorders, 19,* 229–245.

Ambrose, N. G. & Yairi, E. (1995). The role of repetition units in the differential diagnosis of early childhood incipient stuttering. *American Journal of Speech-Language Pathology, 4*(3), 82–88.

Ambrose, N. & Yairi, E. (2002). The Tudor study: Data and ethics. *Journal of Speech, Language, and Hearing Research, 11,* 190–203.

Ambrose, N. G. & Yairi, E. (1999). Normative disfluency data for early childhood stuttering. *Journal of Speech, Language, and Hearing Research, 42,* 895–909.

Ambrose, N. G., Yairi, E., & Cox, N. (1993). Genetic aspects of early childhood stuttering. *Journal of Speech and Hearing Research, 36,* 701–706.

Anderson, J., Pellowski, M., Conture, E., & Kelly, E. (2003). Temperamental characteristics of young children who stutter. *Journal of Speech, Language, and Hearing Research, 46,* 1221–1233.

Andrews, G. & Harris, M. (1964). *The syndrome of stuttering: Clinics in developmental medicine, No. 17.* London: Spastics Society Medical Education and Information Unit in association with WM. Heinemann Medical Books.

Bernstein Ratner, N. (1997). Leaving Las Vegas: Clinical odds and individual outcomes. *American Journal of Speech-Language Pathology, 6*(2), 29–33.

Bloodstein, O. (1958). Stuttering as anticipatory struggle reaction. In J. Eisenson (Ed.), *Stuttering: A symposium* (pp. 1–70). New York: Harper & Row.

Bloodstein, O. (1995). *A handbook on stuttering* (5th ed.). San Diego, CA: Singular.

Bothe, A. (2003). Evidence-based treatment of stuttering: V. The art of clinical practice and the future of clinical research. *Journal of Fluency Disorders, 28,* 247–258.

Braun, A. R., Varga, M., Stager, S., Schulz, G., Selbie, S., Maisog, J. M., Carson, R. E., & Ludlow, C. L. (1997). Altered patterns of cerebral activity during speech and language production in developmental stuttering: An $H_2^{15}O$ positron emission tomography study. *Brain, 120,* 761–784.

Brill, A. (1923). Speech disturbances in nervous and mental diseases. *Quarterly Journal of Speech Education, 9,* 129–135.

Bryngelson, B. & Rutherford, B. (1937). A comparative study of laterality of stutterers and non-stutterers. *Journal of Speech Disorders, 2,* 15–16.

Buchel, C. & Sommer, M. (2004). What causes stuttering? *PLoS Biology, 2*(2), 159–163.

Coriat, I. (1928). Stammering: A psychoanalytic interpretation. *Nervous & Mental Disorders Monographs, 47,* 1–68.

Craig, A., Hancock, K., Tran, Y., & Craig, M. (2003). Anxiety levels in people who stutter: A randomized population study. *Journal of Speech, Language, and Hearing Research, 46,* 1197–1206.

Curlee, R. F. & Yairi, E. (1997). Early intervention with early childhood stuttering: A critical examination of the data. *American Journal of Speech-Language Pathology, 6*(2), 8–18.

Felsenfeld, S., Kirk, K. M., Zhu, G., Statham, D. J., Neale, M. C., & Martin, N. G. (2000). A study of the genetic and environmental etiology of stuttering in a selected twin sample. *Behavior Genetics, 30,* 359–366.

Fox, P. T., Ingham, R. J., Ingham, J. C., Hirsch, T. B., Downs, J. H., Martin, C., Jerabek, P., Glass, T., & Lancaster, J. L. (1996). A PET study of the neural systems of stuttering. *Nature, 382,* 158–162.

Howie, P. M. (1981). Concordance for stuttering in monozygotic and dizygotic twin pairs. *Journal of Speech and Hearing Research, 24,* 317–321.

Ingham, J. C. (2003). Evidence-based treatment of stuttering: I. Definition and application. *Journal of Fluency Disorders, 28,* 197–207.

Johnson, W. & Associates. (1959). *The onset of stuttering: Research findings and implications*. Minneapolis: University of Minnesota.

Jones, M., Onslow, M., Harrison, E., & Packman, A. (2000). Treating stuttering in young children: Predicting treatment time in the Lidcombe Program. *Journal of Speech, Language, and Hearing Research, 43*, 1440–1450.

Kidd, K. K. (1984). Stuttering as a genetic disorder. In R.F. Curlee & W.H. Perkins (Eds.), *Nature and treatment of stuttering: New directions* (pp. 149–169). San Diego, CA: College-Hill.

Mansson, H. (2000). Childhood stuttering: Incidence and development. *Journal of Fluency Disorders, 25*, 47–57.

Paden, E. P., Yairi, E., & Ambrose, N. G. (1999). Early childhood stuttering II: Initial status of phonological abilities. *Journal of Speech, Language, and Hearing Research, 42*, 1113–1124.

Proctor A., Duff, M. C., & Yairi, E. (2002). Early childhood stuttering: African Americans and European Americans. *ASHA Leader, 4*(15), 102.

Salmelin, R., Schnitzler, A., Schmitz, F., Jancke, L., Witte, O.W., & Freund, H-J. (1998). Functional organization of the auditory cortex is different in stutterers and fluent speakers. *NeuroReport, 9*, 2225–2229.

Shames, G. H. & Sherrick, C. E. (1963). A discussion of nonfluency and stuttering as operant behavior. *Journal of Speech and Hearing Disorders, 28*, 3–18.

Sheehan, J. (1953). Theory and treatment of stuttering as an approach-avoidance conflict. *Journal of Psychology, 36*, 27–49.

Sommer, M., Koch, M. A., Paulus, W., Weiller, C., & Buchel, C. (2002). Disconnection of speech-relevant brain areas in persistent developmental stuttering. *Lancet, 360*, 380–383.

Throneburg, R. N. & Yairi, E. (1994). Temporal dynamics of repetitions during the early stage of childhood stuttering: An acoustic study. *Journal of Speech and Hearing Research, 37*, 1067–1075.

Throneburg, R. N. & Yairi, E. (2001). Durational, proportionate, and absolute frequency characteristics of disfluencies: A longitudinal study regarding persistence and recovery. *Journal of Speech, Language, and Hearing Research, 44*, 38–51.

Travis, L. (1957). The unspeakable feelings of people, with special reference to stuttering. In L. Travis (Ed.), *Handbook of speech pathology* (pp. 1009–1033). New York: Appleton-Century-Crofts.

Travis, L. (1978). Neurophysiological dominance. *Journal of Speech and Hearing Disorders, 43*, 275–277. (Originally published in 1931)

Van Riper, C. (1982). *The nature of stuttering* (2nd ed.). Englewood Cliffs, NJ: Prentice-Hall.

Watkins, R. V., Yairi, E., & Ambrose, N. G. (1999). Early childhood stuttering III: Initial status of expressive language abilities. *Journal of Speech, Language, and Hearing Research, 42*, 1125–1135.

Wischner, G. J. (1950). Stuttering behavior and learning: A preliminary theoretical formulation. *Journal of Speech and Hearing Disorders, 15*, 324–335.

Wu, J. C., Maguire, G., Riley, G., Fallon, J., LaCasse, L., Chin, S., Klein, E., Tang, C., Cadwell, S., & Lottenberg, S. (1995). A positron emission tomography [18F] deoxyglucose study of developmental stuttering. *NeuroReport, 6*, 501–505.

Yairi, E. (1997). Home environments of stuttering children. In R. Curlee and G. Siegel (Eds.), *Nature and treatment of stuttering*. Needham Heights, MA: Allyn and Bacon.

Yairi, E. (1981). Disfluencies of normally speaking two-year-old children. *Journal of Speech and Hearing Research, 24*, 490–495.

Yairi, E. & Ambrose, N. (1999). Early Childhood Stuttering I: Persistency and Recovery Rates. *Journal of Speech, Language, and Hearing Research, 42*, 1097–1112.

Yairi, E. & Ambrose, N. (2004). *Early childhood stuttering*. Austin, TX: Pro-Ed.

Yairi, E., Ambrose, N. G., Paden, E. P., & Throneburg, R. N. (1996). Predictive factors of persistence and recovery: Pathways of childhood stuttering. *Journal of Communication Disorders, 29*, 51–77.

Zebrowski, P. (1997). Assisting young children who stutter and their families: Defining the role of the speech-language pathologist. *American Journal of Speech-Language Pathology, 6*(2), 19–28.

Zebrowski, P. M. & Conture, E. G. (1989). Judgment of disfluency by mothers of stuttering and normally fluent children. *Journal of Speech and Hearing Research, 32*, 625–634.

—6—

Treatment of Very Early Stuttering and Parent-Administered Therapy: The State of the Art

Nan Bernstein Ratner
University of Maryland

Barry Guitar
University of Vermont

Early treatment for stuttering: What are the issues?

FIRST: IS IT NECESSARY?

A number of important issues arise in the discussion of appropriate responses to the earliest stages of stuttering in young children. A first concern, recently re-energized in recent debates (Bernstein Ratner, 1997; Curlee & Yairi, 1997; Packman & Onslow, 1998) is whether or not any intervention is necessarily warranted during the first year or so after symptoms have emerged. As Ambrose (chap. 5, this volume) discusses, the discovery of statistical predictors of chronicity and recovery require careful discussion between parents and the SLP. In some, but not all cases, parental concern over the fluency problem greatly exceeds that of the child him or herself, and some period of monitoring may be appropriate before direct therapy is advised or undertaken. This monitoring should take the form of careful diaries of the frequency and quality of dysfluency-related events over time, which we detail. It should not be a dismissal of parental concerns or a simple appointment for follow-up. However, information obtained at first consultation is crucial to diagnosis and counseling.

Because parent counseling is important in setting the foundation for later parent involvement in all aspects of fluency treatment for children, we will briefly review currently available information provided to parents regarding the likelihood that stuttering will spontaneously remit without direct intervention. The first good news that we like to share with parents is that 80% of early stuttering appears to spontaneously resolve (see Yairi, Ambrose, Paden, & Throneburg, 1996, for discussion). As Ambrose (chap. 5, this volume) details, potential prognostic indicators of spontaneous recovery include family history negative for stuttering or positive for spontaneous recovery in childhood. Girls are quite likely, statistically, to recover without direct intervention, as are children who began to stutter before age 3 and have relatively strong standardized language profiles. Because the rate of recovery is highest for those within 1 year to 18 months postonset of symptoms, time since onset can be used to weigh whether or not additional monitoring is reasonable. Perhaps surprisingly, the child's level of awareness, and the severity and profile of the stuttering pattern do not appear to predict the potential for spontaneous recovery (Yairi et al., 1996). However, in making decisions to treat or not to treat, many agree that statistical indicators are "trumped" by obvious child discomfort in speaking, as indicated by degree of struggle, avoidance behaviors, or other evidence that the stuttering is impeding the child's ability to converse comfortably (Bernstein Ratner, 1997; Guitar, 1998). When a child is discomforted by stuttering, choosing to intervene is probably warranted.

The proportion of children who spontaneously remit from stuttering between 2 and 4 years of age is rather strikingly similar to that seen in childhood expressive language delay (ELD; Rescorla & Lee, 2001). This has led some researchers and clinicians to actively develop procedures to enable parents and SLPs to "watch and see" what the child does over a selected window of time before making direct therapy recommendations (see Paul, 2001). Watch and see is distinguished from "wait and see," a more typical earlier recommendation. "Wait and see" implies that therapy is not considered necessary or advisable at a particular point, and reevaluation at a later time is recommended. In a "watch and see" strategy, the child's communicative pattern is actively monitored for signs of change, growth, improvement, or worsening of symptoms. In child language disorder, such monitoring advice is also often paired with recommendations that enable parents to enrich or shape child language gambits at home, a strategy very similar to the ones we discuss for fluency in the following sections of this chapter.

For beginning stuttering, some authors (e.g., Curlee & Yairi, 1997) propose that the suggested wait time from onset to reconsideration of direct therapy options is up to 18 months if the child does not show distress; during this period of time parents are taught how to monitor the fluency pattern and the child's reactions to fluency failure. Adverse changes that either deviate from commonly seen cyclic changes in either dysfluency pattern or the child's reaction to fluency failure should prompt return to the clinic for further evaluation and decision-making.

The bad news that emerges from the new and exciting research on patterns of early stuttering is that prognostic variables such as age of onset, genetic history, and language profiles are defined over the population, and currently do not predict specific cases well: We have no crystal ball (Bernstein Ratner, 1997). For this and other reasons, there is reasonable dispute over whether watching and seeing is the appropriate first approach to a stuttering problem. Put simply, if 80% will get better within 18 months to 2 years postonset, should we intervene with any child before that point, if the child does not appear to be adversely impacted by the dysfluencies? After all, direct therapy entails cost, inconvenience, and muddies the ability to know what proportion of our positive clinical outcomes are due to therapeutic strategies or the "tincture of time." Among the possible benefits and indications of immediate direct intervention in early stuttering are the ability of therapy to palliate parental and child discomfort, which is not trivial, even if a child will eventually recover on his own. As one of us likes to say, most headaches go away on their own, but the sale of aspirin in this country is a big business; most of us would rather intervene than wait out the natural course of painful events.

A second belief that encourages earlier rather than later intervention is the potential that earlier intervention might be more effective, although the debate on this is spirited, with data suggesting multiple interpretations. Thus, although it is attractive to believe that earlier intervention for childhood disorders is always more effective than later intervention, the data to defend this position in treatment of fluency disorders are somewhat limited, particularly for the age range of most concern (2 to 5 years). In fact, recent data conflict on whether outcomes are affected by delayed treatment time. In one study (Starkweather & Gottwald, 1993), treatment delayed by more than 1 year postonset of symptoms was associated with slower progress in treatment, whereas in two others (Jones, Onslow, Harrison, & Packman, 2000; Kingston, Hubert, Onslow, Jones, & Packman, 2003), it was actually found that behavioral intervention was slightly more effective when implemented more than 1 year postonset of stuttering symptoms.

Yet another justification for earlier intervention is the 20% of children who we know will be chronic; in this case, over-treatment is much like mass inoculations for dangerous childhood diseases: the many are treated to prevent the few who would suffer. To this end, we turn to treatment options for children at the earliest stages of stuttering.

The state of the art: A survey of direct and indirect approaches to the treatment of early stuttering

The historical treatment models for the very earliest stages of stuttering are the intellectual legacy of at least two influential founding fathers of the discipline: Van Riper and Johnson. Each contributed to current practice patterns through research and counsel that targeted different concerns in the relationship between parents and the stuttering child. In particular, what are currently termed indirect approaches to stuttering management borrow heavily from the Van Riperian and Johnsonian schools of thought, but in very different ways.

We will start with Johnson (1942, 1959, 1962), because the basic tenet of indirect therapy is the premise that children's fluency may be altered by managing the environment rather than by directly working with the child's speech. This philosophy can be traced rather directly to what has come to be called the *Diagnosogenic Theory of Stuttering,* which reflects Johnson's concern that stuttering emerges as a result of undue parental attention to what may in fact be quite normal disfluency patterns. A logical outgrowth of such a model is that management of the problem is best done without calling further attention to it, directly or indirectly. Although Van Riper had few qualms about direct work on stuttering with young children, he held the belief that children's stuttering could reflect mismatch between the child's ability to achieve adult-like speech and language targets within the system's capacity to produce speech fluently, a precursor to later "Demands and Capacities" models of stuttering (see a full issue of *Journal of Fluency Disorders,* 2000 devoted to lengthy evaluation of the model). Moreover, Van Riper (1973) was quite explicit in his assumption that children attempt to match or imitate relative styles of speech modeled by their parents, and discussed the need to create suitable fluency models: "We need to bombard the child's ears with simple phrases and shorter sentences, all unhurried and fluently spoken ... let us provide simple models for him to imitate if we desire fluency rather than gluency" (p. 405).

Thus, the direct philosophical bases of most current recommendations to the parents of stuttering children can be seen to flow from a desire to first tackle the young child's stuttering symptoms without calling his further attention to them, combined with an assumption that children actively "fine tune" speech attempts to the lexical, syntactic, and rate characteristics of parental models. Later in this chapter, we evaluate whether or not historical and current theories can be defended empirically by the available research data, and suggest ways in which the data we have and novel approaches to treating stuttering that are beginning to emerge can improve our understanding of the relationship between parental behaviors and children's stuttering.

If we intervene, how do we define success?

A less commonly discussed implication of the widespread recovery rate in very young children is how it impacts our evaluation of therapy effectiveness. In any discipline, a therapy that "cures" 80% of cases is considered rather effective, or at least a good starting point for refinement of the treatment approach. However, if 80% will get better with absolutely no systematic intervention, our standard for defining effective therapy must be higher, and must also be based on careful assessment of how recovery was linked to the timing of intervention as well as components of the intervention plan. This important concern is addressed in more detail later in this chapter.

An overview of parents' role in early stuttering treatment

We presume (and hope) that all programs involve parents, at some point, and historically, most have (see Guitar, 1998, and Onslow & Packman, 1999c, for discussion of representative approaches). Our focus in this chapter is more limited, however, and specifically discusses those programs that rely on parents' actions and interactions with their child to achieve therapeutic ends. These include indirect therapy (which may be paired with "watch and see" monitoring); "family-centered" therapy (which often consist of a broad mix of indirect and direct therapy components), and parent-administered direct therapy. The best current example of this last approach is the Lidcombe Programme (Onslow & Packman, 1999a), which is discussed in some detail in this chapter.

There is also a mix of components across therapies. Many include parental input style adjustments (such as rate, turn-taking latencies, and parental language style changes). Many target manipulation of the conversational environment (such as turn-taking and interrupting behaviors). A few instruct parents to directly model fluency-enhancing techniques. And most specify some preferred feedback strategies to be used by parents in responding to the child's fluency or moments of dysfluency. Of these, the primary types divide into acknowledgement strategies (what to do when the child appears distressed by fluency breakdown), and contingent responses to fluency and fluency failure meant to alter their frequency of occurrence (the basis for programmed parent-administered therapy such as Lidcombe).

Parental input and stuttering: Some preliminary observations

In this section, we review typical advice used when indirect therapy is suggested as the sole therapeutic component, as an added feature in melded therapy approaches, or as a component of "watch and see" recommendations. Years ago, Broen (1972) coined the phrase "the verbal environment of the language learning child." A similar construct underlies advice to parents whenever adjustments are recommended in parental speech or language style in the hopes that the child's fluency will be facilitated. It is important to understand that, just as in the overwhelming proportion of cases of delayed or disordered language development, there are no existing data to suggest that underlying deficiencies in input, conversational environment, or feedback patterns trigger the onset of stuttering symptoms. Parental behavior does not cause speech and language disorders in children, and it is important for SLPs to counsel parents to understand this properly. More specifically, it is critically important to recognize that any current recommendation for parental involvement is a palliative or treatment response that does not imply blame. Sometimes parents find this concept difficult to understand, and it is logical for any parent who is told, for example, that slowed parental speech rate may make the child's speech more fluent, to believe that their current speech rate contributed to the child's problem.

One of us uses analogies from other disorders to try to make the point more clearly. Most parents understand that juvenile diabetes does not evolve from bad diet; however, any child with a diagnosis of juvenile diabetes is best not fed foods high in sugar content, and requires careful dietary planning not utilized prior to the child's diagnosis. Similarly, children with severe allergies will do better in homes with less dust and fewer allergens, but mothers who are not "domestic goddesses," to quote comedian Roseanne Barr, do not cause allergies in their children.

Evaluation of the existing indirect therapy approaches

It is very important for SLPs to understand that relatively little research has been done to validate most of the commonly recommended components of indirect therapy. These components typically include parental speech rate and turn-taking adjustments, changes in the form and content of parents' speech to their stuttering children, and certain acknowledgement strategies. Virtually universal in their coverage in major textbooks on stuttering, as well as on major public service websites, in the following sections, we focus more closely on each set of traditional recommendations to clarify its research and efficacy basis. For a more detailed critique of "traditional" indirect approaches to treatment of stuttering in young children, see Bernstein Ratner (2004).

Input style adjustments

RATE

This component seems best supported, though weakly. Although no empirical evidence existed that parents of stuttering children spoke too rapidly before experts made the earliest recommendations that parents reduced speech rate, some later studies do in fact suggest that reduction in maternal speech rate may reduce stutter frequency (Guitar & Marchinkoski, 2001; Guitar, Schaefer, Honahue-Kilburg, & Bond, 1992; Stephenson-Opsal & Bernstein Ratner, 1988; Zebrowski, Weiss, Savelkoul, & Hammer, 1996). However, children's speech rate does not universally entrain to their parents' (see Bernstein Ratner, 2004, for summary). Some rather interesting findings, such as the possibility that stuttering frequency in children may fluctuate as a function of relative difference between the child and adult's speech rate (Kelly & Conture, 1992), have not been extensively explored. More research is needed in this area, especially single-subject design. As we reiterate later in this chapter, evidence-based application of therapy advice will eventually depend not only on trends observed in group studies, but also on assessment of individual children and parents that relates their behaviors to past research to ensure they are representative cases for application of the treatment approach, and careful assessment of changes in the parents' and children's behaviors, both in the target domain and in fluency outcome. One of us has successfully used a brief ABAB design during evaluation to assess whether parental slowing of rate will improve the child's fluency.

TURN-TAKING ADJUSTMENTS

This area of research is particularly limited but has produced promising data, including laboratory study of the relationships between turn-taking latencies and fluency (e.g., Newman & Smit, 1989), linkages between interrupting behavior and fluency breakdown (Meyers & Freeman, 1985a, 1985b; Ryan, 2000), and case studies in which reduction of interrupting behaviors improve fluency (e.g., Winslow & Guitar, 1998).

PARENTAL LANGUAGE STYLE

A more controversial component of many indirect therapy advisements is recommendations to adjust parental language style (e.g., reduce input complexity). The typical targets of these recommendations are parental length of utterance, level of syntactic complexity, and vocabulary style. As more specifically discussed elsewhere (Bernstein Ratner, 2004), this component appears particularly poorly motivated—there is no evident undue challenge placed by parents of stuttering children at onset (Bernstein Ratner & Silverman, 2000; Miles & Bernstein Ratner, 2001). Moreover, changes in parental style do not appear to exert a positive effect on children's language styles or fluency (Bernstein Ratner, 1992), and may have negative impacts on child's language development, using extensions from language acquisition literature (Hoff & Naigles, 2002; Huttonlocher, Haight, Bryk, Seltzer, & Lyons, 1991; Huttonlocher, Levine, & Vevea, 1998; Lacroix, Pomerleau, & Malcuit, 2002; Newport, Gleitman, & Gleitman, 1984; Weizman & Snow, 2001). To summarize concerns, the normal child development literature closely correlates level of parental lexical and syntactic input with subsequent child language facility, and children with reduced levels of input appear relatively disadvantaged linguistically. As one of us elaborates (Bernstein Ratner, 2004), meddling in this domain should give us pause without robust evidence of some empirical benefit to the child, which is currently lacking.

FEEDBACK ADJUSTMENTS

To review, feedback adjustments tend to fall into two basic categories: acknowledgement of the stuttering moment, and contingent responses to stuttering and fluency. Contingent response programs such as Lidcombe obviously also, by nature, include acknowledgement. Acknowledgement is often recognized as an important component in working with early stuttering (Guitar, 1998). In our own experience, we find it very useful in reducing struggle, and have seen cases where simple parental response to a moment of obvious struggle by the child (of the basic sort, "that looked hard for you to say; that's okay, sometimes I have trouble talking, too") appears to diminish signs of stress during stuttering moments. However, the specific effects of acknowledgement are not documented per se by any targeted research studies.

Contingent response programming, however, has received extensive recent scrutiny. The primary parent-administered (as opposed to clinician-administered) program utilizing contingency schedules for responding to stuttered events is the Lidcombe Programme (for full program details, see Onslow, Packman, & Harrison, 2003). Developed by Mark Onslow, Ann Packman, and colleagues at University of Sydney Australian Stuttering Research Centre, Lidcombe has extensively published data on outcomes in a series of articles in peer-reviewed journals. The combined studies on Lidcombe to date are based on a large data set, although most published work has been carried out in Sydney using the original research team (North American work is currently being carried out in Montreal and the University of Vermont, among other places). An overview of the program is provided by a manual and references available at www3.fhs.usyd.edu.au/asrcwww/treatment/lidcombe.htm; highlights of the program relevant to the topic of this chapter are provided in the following section.

An overview of Lidcombe

First, Lidcombe is a highly structured approach utilizing parental verbal contingencies for the child's speech rather than a loosely designed set of feedback recommendations. It requires a high level of parental understanding, learning, and commitment, as well as a high level of clinician guidance, monitoring, and problem-solving. Thus, Lidcombe should not be viewed as a substitute for professional guidance in stuttering treatment, but rather as a cooperative program in which professionals and parents work closely together to create daily, systematic opportunities for responses to the child's fluent and stuttered speech, in the child's natural environment. Lidcombe is categorized by its developers as an operant approach; "feedback sessions" are done at home each day for 10 to 15 minutes in one-to-one parent sessions with the child.

LIDCOMBE PARENT TRAINING COMPONENTS

Parents require systematic training to administer the components of the program. During initial stages of training, parents learn to:

- distinguish normal fluency from unambiguous stuttering;
- develop activities that create fluency and that are fun for the child. This requires parents and the clinician to appraise how language and conversational demands may affect the child's fluency patterns, and establish graded activities that produce a mix of fluent utterances with a smaller proportion of stuttered utterances;
- rate the child's fluency for each day (on a 1 to 10 scale);
- praise fluency (in a ratio of fluent to stuttered utterances suited to the child; a typical ratio is praise for five fluent utterances for each stuttered utterance monitored); in addition to praise of fluency, the parent might ask, after a period of stutter-free speech, "How was your speech just now?"
- acknowledge stutters or request corrections of stutters in a supportive manner (with at least a 5:1 ratio of praise to request-for-correction). Examples include "Oops, that was a little bumpy" and "That word was a little sticky. Do you want to try 'I' again?"

Systematic data collection is a critical component of the Lidcombe program, and has enabled the rapid dissemination of efficacy data. Speech measures used in Lidcombe include daily severity ratings made by parents, and percent stuttered syllables (%SS) taken in clinic visits by the SLP to validate progress.

The SLP's role in the program takes many forms: counselor, coach, consultant, and instructor. It is the responsibility of the SLP to teach parents how to rate the child's speech fluency, how to design activities that scaffold the appropriate level of language to get the desired ratio for feedback opportunities, and how to respond to the child's fluent and stuttered productions. The program is divided into stages.

During Stage 1, parents conduct daily sessions (for 10 to 15 minutes per day, no more, to avoid tiring or boring the child). Parents problem-solve the best time for such sessions, but often find them best done in morning, to give the child a good start on the day. Parents work with the SLP to develop activities for verbal interaction that are fun for the child. Some sites differ in the use of praise and "correction" during the initial phase of the program. For example, in Vermont, the first attempt to use a Lidcombe-like approach used praise alone for roughly 1 in 5 of the child's fluent utterances. Such praise takes the form of comments such as "that was smooth talking," "really nice speech," and so on. We note that this is not the published guidance on the program, which calls for a mix of praise and correction in all phases of therapy. However, there is anecdotal evidence that praise alone tends to reduce severity somewhat; published comparisons of praise only and praise/correction trials are not yet available.

The University of Vermont clinic now uses a standard Lidcombe program, as described in Onslow, Packman, and Harrison (2003). Treatment is individualized to the family so that a parent might begin by using praise for fluency as well as acknowledgement of stuttering and requests for self-correction. In other cases, if the parent is a little hesitant about calling attention to stuttering, the program begins with praise for fluency and, when it is clear the parent is using it effectively, contingencies for stuttering are started. It is crucial that the SLP help the parent to program activities that are fun for the child and that the parent implements feedback to achieve a 5:1 ratio of praise to contingencies for stuttering; a larger proportion of corrections may be frustrating to the child, while a smaller proportion does not appear to produce changes in fluency. As we note, this may call for sophisticated consideration of environments and utterances that promote fluency. Charting of the child's responses is also very critical, and we note that this program is unique in its insistence on parental record keeping. Parents must chart the child's behaviors in response to intervention, as shown in Figure 6-1.

FIGURE 6-1

| Sample daily rating form to be completed by parents participating in the Lidcombe program. |

THE UNIVERSITY OF VERMONT
Daily Fluency Rating Form

Child's name: ___David R.___ Form completed by: ___Mom___

Instructions: Please place an "x" or check mark in the box
representing your child's overall speech for each day.
10 = worst stuttering that you can imagine your child ever having
1 = normal fluency

10							
9							
8						X	
7					X		X
6		X	X	X			
5	X						
4							
3							
2							
1							
RATING							
	3/28	3/29	3/30	3/31	4/1	4/2	4/3
	Day/Date	Day/Date	Day/Date	Day/Date	Day/Date	Day/Date	Day/Date

10							
9							
8							
7							
6							
5							
4	X	X	X				
3							
2							
1				X	X		
RATING						X	X
	4/4	4/5	4/6	4/7	4/8	4/9	4/10
	Day/Date	Day/Date	Day/Date	Day/Date	Day/Date	Day/Date	Day/Date

Reprinted with permission of The University of Vermont.

MOVING TO UNSTRUCTURED SESSIONS

When a few weeks of uniformly lower stutter rates are observed, the SLP and parent prepare to go to less structured settings. This can be done gradually by substituting natural for structured interactions in one of the daily sessions, then another is changed to unstructured, and so on. These unstructured sessions use contingencies as before, but in natural, varied situations, such as in the kitchen during routine activities, in the car, or while playing with the child's sibling. Some families prefer to continue structured sessions for a time after unstructured sessions are phased in because both parents and children enjoy them.

MOVING TO STAGE 2

During the next stage, after percent stuttered syllables measured in weekly clinic meetings fall below 1%, and severity ratings are low (1s and 2s, out of a possible 1 to 10 scale), and if the parent is ready, the parent and child come to clinic less often as long as outcome measures stay low. During this phase, contingencies are gradually faded. As examples of this gradual "weaning" process from direct consultation, the following schedule might apply: the parent and child come once every 2 weeks (two times), then once every 4 weeks (two times), then once every 8 weeks (two times), and once every 16 weeks (once). The program also requires branching and adjustment if the child's profile changes. If the child's stuttering returns, families, in consultation with the clinician, may make more frequent clinic visits or even return to structured and unstructured sessions for a brief period.

Outcome data from Lidcombe

Lidcombe has produced some of the most plentiful peer-reviewed data on stuttering treatment available. Published outcomes are based on approximately 250 cases and growing (Jones et al., 2000). Currently available data suggest that the mean time to zero stuttering is 11 to 12 visits (with a standard deviation of 9.4); children presenting with more than an average of 5% stuttered syllables tend to require slightly more time (these findings are consistent with those reported by Starkweather & Gottwald, 1993, for their preschool program). Relevant to some concerns regarding the timing of early intervention, age and time since onset do not appear to predict time in the Lidcombe program. However, mean time since onset in Jones et al. (2000) was 12 months, well within the active spontaneous recovery window, making the relative contributions of the therapy and spontaneous recovery still an issue for future exploration. Although overall success in the program is high, some children's fluency does not improve as well or as quickly, and it is not clear what other variables targeted by Yairi et al. (1996) as predictors of chronicity might predict less favorable responses to the program, such as genetics, language ability of child, and so on. Future research should target these intake variables to ascertain whether some children are better candidates for Lidcombe than others. For example, no published data seem to have evaluated Lidcombe outcomes as a function of children's history of familial stuttering, or concomitant speech and language function, although a recent small study reported brief descriptions of these two variables for children enrolled in Lidcombe and a delayed treatment group (Harris et al., 2002).

How does Lidcombe work?

Lidcombe has not yet achieved a broad implementation base in the United States. Anecdotal responses to the program often include concern over how any operant program, including Lidcombe, can help children achieve fluency. Indeed, there does seem to be a disconnect between current research regarding the etiology of stuttering, and therapeutic models based on learning theory. Kuhr (1994) noted that operant programs for stuttering have lost favor in many settings over the years. In the United Kingdom, a recent survey by Crichton-Smith, Wright, and Stackhouse (2003) found that the majority of therapists who are not using Lidcombe do not believe that operant programs are effective in treating stuttering, although a growing number of British clinicians use and express strong support for the program. We believe that it will be important for there to be continued dialogue on the theoretical and empirical bases for developing therapeutic components and selecting a therapy approach. Although some feel that an articulated theoretical basis may not be necessary for effective stuttering therapy (Attanasio, 1999), others disagree. In considering the problem facing other fields, such as clinical psychology, some authors warn that bridging between theory and practice is important in validating therapies (Lohr, DeMaio, & McGlynn, 2003). Indeed, the potential need for SLPs to understand the mechanisms of action by which Lidcombe achieves its goals can be seen as a key to broadening its clinical application.

However, pending that dialogue, it is possible for those SLPs not trained in or compelled by operant procedures to view a program such as Lidcombe in broader ways. Viewed from varying perspectives, not everything about Lidcombe is necessarily new or best viewed only as operant. For example, the program has a large and critical parent counseling component. Its primary focus is on the parent, as it gives them more opportunity to express emotion and do something actively for the child than most other approaches to early stuttering treatment. Although data from parents in Lidcombe and other programs are not available for direct comparison, it is possible that programs that involve parents more heavily increase parents' sense of control over a difficult parenting problem, and reduce parental anxiety. Do calmer parents produce more fluent children? We do not know, but it is certainly possible. Across most fields, understanding how parental anxiety affects children's treatment outcomes is an emerging area of interest. A study that incorporated parental anxiety reduction as part of a program to treat children's anxiety showed benefits beyond a control condition in which the child's symptoms alone were treated (Cobham, Dadds, & Spence, 1998). The very act of charting severity ratings may help parents to "bind anxiety"—to feel that they are useful participants, rather than passive bystanders in their children's progress. In fact, Cobham, Dadds, and Spence (1998), in interpreting their parent training module, added that part of their observed favorable outcomes might be due to the nonspecific effects of increased parental locus of control during their children's treatment program.

A second critical component in Lidcombe is acknowledgement of the child's stuttering, which is less systematically done in many other programs. The contingent schedule of praise and correction brings the stuttering out into the open for joint work. This level of cooperation between children and parents is evident in clinical examples: in Vermont, children have asked mothers to bring in toys to work on their bumpy speech and seem very matter-of-fact about working on the stuttering. In his final publication, our late colleague Gardner Gateley (2003) noted that Lidcombe may paradoxically have validated some aspects of Johnson's diagnosogenic theory by "normalizing" dysfluency by paying attention to it, to use another one of our colleague's terms (Murphy, 1997). By normalizing the behavior, fears, anxieties, and reactions that might impede recovery are probably reduced.

The praise component of Lidcombe may also profit from further analysis. Andrews et al. (1983) noted that untangling the putative value of verbal feedback in operant interventions can be difficult. In a recent review of the effects of praise on children's motivation and behavior, Henderlong and Lepper (2002) note that preschool children interpret praise very globally, and fail to distinguish messages about ability and effort that may complicate older children's view of praised behavior. Children additionally read the value of praise based on the presumed sincerity and involvement of the praise-giver. Such findings have important ramifications for a program such as Lidcombe because they imply that the program might work better for younger children than older children, which it does. The fact that Lidcombe parents are very specific in their praise and in targeting the child's speech may additionally explain the program's success. Henderlong and Lepper also imply that modifications to substitute SLPs for parents in administering the program might result in less optimal outcomes if children reinterpret the value of their praise differently, for reasons that the current program modeling cannot explain. Although the current program was based on pragmatic exigencies in serving large numbers of children in an environment where SLPs are in short supply, one might legitimately compare, on empirical and theoretical bases, whether professional "surrogates" would be as efficient as agents of behavioral change.

This view of the "parent bond" as instrumental in achieving desired outcomes may also explain why Lidcombe appears to be one of the very few "operant" programs for young children that appears to quickly produce generalizable effects. Fey (1986) noted that operant paradigms are often lacking in "ecological validity," a claim that certainly makes sense when "teaching" or "training" sessions are conducted outside the child's natural and functional environment. Lidcombe, by contrast, is almost entirely administered in the child's everyday environment, seven days a week, rather than twice a week in the SLP's office. Viewing Lidcombe within multiple potential theoretical frameworks makes it easier to appreciate potential causative agents in its observable outcomes.

OTHER NOTIONS ABOUT HOW LIDCOMBE WORKS

There has been some speculation about the role of language in developing Lidcombe activities and responding to fluency failure. It is not trivial to establish early sessions to maximize the child's opportunity for the right mix of fluency and stuttering to feed the contingency ratio. This is where clinician guidance is paramount because most parents do not have an inherent notion of how to structure the difficulty of elicited conversational gambits. The language component is basic to many other direct therapies that try to manipulate utterance length, complexity, and pragmatics to maximize the child's ability to maintain fluency (see Guitar, 1998, for review of traditional childhood therapies, many of which include components of GILCU (Ryan, 1974): Gradual Increases in Length and Complexity of Utterance). Arguably, because the program depends on an optimal proportion of fluent and dysfluent responses by the child for praise and correction, participants in the program problem-solve this important variable more carefully and systematically than other therapy approaches.

Another potential mechanism by which linguistic variables may play a role in Lidcombe's success is the intrinsic relationship between children's disfluency and the linguistic complexity of their conversational utterances, a well-known phenomenon (see Bernstein Ratner, 1997). There is an established correlation between the likelihood of early childhood stuttering and the length and linguistic complexity of the child's output. This allows for some ambiguity in the child's interpretation of parental feedback. For example, Bonelli, Dixon, Bernstein Ratner, & Onslow (2000) analyzed pre- and postintervention variables for a subset of mothers and children enrolled in Lidcombe therapy. The intent of the study was to explore whether mothers and children who were engaged in Lidcombe activities instinctively adjusted conversational styles in ways not specifically targeted by the program. A large number of variables, including mother and child speech rate, turn-taking, and conversational contingency were examined. None changed during the course of therapy. However, a main significant finding was that children started the program with above age-level expressive language tendencies and reduced relative complexity of expressive conversational turns by end of program. That is, given the length of time enrolled in the program, beginning expressive language profiles (as measured by mean length of utterance, vocabulary diversity, and Developmental Sentence Score), expected growth rate, and postintervention language sample scores, children appeared to use more age-appropriate and less "ambitious" expressive language following therapy. We wish to emphasize that this does not suggest a "loss" of language skills, but rather a more adaptive mix of expressive language gambits and sentence production skills on the child's part. Children were using simpler language but had not lost any measurable language skills. Although we cannot verify this, one potential explanation is that children may intuit that long, complex (and statistically, more likely to be stuttered) utterances are likely to be followed by requests for rephrase. Having discerned this, they may adopt a strategy of conversing in shorter and simpler utterances, which in turn aids their ability to generate more fluent speech. Concurrent data in progress from Watkins et al. (in review) suggest that modifying children's expressive language tendencies may be a factor in remission from early stuttering. Their data are consistent in identifying a potential risk factor for persistent stuttering: a tendency for children to attempt relatively advanced language output, which presumably is not buttressed by adequate lexical retrieval and sentence assembly abilities to assure speech fluency. In this regard, we note that direct reinforcement of the children's utterances may shape their fluency-enhancing potential, and do so more effectively than parental modeling of simpler language, which does not appear to influence children's lexical and syntactic preferences.

Considerations in using Lidcombe

This program requires a large commitment from parents and children. It requires knowledgeable and warm, supportive feedback from parents. As with other interventions, when it works well, it is tempting to stop. The parent needs to be taught how to do it and how to stick with it; that is why the ratio of return visits is important. Although the program has not yet be microanalyzed for factors critical to its success, adopting parts of the program is not likely to work; it is not clear what the key components are, but partial implementation does not appear to be successful by anecdotal report.

Considerations when using parents to provide feedback and administer therapy

In this section, we address some overarching considerations when using parents as direct or indirect aides in therapy. Among them are the child's age.

For preschool children, among the positive considerations in utilizing parents to administer a program of therapy are the beliefs that, presumably, the children do not have an entrenched fear of stuttering, that they do not typically have entrenched negative attitudes toward speech, and that their main (and perhaps exclusive) source of approval and acceptance is their parents. The same cannot be said of school-aged children, who are more likely to have fear of stuttering and therefore avoidance behaviors which may require direct work on confronting stuttering. For older children, peers are important sources of approval and acceptance. Parents may be less acceptable for the older child as a therapist. Earlier, we mentioned newer studies of children's responses to praise and correction, which are more complicated in older children than in preschoolers (Henderlong & Lepper, 2002). Specifically, some older children view feedback as critical variably of ability or motivation, which can complicate the power of praise to produce desired outcomes. Finally, with older children, parents may not be able to provide the encouragement and support for open stuttering that may appear to worsen during some types of stuttering therapy, such as stuttering modification or avoidance-reduction. Thus, there is some theoretical and clinical basis for not relying on parents as administrators of fluency therapy for older children.

Using parents increases the complexity of treatment by essentially giving the SLP two clients, and can offer the opportunity for abuse/misuse of techniques by parents. For preschoolers, we have found that changing parent–child interaction patterns can be straightforward but benefit from training. Even conversational slowing, scheduling of protected one-to-one time, and reducing the frequency of interrupting may need instruction, modeling, evaluation, and shaping through clinicians' feedback. Particularly when an operant program is used that incorporates "punishment" for stuttering, parents may misapply or misuse the program. (Years ago, Costello [see Guitar, 2003] expressed reluctance to let parents do consequation of stuttering, rather than reinforcement of fluency.) It is noteworthy that "correction" in Lidcombe is modeled as a gentle and facilitative response rather than what is sometimes envisioned when a response is considered to be "punishment" within the operant framework. Indeed, some observers of ongoing parent–child sessions have commented on their almost Rogerian nature of quiet, cooperative, and reflective interaction. Finally, the Lidcombe program is careful to limit the amount of time per day initially spent in establishing fluency; there is a tremendous tendency for parents to reach the conclusion that, if a small amount of time spent on a communicative goal is productive, more time would be more productive. Unfortunately, children may become frustrated when a focus on speech dominates daily interactions.

Things we still need to learn about both indirect and direct therapy options for very young children

RISK FACTORS AND OUTCOME

It is increasingly clear that some children are predisposed to recovery more than others; when these children enter therapy trials, we need to be able to appraise whether or not the majority of successful cases were already likely to have recovered without intervention. Virtually *no* currently published evaluations of therapy programs break down their child clients in such a way. Important variables that will need to be disclosed will include gender, family history of recovered or persistent stuttering in first degree relatives, concurrent appraisal of language ability, time since onset of stuttering symptoms, and presenting profile of fluency that includes affective and cognitive components. The recent Lidcombe replication study (Harris et al., 2002) is a good first step in this direction, although still less detailed than may be necessary to link children's presenting profiles with statistically likely outcomes.

Which components of our therapeutic approaches or recommendations do the work? At this point in time, it appears quite fair to say that no one knows, for most of the indirect and the direct therapies such as Lidcombe. To distinguish among possible hypotheses, we could consider asking the following questions: Does development of carefully designed daily sessions and conscientious charting in Lidcombe increase parental awareness of fluency aggravators? Does the program shape adjustments in the child's tendency to attempt fluency-challenging utterances? What are the roles of acceptance and teaming to solve the child's problem? We just don't know. The answers to these questions will require careful "dismantling" designs to discover which features of intervention programs with young children are "active agents" of change (Lohr, DeMaio, & McGlynn, 2003) and which are incidental features. Active agents of change may or may not correspond to the theoretical bases on which intervention programs are based (Ahn & Wampold, 2001).

However, there are some things we have definitely learned about parents and early stuttering from programs such as Lidcombe. Among the lesser discussed outcomes of Lidcombe may be its lessons on the role of feedback in early stuttering. The Johnsonian legacy not to pay attention is clearly contradicted by the reported success rates of programs such as Lidcombe. If open acknowledgement of the child's stuttering by parents played a role in creating or aggravating initial patterns of stuttering, such success rates would be inconceivable. The Lidcombe Programme has offered us the opportunity to bury the misconception that adult attention to the child's distress in speaking is dangerous. Indeed, gentle, non-evaluative, and other appropriate responses to the problem, such as the joint problem solving that underpins Lidcombe may be infinitely preferable to some forms of parent advice, such as those that urge the child to "slow down and relax" (still a popular response, as a recent study sponsored by the Stuttering Foundation discovered).

Challenges in the future of parent-administered intervention

MOTIVATING THE COMPONENTS OF INTERVENTION THROUGH DATA AND THEORY

Many of the published parent involvement and advice programs consist of components that do not appear to be optimally motivated by either theory or data. Furthermore, in the case of indirect therapy components, application of advice is often a "bundled" affair, with multiple adjustments targeted simultaneously. This makes exploration of the effective, or less effective and potentially counterproductive components extremely difficult. Without such microanalysis, refinement of whatever components in indirect therapy are efficacious to improve the mix is not possible. There is a dearth of data on parents' systematic implementation of prospective targets and a lack of systematic data collection. When viewed in the context of traditional parent involvement recommendations, Lidcombe suffers from slightly complementary problems. Although cases of successful outcome abound, the mechanisms by which fluency is attained by Lidcombe children remain elusive. Although Lidcombe is rapidly being positioned as an example of evidence-based practice in speech-language pathology, evidence-based practices also require some attempt to determine how effective therapy achieves its goals. Rosen and

Davidson (2003) expressed concern that we should not confuse empirically supported treatments with empirically supported principles of change, which many programs cannot successfully or unambiguously document. Among the skills that Rosen and Davidson would teach is how to "dismantle" therapies to identify their process mechanisms and how to match therapies to individual client characteristics. Thus, specific information about children's predisposing factors for chronic stuttering such as family history and concomitant developmental profile will greatly add to our interpretation of Lidcombe outcome data and allow further refinement of the program. Additionally, although an operant model may superficially account for the data, it is in turn inconsistent with growing scientific and popular conceptualization of the underlying deficit that produces the disorder. If stuttering is in fact the outgrowth of speech motor and linguistic encoding imbalance, or any other physiological deficit, as many clinicians believe (Cooper & Cooper, 1996; Crichton-Smith, Wright, & Stackhouse, 2002), how does simple encouragement to the child to re-attempt dysfluent utterances produce lasting fluency? This gap may need to be bridged if the program's success is to be enlarged by broader adoption, and if the program's success rate is to be improved by refinements to the therapy protocol. As noted earlier, we have not conducted many meta-analyses of data to refine and extend original hypotheses about the role of parental behaviors in affecting children's fluency. All of these are valuable and necessary future goals.

A final thought about existing clinical guidance

Right now, efficacy of early intervention for stuttering and the utilization of parents in achieving therapy goals is a lot like the weather—everybody talks about it, but few either do it systematically or document it in ways that allow us to evaluate its efficacy or understand its mechanisms of action. At some level, efficacy of any approach will be a slow numbers game: the relatively low incidence of stuttering, its high and rapid remission rate, unknown levels and styles of parental implementation of recommendations, and the common tendency for parents to lose contact with professionals when the child spontaneously recovers fluency all impede our collection of needed data. We also need to more carefully evaluate existing models and data with an eye toward establishing reasonable input-output relationships in parent–child interaction and then explore when to look for effects (e.g., within a session, within days, weeks, etc.). In this regard, case studies continue to be useful when properly documented (e.g., single subject design). We may also wish to consider design issues in the many studies of parent–child input and interaction that have deepened the study of normal child language acquisition (see Schwartz & Camarata, 1985). An end result of model and data evaluation across stuttering and child development literature could lead to the development of evidence-based "unified theories of practice" such as those being proposed for early intervention/early childhood special education (Odom & Wolery, 2003). The resulting framework would encourage multiple effective approaches to remediation using identified agents and principles of behavior change.

In closing, we wish to note that we now know more about the onset and development of childhood stuttering than ever before. Although the level of evidence currently guiding clinical intervention seems bleak to some (Ingham, 2003), this real problem has spurred increased attention to the types of information needed to improve clinical care for children who stutter. Our growing body of information has helped us counsel parents and involve them more meaningfully in decisions regarding their children's fluency therapy. We are very optimistic about research advances being made in the use of both indirect and direct therapy approaches in the treatment of the earliest stages of fluency disorder, and their potential for improved outcomes for all children referred because of stuttering of recent onset.

References

Ahn, H. & Wampold, B. (2001). Where, oh, where are the specific ingredients? A meta-analysis of component studies in counseling and psychotherapy. *Journal of Counseling Psychology, 48,* 251–257.

Ambrose, N., Cox, N., & Yairi, E. (1997). The genetic basis of persistence and recovery in stuttering. *Journal of Speech, Language and Hearing Research, 40,* 567–580.

Andrews, G., Craig, A., Feyer, A-M., Hoddinott, S., Howie, P., & Neilson, M. J. (1983). *Journal of Speech and Hearing Disorders, 48(3),* 226–246.

Attanasio, J. (1999). Treatment of early stuttering: some reflections. In A. Packman & M. Onslow (Eds.), *The handbook of early stuttering intervention* (pp. 189–204). San Diego: Singular.

Bernstein Ratner, N. (1992). Measurable outcomes of instructions to modify normal parent–child verbal interactions: Implications for indirect stuttering therapy. *Journal of Speech and Hearing Research, 35,* 14–20.

Bernstein Ratner, N. (1997). Leaving Las Vegas: Clinical odds and individual outcomes. *American Journal of Speech-Language Pathology, 6,* 29–33.

Bernstein Ratner, N. (1997). Stuttering: A psycholinguistic perspective. In R. Curlee & G. Siegel (Eds.) *Nature and treatment of stuttering: New directions, 2nd edition* (pp. 99–127). Boston: Allyn & Bacon.

Bernstein Ratner, N. (2004). Caregiver–child interactions and their impact on children's fluency: Implications for treatment. *Language, Speech and Hearing Services in Schools, 35,* 46–56.

Bernstein Ratner, N. & Silverman, S. (2000). Parental perceptions of children's communicative development at stuttering onset. *Journal of Speech, Language, and Hearing Research, 43,* 1252–1263.

Bonelli, P., Dixon, M., Bernstein Ratner, N., & Onslow, M. (2000). Child and parent speech and language and the Lidcombe Program of early stuttering intervention. *Clinical Linguistics and Phonetics, 14,* 427–446.

Broen, P. (1972). *The verbal environment of the language-learning child.* Monographs of the American Speech and Hearing Association, 17.

Cobham, V., Dadds, M., & Spence, S. (1998). The role of parental anxiety in the treatment of childhood anxiety. *Journal of Consulting and Clinical Psychology, 66,* 893–905.

Cooper, E. B. & Cooper, C. (1986). Clinician attitudes toward stuttering: two decades of change. *Journal of Fluency Disorders, 21,* 119–135.

Crichton-Smith, I., Wright, J., & Stackhouse, J. (2003). Attitudes of speech and language therapists toward stammering: 1985 and 2000. *International Journal of Language and Communication Disorders, 38,* 213–234.

Curlee, R. & Yairi, E. (1997). Early intervention with early childhood stuttering: a critical examination of the data. *American Journal of Speech-Language Pathology, 6,* 8–18.

Fey, M. (1986). *Language intervention with young children.* San Diego: College-Hill Press.

Ellis Weismer, S. (1991). Child language intervention: Research issues on the horizon. In J. Miller (Ed.), *Research on child language disorders: A decade of progress* (pp. 233–242). Austin, TX: Pro-Ed.

Gateley, G. (2003). Johnson's diagnosogenic theory of stuttering: An update. *ETC: A Review of General Semantics, 60,* 22–28.

Guitar, B. (1998). *Stuttering: an integrated approach to its nature and treatment.* Baltimore, MD: Williams & Wilkins.

Guitar, B. & Marchinkoski, L. (2001). Influence of mothers' slower speech on their children's speech rate. *Journal of Speech, Language, and Hearing Research, 44,* 853–861.

Guitar, B., Schaefer, H., Donahue-Kilburg, G., & Bond, L. (1992). Parent verbal interactions and speech rate: a case study in stuttering. *Journal of Speech and Hearing Research, 35,* 742–754.

Harris, V., Onslow, M., Packman, A., Harrison, E., & Menzies, R. (2002). An experimental investigation of the impact of the Lidcombe program on early stuttering. *Journal of Fluency Disorders, 27,* 203–214.

Henderlong, J. & Lepper, M. (2002). The effects of praise on children's intrinsic motivation: a review and synthesis. *Psychological Bulletin, 128,* 774–795.

Hoff, E. & Naigles, L. (2002). How children use input to acquire a lexicon. *Child Development, 73,* 418–433.

Huttenlocher, J. (1998). Language input and language growth. *Preventive Medicine, 27,* 195–199.

Huttenlocher, J., Levine, S., & Vevea, J. (1998). Environmental input and cognitive growth: a study using time-period comparisons. *Child Development, 69,* 1012–1029.

Huttenlocher, J., Haight, W., Bryk, A., Seltzer, M., & Lyons, T. (1991). Early vocabulary growth: Relation to language input and gender. *Developmental Psychology, 27,* 236–244.

Ingham, J. (2003). Evidence-based treatment of stuttering: I. Definition and application. *Journal of Fluency Disorders, 28,* 197–207.

Ingham, R. & Cordes, A. (1998). Treatment decisions for young children who stutter: Further concerns and complexities. *American Journal of Speech-Language Pathology, 7,* 10–19.

Johnson, W. (1942). A study of the onset and development of stuttering. *Journal of Speech and Hearing Disorders, 7,* 251–257.

Johnson, W. (1962). *An open letter to the mother of a "stuttering" child.* Danville, IL: Interstate Publishers.

Johnson, W. and Associates (1959). *The onset of stuttering.* Minneapolis, MN: University of Minnesota Press.

Jones, M., Onslow, M., Harrison, E., & Packman, A. (2000). Treating stuttering in young children: predicting treatment time in the Lidcombe program. *Journal of Speech, Language and Hearing Research, 43,* 1440–1450.

Kelly, E. (1994). Speech rates and turn-taking behaviors of children who stutter and their fathers. *Journal of Speech & Hearing Research, 37,* 1284–1294.

Kelly, E. & Conture, E. (1992). Speaking rates, response time latencies, and interrupting behaviors of young stutterers, nonstutterers, and their mothers. *Journal of Speech & Hearing Research, 35,* 1256–1267.

Kingston, M., Hubert, A., Onslow, M., Jones, M., & Packman, A. (2003). Predicting treatment time with the Lidcombe Program: Replication and meta-analysis. *International Journal of Language and Communication Disorders, 38,* 165–177.

Kuhr, A. (1994). The rise and fall of operant programs for the treatment of stammering. *Folia Phoniatrica and Logopaedia, 46(5),* 232–240.

Lacroix, V., Pomerleau, A., & Malcuit, G. (2002). Properties of adult and adolescent mothers' speech, children's verbal performance and cognitive development in different socioeconomic groups: A longitudinal study. *First Language, 22,* 173–196.

Lincoln, M. & Onslow, M. (1997). Long-term outcome of an early intervention for stuttering. *American Journal of Speech-Language Pathology, 6,* 51–58.

Lohr, J., DeMaio, C., & McGlynn, F. (2003). Specific and nonspecific treatment factors in the experimental analysis of treatment efficacy. *Behavior Modification, 27,* 322–368.

Meyers, S. C. & Freeman, F. (1985a). Mother and child speech rates as a variable in stuttering and disfluency. *Journal of Speech and Hearing Research, 28,* 436–444.

Meyers, S. C. & Freeman, F. (1985b). Interruptions as a variable in stuttering and disfluency. *Journal of Speech and Hearing Disorders, 28(3),* 428–435.

Miles, S. & Bernstein Ratner, N. (2001). Parental language input to children at stuttering onset. *Journal of Speech, Language & Hearing Research, 44,* 1116–1130.

Murphy, B. (1999). A preliminary look at shame, guilt, and stuttering. In N. Bernstein Ratner & E. C. Healey (Eds.), *Stuttering research and practice: Bridging the gap* (pp. 131–144). Mahwah, NJ: Lawrence Erlbaum Associates.

Newman, L. & Smit, A. (1989). Some effects of variations in response time latency on speech rate, interruptions, and fluency in children's speech. *Journal of Speech and Hearing Research, 2,* 635–644.

Newport, E., Gleitman, H., & Gleitman, L. (1977). Mother, I'd rather do it myself: Some effects and noneffects of maternal speech style. In C. Snow & C. Ferguson (Eds.), *Talking to children: Language input and acquisition* (pp. 109–150). Cambridge: Cambridge University Press.

Odom, S. & Wolery, M. (2003). A unified theory of practice in early intervention/early childhood special education: Evidence-based practices. *Journal of Special Education, 37,* 164–173.

Onslow, M. & Packman, A. (1999a). The Lidcombe Program of early stuttering intervention. In N. Bernstein Ratner & E. C. Healey (Eds.), *Stuttering treatment and research: Bridging the gap* (pp. 193–210). Mahwah, NJ: Laurence Erlbaum Associates.

Onslow, M. & Packman, A. (1999b). Recovery from early stuttering with and without treatment: The need for consistent methods in collecting and interpreting data. *Journal of Speech, Language and Hearing Research, 42,* 398–401.

Onslow, M. & Packman, A. (Eds.). (1999c). *The handbook of early stuttering intervention.* San Diego: Singular.

Onslow, M., Packman, A., & Harrison, E. (2003). *The Lidcombe Program of early stuttering intervention: A clinician's guide.* Austin, TX: Pro-Ed.

Packman, A. & Onslow, M. (1998). What is the take-home message from Curlee and Yairi? *American Journal of Speech-Language Pathology, 7,* 5–9.

Paul, R. (2001). *Language disorders from infancy through adolescence, 2nd edition.* St. Louis: Mosby.

Rescorla, L. & Lee, E. (2001). Language impairment in young children. In T. Layton, E. Crais, & L. Watson (Eds.), *Handbook of early language impairment in children: Nature.* Albany, NY: Thomson Delmar Learning.

Rosen, G. & Davidson, G. (2003). Psychology should list empirically supported principles of change (ESPs) and not credential trademarked therapies or other treatment packages. *Behavior Modification, 27,* 300–312.

Ryan, B. (2000). Speaking rate, conversational speech acts, interruption, and linguistic complexity of 20 pre-school stuttering and non-stuttering children and their mothers. *Clinical Linguistics & Phonetics, 14,* 25–51.

Schwartz, R. & Camarata, S. (1985). Examining relationships between input and language development: some statistical issues. *Journal of Child Language, 12,* 199–207.

Starkweather, C. & Gottwald, S. (1993). A pilot study of relations among specific measures obtained at intake and discharge in a program of prevention and early intervention for stuttering. *American Journal of Speech-Language Pathology, 2,* 51–58.

Stephenson-Opsal, D. & Bernstein Ratner, N. (1988). Maternal speech rate modification and childhood stuttering. *Journal of Fluency Disorders, 13,* 49–56.

Van Riper, C. (1961). *Your child's speech problems.* NY: Harper & Row.

Van Riper, C. (1973). *The treatment of stuttering* (2nd ed.). Englewood Cliffs, NJ: Prentice-Hall.

Watkins, R. & Johnson, B. (2004). Language Abilities in Children Who Stutter: Toward Improved Research and Clinical Applications. *Language, Speech & Hearing Services in Schools,* 82–89.

Weizman, Z. & Snow, C. (2001). Lexical input as related to children's vocabulary acquisition: Effects of sophisticated exposure and support for meaning. *Developmental Psychology, 37,* 265–279.

Winslow, M. & Guitar, B. (1994). The effects of structured turn-taking on disfluencies: A case study. *Language, Speech and Hearing Services in Schools, 25,* 251–258.

Woods, S., Shearsby, J., Onslow, M., & Burnham, D. (2002). Psychological impact of the Lidcombe Program of early stuttering intervention. *International Journal of Language and Communication Disorders, 37,* 31–40.

Yairi, E., Ambrose, N., Paden, E., & Throneburg, R. (1996). Predictive factors of persistence and recovery: Pathways of childhood stuttering. *Journal of Communication Disorders, 29,* 51–77.

Zebrowski, P., Weiss, A., Savelkoul, E., & Hammer, C. (1996). The effect of maternal rate reduction on the stuttering, speech rates and linguistic productions of children who stutter: Evidence from individual dyads. *Clinical Linguistics and Phonetics, 10,* 189–206.

— 7 —

Therapeutic Change and the Nature of Our Evidence: Improving Our Ability to Help

Walt Manning, Ph.D.
The University of Memphis

My comments are based on nearly 60 years of experience as someone who stuttered during the first 25 to 30 years of my life and gradually less so since then. The experience of being someone who once stuttered brings with it some useful insights that I have shared with those whom I have helped in the past and hope to share with those I help in the future. I am also speaking as a clinician who, for more than 30 years, continues to try to improve my ability to help people who stutter. I bring the perspective of someone who enjoys conducting research, writing, and speaking about the phenomena of stuttering—how it is that humans are able to speak more, and sometimes less, fluently. I believe that when you study anything for many years, especially if you have some enthusiasm for the task, you can become reasonably proficient. Or, at the very least, you begin to form some definite opinions about the experience and the phenomena.

A (very) few comments about traditional treatment

In order to place the majority of my comments into perspective I would like to begin by commenting about "traditional treatments for stuttering." However, I say relatively little about these, for most readers already have some sense of the history of thinking in fluency disorders. The zeitgeist has swung back and forth among different ways of considering and treating the problem: physiological, psychogenic, learning theory, behavioral. The literature indicates that many of the current opinions can be described as multifactorial and somewhat eclectic (Conture, 2001; Cooper

125

& Cooper, 1992; De Nil, 1999; Guitar, 1998; Riley & Riley, 2000; Smith & Kelly, 1997), which I think is a good way to view stuttering and its treatment. In this volume, Montgomery (chap. 8, this volume) discusses the basic strategies that incorporate stuttering modification and fluency shaping techniques and about the importance of counseling—although I know there are a few people who do not think counseling skills are necessary for successful change. In some cases they are not.

In thinking about what are called "traditional treatments," it is fascinating to think about what we were taught and some of the things we then taught our students only a few decades ago. In discussing treatment of children, it was common to see opinions such as:

> *Do nothing at any time, by word or deed or posture or facial expression, that would serve to call Fred's attention to the interruptions in his speech. Above all, do nothing that would make him regard them as abnormal or unacceptable.* (Johnson, 1962, p. 3)

> *Do not permit the child to hear the word stuttering used about his speech. Do not ... do anything that makes it necessary for him to think about speaking or to conclude that he is not speaking well.* (Eisenson & Ogilvie, 1963, p. 323)

Admonitions not to intervene, at least directly, with young children were frequent:

> *The way to treat a young stutterer in the primary stage is to let him alone and treat his parents and teachers.* (Van Riper, 1939, p. 2)

We taught our students that most or all children moved from "primary" to "secondary" stuttering as they progressed through the development of the disorder, something we now know not to be the case with many children, based on the longitudinal research of Yairi and his colleagues (e.g., Yairi & Ambrose, 1992a, 1992b, 1999; Yairi, Ambrose, & Niermann, 1993; Yairi, 2004; see also Ambrose, chap. 5, this volume).

Many changes have occurred as we have studied and continued to develop an understanding of stuttering phenomena. During the later part of the past century, we became much more direct in how we treated people who stutter. As a field, we have made dramatic, and I think useful, changes in our views of what we should be doing—especially with young children (Onslow, Packman, & Harrison, 2003). For a variety of reasons we became less inhibited about using the word *stuttering* and more confident that we could successfully change speaking behaviors by identifying and systematically modifying them. New models of language acquisition, as well as new technology for understanding the characteristics of fluent speech, have helped us make better decisions concerning assessment and intervention in fluency disorders.

Nevertheless, obstacles remain to the development of unambiguously "best practices" in fluency, and not all of them are directly related to the evidence base for assessment and therapy recommendations. One is the representativeness of people who participate in basic and clinical research programs. I have commented on other occasions (e.g., Manning, 1999, 2001) about how few people from the overall population of people who stutter we are able to connect within our clinics and laboratories. Based on the prevalence of stuttering, particularly in early childhood (Yairi, 2004), and the total current population of the United States of 294 million people (Population Reference Bureau Report, 2004), there are likely to be at least 3 million people who stutter in the United States. It's clear that clinicians have contact with small fraction of this total. We know very little about the hundreds of thousands of people who do not or cannot ask for our help. We don't know for certain, but it is likely that more than 90% of the people who stutter manage as well as they can without any professional help (see Reeves, chap. 11, this volume). Some do pretty well on their own and find creative (although occasionally maladaptive) ways to survive and even succeed in spite of their stuttering. They find assistance in the form of supportive friends, mentors, and self-help organizations. It could be that the people we do have contact with in our clinics and laboratories are representative of the larger population of people who stutter. Or perhaps they are not. In any case, it would seem wise for us to keep in mind that our understanding of stuttering phenomena is based on a highly select, extremely small, and possibly biased sample of people who experience this problem. Of course, even for those people we are able to see, there are several other factors that come into play that sometimes lead to disagreements about what we should be doing and the nature of successful therapy.

People believe that they are helping, but not all agree on how: Current concerns in evidence-based practice

At the risk of sounding naïve, I believe that nearly everyone who is in this field believes that the therapeutic approach and associated techniques they advocate are helpful. Even people who are not in this field think that what they suggest to people who stutter is helpful. They think this because, in many cases, the speaker tends to stutter less when they suggest various things. As we know, nearly anything that serves to highlight stuttering events will result in a decrease of the behavior.

I tend to have a difficult time understanding people who advocate simple or effortless techniques for helping humans to change—especially when they are trying to sell you a device or product (see Bakker, chap. 9, this volume). Furthermore, when it is stuttering that they are trying to change and if the device or technique is focused solely on reducing the frequency of stuttering, I am usually suspicious. I believe that effective treatment is about far more than decreasing the number of times that someone stutters. Successful therapy is also closely tied to the quality of stuttering, the quality of fluency, and the speaker's ability to communicate and problem solve. Successful therapy also has to do with being able to live a life that is unrestricted, even if it occasionally involves stuttering. As it turns out, many people who stutter can become better communicators than nonstuttering adults. They can, for example, have better than average scores on measures of communicative effectiveness (Hillis & Manning, 1996).

Our field has diverse and differing opinions, even about the few things I have said so far (Ingham & Cordes, 1999; Ryan, 2001). And although working with people who tend to disagree with your perception of a phenomenon can be frustrating at times, I must admit that I sometimes enjoy the disagreements. For example, one area of disagreement that lies at the core of assessing the effectiveness of stuttering therapies is the relationship among behavioral, cognitive and affective components of the disorder (the so-called "ABC's of stuttering") and the "directionality" of treatment effects across these domains. Does improving fluency improve the speaker's cognitive and emotional responses to speaking demands? Does addressing these responses provide any fluency benefits? In order to answer these questions, I believe that people will need first to agree that stuttering is more than speech dysfluencies, and it is not clear we have come to any consensus on this issue.

To illustrate this, following Bill Murphy's presentation about stigma and shame (some of the affective and cognitive features for many who stutter) at the Division 4 Leadership Conference in Monterrey, California (later published as Murphy, 1999) I overheard some of the attendees saying things like "What's this thing about stigma?", "What's the big deal about shame?", and "What does shame have to do with stuttering?" Such expressions support comments by Bob Quesal (2002), who was of the opinion that some professionals do not seem to "get it" when it comes to stuttering. They insist on viewing stuttering primarily or only in terms of its overt behavioral features. Most of the general public does not "get it" and, of course, that is not surprising. But if someone is a professional in the field, I think that they should "get it." It is a big part of our job to help our students "get it" (Manning, 2004). If you do not understand, you are unlikely to provide help, or the help you provide may not fully address the scope of the problem the client brings to us.

In 1971, Wingate suggested that many professional clinicians have a fear of stuttering, and I believe he was correct, although he and I have viewed many other topics about the nature and treatment of stuttering quite differently. I think that some clinicians and researchers in the field need more therapy than their clients when it comes to being able to tolerate stuttering. Furthermore, I suspect that too many clinicians view fluency in a categorical manner and verbally (or nonverbally) convey the notion of fluency as "good" and stuttering as "bad."

A fluent speaker is assumed to be a good speaker and a good clinical outcome; a stuttering speaker is judged to be something less. The speaker and their parents take this set of values home with them. Everything else being equal, although they never are, fluency *is* generally better and stuttering does get in the way of communicating. It is nice to be fluent, and I, for one, really enjoy it. Fluency-facilitating behaviors can be effective and I use them myself and I do my best to get my clients to use them. But that is very different than communicating the categorical and judgmental attitude about the "goodness" of fluency and the "badness" of stuttering. It is far from that simple. It is possible to stutter and, by doing it well, to become a very good communicator.

Likewise, while I disagree with Ingham & Cordes (1999) that inducing fluency "cures" the basic problem in stuttering (see also Ryan, 2001), I absolutely agree with their assessment (Ingham & Cordes, 1997) that,

> One reasonable goal for stuttering treatment, therefore, might be self-judged acceptability of fluency, a goal that would depend on self-judgments of stuttering and of related behaviors and perceptions. (p. 430)

Such comment recognizes that the speaker's opinion of the stuttering experience often provides more useful and valid information than the clinician is able to glean from the behaviors that are so obviously apparent on the surface. What the clinician can observe from overt stuttering behavior is obviously useful, but often it does not carry the depth of information available from the speaker's perceptions. In fact, the surface features that we spend so much effort measuring often provide information that is contradictory with the speaker's self-judgments and perceptions (e.g., word avoidances and substitutions). That is, a person may seem more fluent than is clinically relevant by avoiding the stuttering moment altogether through circumlocution or word-choice changes. Ingham and Bothe (1997) included another sentence that I also think is a good suggestion:

> ... fluency might be usefully defined by the speaker's private sensation of acceptable, or acceptably effortless, speech production. (p. 431)

I think that is exactly correct. We should be paying more attention to what our clients are telling us; certainly to their judgments of their fluency, but also to their reports of experiences as a person who does or does not stutter. Their descriptions will help us to better understand their circumstances and the ways in which we can provide assistance that will enable them to make the changes that *they* need. Not necessarily what *we* want them to do, but what *they* need to do. Continuing along a related line of thinking I would like to briefly discuss some ...

Unique aspects about our field of fluency disorders

ETIOLOGY "WARS"

Some of the unique characteristics of our field make our professional lives difficult. For example, stuttering is unique in the field of communication disorders because there have been and continue to be a wide variety of (often controversial or diametrically opposed) proposed etiologies, including the persisting notions that stuttering evolves from environmental stressors or is learned. And because of its overt symptomology, unlike Specific Language Impairment, for example, throughout history, nonprofessionals observing people who stutter have been willing to join in with professionals to suggest both causes and remedies. The willingness of people to offer theories about causes and related cures may be due to such things as the apparent simplicity of the problem (we all get stuck on words and sounds now and then), the natural variability of the surface features of stuttering (sometimes the speaker is fluent and sometimes he is not), and the rather sudden fluency-enhancing (or disrupting) properties of a multitude of speaker as well as listener responses. The confusion continues today, particularly on the Internet, and not only across cultures but even within them. And because we don't know precisely what combinations of intrinsic and extrinsic factors precipitate and maintain stuttering, we often find it difficult to explain this to people who call on us. When we receive calls from the local newspaper or television station seeking simple answers to questions about stuttering, it can be difficult to provide easy explanations about the nature of the problem and ways we are able to help. As with many multifaceted human problems, an informed clinical response depends on the person sitting in front of us, his environment, needs, and concerns. Thus, easy, standardized answers don't do the job. The variety of ways that we might appropriately respond may lead to confusion and even the notion that we, as professionals, don't have answers. Throughout history, whenever anyone said they knew what caused stuttering and, especially, how to fix it, everyone listened. These days, talk show hosts seem to be particularly susceptible to claims that the cure for stuttering is at hand (see, e.g., archives of "miracles" performed on popular daytime programs, such as "Oprah" or "Montel Williams," www.oprah.com/tows/pastshows/200302/tows_past_20030203.jhtml; www.montelshow.com/show/past_detail_8_4_2003.htm).

VARIABILITY

Because fluency, even in nonstuttering speakers, is so variable (Goldman-Eisler, 1961) it's easy to make the argument that stuttering is the most variable of all human communication disorders. The natural variability of both the quantity and quality of stuttering behavior combined with the many ways that individuals respond to the problem make it especially difficult to assess and to obtain good measures of progress and valid indicators of treatment efficacy (see St. Louis, chap. 4, this volume). Certainly people with other communication problems reach plateaus in their progress during and following treatment, but they rarely experience the extreme variability associated with fluency. Closely related to variability is the issue of ...

RELAPSE

Stuttering is also unique among communication disorders because, given the current state of our understanding and therapeutic skill, relapse following "successful" intervention is common, particularly in adolescents and adults. In the past few decades, several authors have conducted good research addressing this problem, but relapse continues to be unique to stuttering (Boberg, 1981; Craig, 1998; Craig & Calver, 1991; Craig & Handcock, 1995; Culatta & Goldberg, 1995; Perkins, 1983; Silverman, 1992). In my opinion, the pervasive nature of relapse is an indicator that good therapy is about considerably more than changing the surface features of the problem (DiLollo, Neimeyer, & Manning, 2002).

STIGMA

Stuttering is unique because people often assign a high level of stigma to the behavior. Many investigators have documented negative reactions from listeners to people who stutter; St. Louis and his colleagues (2001) have shown that stuttering is as much or more stigmatizing than a wide variety of other problems and characteristics that people may possess. It is no wonder that people who stutter quickly develop a wide and often creative variety of covert responses to their circumstances (Blood, Tellis, Gabel, Mapp, et al., 1998).[1] They naturally develop high levels of fear, quickly learn to avoid situations and people, and learn how to escape from a variety of feared stimuli. Their response to even the *possibility* of stuttering can result in restriction of their lives and contribute to the handicap associated with the problem. The stigma associated with stuttering makes it difficult to get people to come to treatment and often inhibits progress during treatment, especially when treatment is conducted in the real world. Stigma and fear make it extremely difficult to disclose the problem to others and to experiment with and modify stuttering behaviors. Our clients who have success in working against the inertia of stigma and fear have done so by taking risks and showing great courage.

THE PSYCHOTHERAPEUTIC COMPONENT

Stuttering is at least somewhat unique among the disorders of our specialty area because successful therapy often includes a strong psychotherapeutic component—either intended, as in a stuttering modification pro-

---

[1]Note, however, that Blood, Blood, Tellis, & Gabel (2003) found that the majority of the 48 adolescents they studied did not perceive stuttering as a stigmatizing condition. This was especially the case for older adolescents (ages 16–18) who were less likely than younger adolescents (ages 13–15) to interpret stuttering as a stigmatizing condition. However, the majority of these adolescents, particularly the younger group, attempted to conceal their stuttering.

gram ("It really is okay to stutter"), or peripheral, as in the Lidcombe Program (Onslow, Packman, & Harrison, 2003), where parents spend lots of quality time talking openly with their children about "bumpy" and "easy" speech (i.e., "You're okay when you stutter. So let's do it this way"; see Bernstein Ratner & Guitar, chap. 6, this volume.) If a supporting and understanding therapeutic relationship is part of the program, psychotherapeutic change is likely to occur. If we go beyond working on the surface features of the problem, we are helping people to better manage their lives, to make better choices, to change the way they view themselves and their world, and to live improved lives. Ways to do this include selflessly listening (Luterman, 2001), understanding, modeling new ways of conceptualizing or re-framing the client's situation, and encouraging risk-taking behavior. We can also do this by helping the speaker to become at least somewhat desensitized to the experience of stuttering. Some people need fewer (or more) of these components than others and that is one reason why some people have good success in programs that exclusively emphasize fluency shaping techniques, and others do not.

Professionals in the field who stutter

The specialty practice of stuttering treatment is also unique in that there are many people working in the field who have personally experienced the problem, something that is rarely the case in other areas of communication disorders. I do not know if anyone has counted but it would be interesting to know how many of the professionals in our field have a history of stuttering. Certainly, a number of our most visible researchers and master clinicians do. Outside of our field, one area of helping where this is also common is in drug and alcohol rehabilitation programs. If you have seen those people in action, you know that they cannot be fooled by some of their clients' actions and comments since they have heard it all before. They have been there, taken the journey, and they know the deal. They say things like, "If an alcoholic is moving their lips they are lying." That is a difficult thing to hear, but it is true.

Some would say that having so many researchers and clinicians in our field who have stuttered, or to some degree still do, is a bad thing. It is true, of course, that being a person who stutters may filter one's view, influence the research questions that one asks, and possibly even skew the interpretation of data. Others would argue that the person with a history of stuttering has a unique perspective for such people have lived the experience. They have played the game.

I played adult league soccer for 20 years and I could always tell when we had a referee who had not played the game. These referees knew the manual and could blow a whistle when they thought someone had violated a rule. But it was often apparent that they did not fully understand the game and would make the incorrect interpretation of a rule because they did not have the deeper and sophisticated understanding of what was occurring. They were calibrated to the manual but not necessarily *this* particular game, the level of skill for the players, and the physical and psychological context of the competition. Because they lacked such understanding, these referees rarely made an outstanding no-call—that is, not blowing the whistle and stopping the action when that would have been an incorrect response. Furthermore, the referees who had not played were less likely to appreciate the dynamics of the game and rarely seemed to sense the flow and beauty of the action. I suppose the same is true for all of us who do not fully understand such activities such as soccer, opera, art, or ballet. In stuttering, this phenomenon is similar to a clinician's lack of appreciation for the degree of courage that it takes for a client to enter into an everyday, but much feared, speaking situation, or to attempt to try a newly learned therapy technique for the first time. It can be more difficult to have empathy if you have not been on the journey. But, it is not impossible. There are many people who have never stuttered who obviously "get it." In our field, there is a long line of such people based on what I have heard them say and what they have written.

EVERYTHING WORKS!

One final unique aspect of stuttering that I mention is the fact that nearly anything and everything works to get people to be fluent, at least for a while. This may seem like a positive attribute for a disorder, and as we have mentioned, likely contributes to the variety of well-meaning suggestions offered by people who don't fully understand the phenomena. Those of us who logged on to the International Stuttering Awareness Day interactive computer conference in October 2002 (www.mnsu.edu/comdis/isad5/isadcon5.html), organized by the incredibly able and affable Judy Kuster, found that some people believe that elephant dung works pretty well. Those of us who were able to watch *The Oprah Winfrey Show* in February 2003 saw that the *not* very new idea (if one has been following the literature over the years) of using altered feedback "works" for some people who stutter (see also Bakker, chap. 9, this volume). Years ago, Bloodstein (1949) provided a listing of at least 150 things one could do to temporarily suspend even severe stuttering. This unique aspect of stuttering is especially difficult to explain to people who do not understand the essential structure of the problem. Of course, the problem with quick, and often enigmatic, "fixes" is that the repair is also of short duration, as Bakker (chap. 9, this volume) notes.

Even people who have no idea what they are doing and do not have a clue about the phenomena of stuttering are able to do and say things that result in brief periods of increased fluency. I recently corresponded via e-mail with an economics student in Sarajevo. He describes how shortly after the war in his country ended in 1992 he began to be optimistic about the future. The fact that English is not his primary language adds to the poignancy of his comments:

> Somewhere during this time I experienced one moment of, I can say, full absence of Stuttering. That was during a few treatments with one, so called, mystic (spiritualist) who used technique of rising self-confidence with his suggestive power (suggestive speech) in combination with some objects that radiate some energy (some kind of metals). No matter how this method sounds strange, it really helped me, and after treatment I felt self-confident and I didn't think on Stuttering anymore. The way I think totally changed in the way that I wasn't making decisions on possibility of appearance of Stuttering anymore. But that period passed quickly.

There is no shortage of such help around the world, including in the United States. And most professionals understand why such approaches do not produce lasting benefits. But even for good clinicians, including those using a comprehensive and well-documented program with lots of efficacy data to back it up, there are abject failures. It is common for many clients to drop out of the treatment program prior to its completion (O'Brian, Onslow, Cream, & Packman, 2003), something that is rarely reported in studies of treatment outcome (see also Quesal, 2003). Thus, although it is easy to see why elephant dung doesn't work, we also need to understand why some well-reasoned and well-documented programs fail some very motivated clients.

One final comment about things that "work." What is usually meant by "working" (by some researchers and by many clinicians) is that the frequency of stuttering decreases. I was often able to decrease my stuttering a lot during my high school and college days. I did this by choosing not to talk or avoiding certain words. The more I avoided and changed words, the less I stuttered. Such strategies do not work well for everyone who stutters, but they worked great for me. Few people had any idea what was going on and, at the time, I felt pretty good about that. On occasion, I could also be fluent by talking in a slightly unique or artificial way (using a slight accent, speaking slowly, or pretending to be angry). No one knew that I was sneaking around my stuttering, although I suspect that some people thought I was weird. I would sometimes pretend not to know the answer to certain questions. For example, someone would ask me where I lived and I would fluently say, "A small town in Pennsylvania." They would look at me for a moment and say "Where?" I would respond with, "Ah, it's about 85 miles north of Harrisburg." My listener might then guess and say "Lock Haven?" "A little east of there," I would respond. They would make another attempt and guess "Bloomsburg?" "About halfway between Lock and Bloomsburg," I would answer. This would go on until someone guessed "Williamsport" and the riddle would be solved. Although few thought I was someone who stuttered, I am quite sure that some listeners thought I was stupid or strange. I think that is how a lot of people who stutter survive—those who do not receive any treatment, decent treatment, or treatment that overemphasizes complete and total fluency.

Of course, these are all examples of why it is unfortunate that the frequency of stuttering is the dependent variable, often the only one, in the vast majority of the research conducted in our field. I believe that decreasing the frequency of stuttering is *necessary* but *not sufficient* for helping most school age children, adolescents, and adults who stutter.

STUTTERING AND THINGS YOU CAN STICK IN YOUR EAR

One of my problems with assistive devices that you stick in your ear is that such approaches encourage the person who stutters to take a passive role in working with stuttering. It tends, I think, to inhibit the possibilities for taking an active role and experimenting with possibilities, risk-taking, and elaborating who you can become, especially if you are still a young person.

On the other hand, there is some interesting research on placebo effects that has relevance to stuttering. Herbert, Lilienfeld, Lohr, Montgomery, O'Donohue, et al. (2000) suggested that medicine prior to the 17th century is really a history of placebo effects. These authors also make a convincing argument that what we term "placebos" are not therapeutically inert variables (see also Wampold, 2001). For example, research participants (and the experimenters) often figure out who is getting the real medicine and who is getting the placebo. Research indicates that placebos play an active role in psychotherapeutic change in that they influence patients' thinking about their ability to change. Herbert et al. (2000) found that many investigators have found little difference in efficacy between placebos and drugs for adults. This remained the case even when the experimental and control participants knew what they are receiving.

I am mentioning the placebo effect here because it happens in our therapy and it most certainly happens when you are using elephant dung and electronic devices. These approaches "help" in the same way as our suggestions to the client about what to do help. That is, it helps them to achieve agency—"The extent to which individuals can act for themselves and speak on their own behalf" (Monk, Winslade, Crockett, & Epstein, 1997, p. 301). As individuals are able to position themselves as an agentic person, good things generally happen. People can do this either with or without our help. The support provided by self-help groups can facilitate this change (see Reeves, chap. 11, this volume). I suspect that is what occurs for some people when they take part in the McGuire program (McGuire, 2000) and even, for a few, when they use fluency-enhancing electronic devices. It may be that nearly anything that helps a person to change their "old story" and see the possibility that they have alternative ways of living can be useful.

Treatment efficacy

It is good for us to be able to demonstrate that what we do when we try to help people really does work (see *Guidelines for Practice in Stuttering Treatment*, ASHA, 1995). But in order to do efficacy research, things must be controlled and variables must be standardized. I would argue, however, that the very act of such control and standardization makes therapy, especially stuttering therapy, less effective. The less spontaneous, dynamic, and evolving the relationship is, the less effective the therapy is likely to be. If we package the therapy into a protocol or manual that follows a prescribed sequence for each person, the flow of therapy is likely to be grotesquely distorted. Standardizing a treatment may make it easier to "teach" and easier to evaluate statistically to justify support from agencies who are paying for therapy. But it does not make it better (see Wampold, 2001). In the area of psychotherapy, there is evidence suggesting that adherence to a clinical manual suppresses the effect of what has been demonstrated to be the most powerful variable contributing to treatment success: clinician competence (Shaw, Elkin, Yamaguchi, Olmstead, Vallis, et al., 1999).

A number of years ago (Manning, 1999), I compared arguments about which therapy strategy is "best" to discussions that some of my teenage friends used to have about which car is best (Chevy vs. Ford type of arguments). I believe that people who spend time arguing about which treatment is the most efficacious reflects the same level of sophistication as teens driving around in pickup trucks (perhaps with a kid doing something inappropriate to the word Ford or Chevy stenciled on the back window). The field of clinical psychology has recognized that comparative efficacy is difficult to evaluate given the range of patient and clinician variables that must inevitably be considered meta-analyses of treatment effects (Westen & Morrison, 2001). Studies that pit one approach to solving a clinical problem against another have sometimes been referred to as "racehorse research." Sometimes one horse wins, sometimes another. Aside from being so obviously egocentric (as in "my program is better than yours"), spending a lot of effort on such research suggests that a field of study is still in its adolescence, since more highly developed disciplines have discovered that many therapeutic approaches are equally effective.

One of my basic take-home messages is that the treatment approach that "works" is most likely determined by the characteristics of the client rather than by clinicians or the dogma of a particular therapy program. If given the opportunity, people will inform us of the tools they need. As an example, Brad Sara was 14 years old when he wrote the following about what he learned while rock climbing:

> When I was climbing, my partner and I were giving each other advice about which way to go and which rock might be the best one to go to next. In learning to manage my stuttering, I have found that I need to find the things that work for me. I need to use my own best words to express myself, find my best chances or opportunities to talk and to discover which tools work best for me. Other people can guide me, but I have to find my own "right rocks." (see Manning, 2001, p. 267)

The process of therapeutic change

Regardless of the treatment approach that is used, there are some basic characteristics of the change process. From observing successes and failures over the years (my own as well as others') and what I have read, I think these things are true for learning about and changing one's speech as well as just about everything else that humans endeavor to do.

READINESS FOR CHANGE

Research has indicated that successful treatment is related to the clinician's ability to connect with the client's readiness for change (Prochaska, DiClemente, & Norcross, 1992). For some time, I have believed that the most critical factors in the success of treatment have to do with the *readiness of the speaker for change*, the *competency and experience of the clinician*, and the *timing* of when and how these two people intersect (see also chap. 6 in Manning, 2001). These factors may be less influential if the person is a young, preschool child. The success of early intervention programs suggests this to be the case. Using the Lidcombe program (Onslow, Packman, & Harris, 2003) as an example, the parents involved in that program are as motivated as people can be—in this case, to help change their child's fluency (see Bernstein Ratner & Guitar, chap. 6, this volume). As Mark Onslow and his colleagues pointed out, stuttering may not be so terribly complex before age 6. What they are doing works because the parents, especially the mothers, make it work. Changing their child's speech is extremely important to them and most are willing to do whatever it takes. They make it fun for the child. They model and develop a good relationship during the process. They reward fluency more than they highlight stuttering. They empower the child with the process of change (see Guitar, 2003). And for these children, the percentage of syllables or words stuttered is likely to provide good, valid, and efficacious information. For older speakers, there are other things that are likely to have greater validity (see chap. 6 in Manning, 2001).

CHANGE IS USUALLY CYCLICAL

In the past few years, I have had the opportunity to interact with an international scholar in psychology at the University of Memphis. Robert Neimeyer's area of study has to do with loss and the grieving process. Among other things, he has found that when dealing with things such as the loss of a loved one, the process is cyclical. It is not necessarily, as Kubler-Ross (1969) and her model suggested, linear and step-wise. Anyone who has ever worked through the loss of a loved one, a relationship, or a job knows that you often revisit different stages of the process, stages that you thought you were finished with. In many ways you do this for the rest of your life. It takes continual effort to do the work necessary for fluency change at many levels, including behavioral, emotional, and cognitive. This cyclical view of the change process corresponds to consistent findings by authors such as Prochaska and DiClemente (1992) and Prochaska, DiClemente, and Norcross (1992). With this process, things are never quite "back to normal" as implied by the linear model where you work through your grief, eventually reaching a stage called "acceptance."

The same could apply to changes made during therapy for stuttering. As the speaker engages in the process of separating from a lifelong relationship with stuttering, many things are never the same again. The speaker is not likely to move in a linear pattern from a life of stuttering to one of recovery. It is much more likely to be a pattern of cyclical movement through a process of gradually more successful management of stuttering-related behaviors and choices. As techniques for modifying stuttering and enhancing fluency are developed they must be practiced in progressively more difficult speaking situations. The new ways of talking (and thinking) are unstable; they sound and feel peculiar, even more than the stuttering patterns that are so familiar and well-practiced. The new ways of speaking and making choices are strange, and for some time, life is considerably less predictable than the more familiar world of stuttering. The lack of predictability may even result in a significant degree of (cognitive) anxiety (see DiLollo, Manning, & Neimeyer, 2003). To the extent that the new behavioral and cognitive changes that accompany increased fluency are effortful and threatening, the speaker may find that the more attractive alternative is to return to what most familiar—stuttering.

CHANGE TAKES A LOT OF PRACTICE

It is obvious, I think, to anyone in the helping professions (not to mention teachers, coaches, and parents) that it is very difficult to change complex human problems and conditions. Furthermore, in order to become accomplished at anything, we need to practice a lot. When we conduct therapy we meet our clients for a few hours a week. Among other things, we demonstrate a variety of techniques, and clinician and client practice the techniques both in and beyond the clinic setting. When we see the client for a subsequent session, we may experience the following dialogue.

Client: "I tried that technique and you know what? It didn't work."

Clinician: "How many times did you try it?"

Client: "Two or three times!"

When we get that response, perhaps we should then say something like: "Well, try it *500 times* and come back." Obviously, when learning anything, it is necessary to work through a hierarchy of gradually increasing difficulty. But the bottom line is that you have to practice a lot.

Research concerning the development of expertise in a variety of activities (sports, dance, chess, and a variety of other domains across the arts and sciences) suggest that 10 or more years of intensive preparation are necessary to attain an international level of performance (Ericsson & Smith, 1991; Simon & Chase, 1973). In summarizing the literature on the development of expertise, Berliner (1994) found agreement with the opinion that 10,000 to 20,000 hours of practice are required in order to perform an activity appropriately and effortlessly: hallmarks of exemplary performance. Although natural ability plays a part in the development of expertise, empirical evidence indicates that training and preparation are necessary prerequisites for superior performance (Ericsson & Smith, 1991).

Anyone who has worked at learning a complex physical or mental activity begins to realize that it will be necessary to practice to the point where the activity is overlearned and habitual. Only when such a level of performance is achieved will you be able rely on a technique under stress or time pressure (or threat to your physical or psychological well-being). Once a technique has been integrated, you will use it because you begin to trust your ability to use it. Just as Brad wrote about rock climbing, I have written (Manning, 2001) about the experience of dealing with fear while kayaking and the need to overlearn techniques, such as rolling back to the surface, to conquer those fears. If you are unwilling to practice and incorporate the techniques to the extent that they become part of you, you will not even attempt the technique when you are under stress.

In addition, many of the things we are taught to do, at the outset at least, seem terribly counterintuitive. I believe it would be fun to sit around a table with several friends and think of the long list of things that are counterintuitive until you "learn" how to do them. For example, "When driving, steer in the direction of a skid." It makes no sense until you practice and master it and then it seems perfectly reasonable. Once you learn to respond to that situation in that way it seems the only logical way. But you have no understanding of this at the outset. When you are kayaking, you learn that leaning into a standing wave or a rock is by far the best thing you can do. But, until you receive instruction and practice, it is the last thing that would occur to you. When traveling at even a moderate rate and turning a motorcycle to the *right* you push on the *right* handgrip; when turning to the *left* you push on the *left* handgrip. It's called countersteering and it allows the bike to lean in the direction you want to go. It is often appropriate in various forms of karate to step toward rather than away from the attacking person. Similarly, as a person who stutters, voluntarily stuttering is the last thing you would think of doing. It's the least intuitive thing imaginable, but if you are willing, the experience can get you going in the right direction. That is, rather than reflexively trying to avoid or escape the experience, it is counterintuitive to make the choice to stay in the moment of stuttering. But staying in the moment allows the speaker to experiment with stuttering rather than reflexively being afraid and running from it.

Finally, the importance of practice, or you might say persistence, is underappreciated. Smith (1999), Guitar (1998), and others have reported data indicating that what we do when we practice, even as adults, is to reform parts of our central nervous system (De Nil & Kroll, 2001). It feels like that is what happened to me and my speech. It feels that way to me as I begin to master some new, relatively complex activity. It feels like the new skills, new motor sequences, and new understanding become part of you. It reminds me of David Luterman's (2003) comments about the techniques of counseling: "The key to counseling is the congruence of the counselor: as congruence increases, technique slips away or more accurately becomes infused into personality" (p. 20). Practice makes that happen.

Time spent in formal therapy involves some learning and some practice, but mostly I think it should be spent refining these new ways of thinking and doing. I have stated (Manning, 2001) that many of the techniques that we use in therapy are not rocket science and that they are easily understood. I have recently begun to adjust my opinion about this for I have come to realize that, in order to be of value, a technique needs to be practiced with precision. I believe that as clinicians, we need to be rigorous in our judgments of what we accept as satisfactory when clients are learning and practicing techniques. If a technique is not done precisely right, it is not as likely to be useful during the challenge of everyday speaking situations. Most of us believe we have mastered a technique well before we really have and it is not until we have a really good instructor that we realize that we can benefit from further improvement. If you do not think this is true, enroll in a yoga or karate class. A clinician who understands this will challenge the client to achieve the highest degree of skill possible and will improve the client's accuracy, speed, confidence, and success.

BEYOND THE TECHNIQUES

Although I have argued for the importance of techniques, I want to suggest that therapeutic success goes well beyond the mastery of technique. People have come up to me at meetings such as the National Stuttering Association to say something like "You are fluent, what is your secret? What technique should I use?" It has always struck me as a form of "magical thinking" to suggest that there is a technique (or even a set of behavioral techniques) that, by themselves, will solve the problem of stuttering. I've often had the thought that some clinicians who attend workshops are searching for such techniques as well. Although techniques are an important part of therapy, they are like so many carpenters' tools. The experienced clinician must sense what tool is the best one for the job and choose the timing for when the tool should be used. As a clinician, we can demonstrate tools and techniques, but unless people are ready for them they will not be effective, even if they are done correctly. Until the client is desensitized and experienced enough to know how and when to use the technique it will have little meaning.[2] I have had clients tell me, "You know, I never understood that technique even though we talked about it and practiced it a lot. I did not even try it for several years. But a couple of weeks ago I began using it again and it really works!"

As we have mentioned, sometimes the techniques do *not* work. Adolescents sometimes feel the things you ask them to do are childish or silly, especially if they resemble things a clinician had asked them to do when they were younger. Techniques do not work if the physiologic and linguistic components of speaking are a mystery or if the speaker continues to be scared to death of stuttering. One of my clients was like that.

---

[2]See Allard & Starkes (1994) for a discussion on the distinction between "knowing" (cognitively responding to relevant environmental information) and "doing" (executing well-practiced actions and techniques) in the performance of expert athletes.

On two different occasions he went through a 3-week intensive fluency shaping program. Each time he did reasonably well during the first 2 weeks of practice in the clinical setting. During the third week, he moved into a more worldly setting in order to transfer skills—mostly at a shopping mall. He was overwhelmed and both times he spent his entire third week in a men's room of the mall. Certainly boring, possibly dangerous. It is clear that he needed some desensitization about stuttering. It is difficult or impossible to walk across a 6-inch beam 40 feet above the ground until you have had some experience at 15 feet or 20 feet. I asked this same client to use that metaphor with what it was like to use his techniques with me in therapy. He said it was like walking a board 5 feet above the ground. I asked him what it was like to do that in a college class and he said 100 feet! As clinicians, we need to attend to these genuine and influential perceptions by the speaker. The initial work using self-efficacy scaling (Hillis, 1993; Hillis & Manning, 1996; Manning, 1994; Ornstein & Manning, 1995) appears to provide one way to quantify and predict success for approaching and achieving improved levels of fluency beyond the safety and security of the treatment setting.

Sometimes the techniques require a different, often unique way of talking that sounds unnatural and feels strange. Talking in a new way, even if it results in fluency, feels like a facade and it is not who you are. You feel like you are not being honest to yourself and that adds to the anxiety when you try to communicate. Unless a person is desperate and totally committed to a program, they are not likely to use such techniques, at least for long. And clients are not always willing to use techniques if the clinician is not willing to use them as well. Every person who stutters who is in therapy should, at least one time during the process, look their clinician in the eye and say something like, "If you are so good, let's see you do it!"

Many of the things I have learned over the years seem to be related to the principles of the cyclical nature of change, persistent practice, and "becoming one" with the techniques. My experiences as a swimmer in college, as a parent, as a soccer coach, while learning to kayak, and, most recently, while taking classes in karate have taught me that the processes of change and learning are similar during all of these activities. Sometimes I use examples from these experiences in my classes. Often, 22-year-old students, who only a year before were more concerned with whether or not they were going to ride on the homecoming float, do not understand why I am talking about these nonprofessional experiences. On the other hand, the people who are in their 30s or 40s, who have done some of these things—most often parenting—are nodding their heads "yes" and looking at me with subtle but knowing smiles. They have applied many of these same principles to their various life experiences.

So how do we continue to improve as clinicians? We usually begin by conducting therapy the way we are taught to do it. As our mentor provides us with a philosophy and shows us an accompanying series of techniques, we gradually become knowledgeable about a particular approach. We are content to have an approach that will give us a sense of direction and activities we can do in the therapy setting. We believe that this approach will work for many reasons (our mentors have demonstrated that it does; we have some experience making it work with a few clients; we have seen data indicating the success of the approach). After having success with the approach, we may come to believe that this is the best approach and that followers of other views are less sophisticated or downright wrong.

Hopefully, either because of professional continuing education requirements or, better yet, our natural curiosity, we obtain additional experience and new information. We connect with others who are experimenting with new and different approaches. If we are open to these ideas, we find that some of them appeal to us and we begin to experiment ourselves and possibly incorporate these techniques into our treatment. We incorporate ideas and techniques from many sources and begin to develop our own style that resonates with who we are and thus become more effective clinicians. We find our own "right rocks" as we develop philosophical and practical responses that coincide with who we are and who we are becoming. I suspect that this is when we start to become our best and the most effective as clinicians.

Challenges and some suggestions

HOW DO WE PROPERLY PREPARE CLINICIANS?

It has been well documented for many years that many clinicians need help in understanding and treating stuttering (e.g., Ainsworth, 1974; Brisk, Healey, & Hux, 1997; Cooper, 1985; Wingate, 1971; Yaruss & Quesal, 2002). The new ASHA continuing education requirements will certainly help to "retool" and fix the gaps in the backgrounds of some clinicians, but are clearly not a solution to the basic problem. CEUs do not necessarily have to be related to anything having to do with fluency unless you have specialty recognition in that area (see www.stutteringspecialists.org). Then you need to accumulate 45 hours over 3 years (10 hours in "related" areas), and even that is liberally interpreted. It is clear to anyone who has site-visited or spoken at many programs that there is a profound lack of good instruction at academic programs across the country. Even under ideal conditions, graduate students are likely to have no more than a single course devoted to stuttering. They will have one semester, two at the most, of clinical experience. They will see one or two clients at various stages of the change process. They will see only a small window of change for a very few clients.

Of course the master's degree is just a beginning anyway. But in too many cases it is not a very good start. A few years ago a new student in our graduate program told me that one of her undergraduate instructors had said to her, "Don't spend any time with people who stutter. Work with those you can help."

DEVELOPING EXPERT PERFORMANCE

Referring back to my earlier comments about the importance of practice on the part of the speaker, it is important to recognize that practice and experience is also critical for the clinician. A good example of this concept may be found in Wampold's (2002) studies of the common factors across the many approaches which result in successful therapeutic outcomes in psychotherapy. Meta-analysis by Wampold and his colleagues indicated that the major factors accounting for successful outcome included the *working alliance* between the client and the clinician (accounting for 5%), *clinician allegiance* to the treatment protocol (accounting for 10%) and *clinician competence* (accounting for 22%).

These results suggest that if we are concerned about the efficacy of our treatment we might do well to focus less on comparisons between specific treatments (at least those that are empirically informed if not always empirically validated, which few are) and more on the attributes of effective clinicians, whoever they may be. Berliner (1994) provided an intriguing explanation of expert performance in his description of a five-stage model proposed by Dreyfus and Dreyfus (1986).

Novices who are new to an activity spend the majority of their time labeling and attaching terms to their activities. They tend to act deliberately, paying close attention to context-free rules (e.g., shifting at 2,500 rpm when driving a car). Novices tend to be relatively inflexible and are likely to strictly follow these context-free protocols and rules. These attributes are characteristic of SLP graduate students and first year professionals (such as CFY's).

The *Advanced Beginner* is similar to the novice in that they tend to set up barriers to keep authority in their own hands. Although they now know the rules, they are still unsure what to do or not to do when new or unusual circumstances occur (as in being uncertain about when to shift when driving on ice or snow). The advanced beginner begins to learn when to ignore or to break the rules when that would be the better thing to do. However, because they are likely to be uncertain about the important indicators and patterns that guide them in their decision making, they are likely to respond to new situations by following rules and classifying and describing events rather than responding creatively or problem solving. These attributes are characteristic of second- and third-year professionals.

People who have become *Competent* (and not all reach this level) have more than the usual motivation necessary for gaining additional experience. Competent performers begin making their own choices and developing their own priorities and strategies. Because they are achieving agency, they tend to have a greater appreciation concerning success or failure of their decisions and take more responsibility for the outcome of their actions. They refine their understanding of the important indicators and patterns that enable them to make wise decisions. Correspondingly, they are able to develop a better sense of timing and know not only what to do but when to do it. These attributes are characteristic of professionals with more than three years of experience.

Proficient performers develop an intuitive sense of situation and are able to make micro-adjustments (as when making small balance corrections while riding a bike) that less proficient individuals are unlikely to notice. They begin taking a holistic approach to their performance. This holistic view allows them to recognize reoccurring patterns that others are unlikely to see and thus they are able to predict events with greater precision. These attributes are characteristic of professionals with more than 5 years of experience.

In order to become an **Expert**, it is usually necessary to focus on one or a very few specific domains with great dedication and persistence. As we discussed earlier, it will take many thousands of practice hours (10 to 20 thousand hours of playing chess; 10 to 15 thousand hours of teaching; reading 100,000 x-rays) to approach this level of expertise. Experts appear to have an intuitive grasp of the situation and seem to perform effortlessly, "becoming one" with the activity (the car they are driving, the instrument they are playing, the tools or techniques they are using). They appear to be nonanalytic and nondeliberative, as vividly demonstrated by the pianist or the expert martial artist; the individual parts of the activity are not easily described as deductive or analytic behavior. They are able to respond in a rapid and fluid manner. Berliner cites the vivid example of when hockey player Wayne Gretsky was asked the reason for his success. He responded, "I don't know; I just go to where the puck is going to be."

Berliner (1991) was particularly interested in understanding expert performance as it applied to exceptionally adept teachers. He found that expert instructors were flexible in approach, apt to consider alternative responses to a situation, unlikely to follow a manual, opportunistic about ways to connect with their students (rather than following a preplanned approach), and often followed the lead of the student. These experts had become integrated individuals who focused less on themselves and more on the student. Additionally, they were unusually sensitive to the affective concerns of their students.

These characteristics of the expert teacher are remarkably similar to the characteristics and the dynamic therapeutic relationship often aspired to in many fields. Furthermore, and particularly important for our discussion, many of the attributes of expert performers would have been predicted by the contextual model of treatment. That is, there are no specific ingredients that are both necessary and sufficient for success. In Berliner's analyses, although experts imparted information and techniques, they did so by responding in nondogmatic and creative ways to the unique characteristics of the person and the situation rather than forcing their own agenda. They made use of their extensive experience and insight by allowing themselves the flexibility to experiment with procedures rather than following a preplanned approach; they considered alternative responses. Their focus was on the client rather than on themselves or the techniques. They were particularly attuned to the affective concerns of the other person.

Related to the characteristics of the expert performer are the concepts of *rules and principles*. As described in a recent manuscript by Levitt, Neimeyer and Williams (2004), rule-based approaches have evolved in many areas including business, education, law, and athletics. *Rules* are created and serve as specific prescriptions for evaluating an experience, whether or not something was accomplished or how well something was done. The rules are formalized, unequivocally applied, mechanistic, algorithmic, and often quantitative. *Principles* are less clear-cut and specific. Principled judgments emphasize expert discretion, intuition, personal knowledge, and are often qualitative and contextual.

For our purposes, a *rule-governed approach* is associated with the application of a particular treatment methodology (and possibly prescribed techniques) to a particular problem. The nature, setting, duration, and timing of the sessions are prescribed (or programmed) and rigorously maintained. Manuals are often developed to ensure the consistency of the treatment. Change is often determined in a quantitative manner. A *principled* approach would allow the clinician any number of methodologies and associated techniques. The clinician and the client are free to respond in creative ways to the dynamic nature of the change process. Change is often determined in a qualitative manner.

Levitt, Niemeyer, and Williams (2004) cite author John Braithwaite (2002) who discussed the rules-principles continuum. Braithwaite suggested that the application of explicit standards without regard to the context of the situation or action works best when the type of action to be regulated is relatively simple and stable. In such cases, rules tend to regulate with greater certainty than principles. A good example might be the rules of driving (what speed to maintain, when to turn on red, when to pass or not). However, Braithwaite (2002) made a convincing case that when the type of action to be regulated is complex and dynamic (such as driving when there is snow on the road), principles tend to regulate with greater certainty than rules (speed limits, turning, and passing guidelines are likely to be adjusted). He argued that using rules to regulate complex procedures results in lower consistency and validity when determining effectiveness. It also results in "gaming" the rule book by providing the evaluators what they want to see and hear.

HOW DO WE IMPROVE OUR CLINICAL EFFECTIVENESS?

It may not be that we can all become experts, but to the degree that we can continue to improve our abilities, we can improve the efficacy and effectiveness of our treatment. We clearly need much better instruction in the area of fluency disorders. A few years ago at an ASHA meeting, someone on a panel suggested that one of these days those interested in helping people who stutter will choose from a list of master's degree programs that specialize in stuttering because such courses will not be offered in all schools. If a student is interested in another area, he or she will select another program. It may be worthwhile for us to create a list of programs where courses in fluency disorders are taught by people who are characterized by one or more of the following features:

- Are active participants in the field of fluency disorders
- Have their ASHA Certificate of Clinical Competence
- Are members of Special Interest Division 4 (Fluency and Fluency Disorders)
- Have written *something* that has contributed to the knowledge in the field
- Have specialty recognition in fluency disorders.

Note that I did not include having a PhD on the list, although in some cases that would be useful for mentoring future clinical researchers. I also think it would be helpful to have some indication that the instructors are doing something in their classes that helps to decrease the fear that students have about stuttering. It would be good to know that the instructors are doing something to increase understanding of the problem of stuttering, so that clinicians are able to make clinical decisions that are not naïve.

We can at least do all we can to help students understand the essential nature of the problem. If you do not understand, you are going to say things to the person who stutters that reveal that you really do *not* "get it." I tell my students in a class or in a workshop, "Don't ever let a person who stutters tell you that because you do not stutter, you don't understand." On one level, they are correct, of course, but you can understand even if you don't stutter. In my case, I am not a woman, I am not African American, I am not Muslim. And so I probably do not completely understand everything that is relevant to their individual experiences. But I can try to understand because I am a human. Tell me and I will listen. I have no doubt that it is possible for someone who has never stuttered to enter into the world of stuttering, and help.

In their article, Levitt et al. (2004) pointed out that the underlying ethos which guides the evidence-based practice movement is the pursuit of rules for treatment that are constrained, and thus consistent and replicable (Held, 1995). This quest for consistency of treatment is reflected in the development of manuals as well as the *DSM-IV* system. Levitt et al. (2004) suggested that, for many reasons, a better approach is the development of *principles* that guide our therapeutic decision-making. It would seem that investigating the principles used by expert clinicians *across* rather than *within* treatment approaches may inform us about the process of successful stuttering management and elevate our ability to help. Because what we do is relatively complex, indeed because humans are complex, I believe our approach to treatment is best guided by principles, perhaps common factors across treatment approaches, rather than rules that are uniformly applied in a noncontextual manner. I believe that we can measure change both quantitatively and qualitatively. I also believe that we need to do all that we can do to enhance the creativity of the clinician for knowing how and when to respond to the client.

I have already mentioned the basic problem that too many people—clinicians, instructors, as well as some researchers—appear to not fully understand the phenomena of stuttering. In order for us to be the best we can be and to be maximally helpful, we need to have an understanding of the essential structure of our clients' unique stuttering experience. Unless we achieve this understanding with each individual, we will be less able to precisely assess and effectively respond to their problem. As we are able to understand and appreciate their successes we will be better prepared to assist them as they work through *their* process of change.

For these reasons, my colleagues and I have become interested in the area of constructivist psychology (e.g., Kelly, 1963, 2003; Neimeyer & Raskin, 2000). Our interest has required that we also become familiar with the concepts of qualitative research, including phenomenology and content analysis. Venturing into the areas of qualitative research is daunting, even risky, for it is not the way we were trained to approach research. We were trained in quantitative methods where we have to know what we are measuring before we do it.

With a qualitative approach, the emphasis is not so much on measuring and quantifying things, although some of that does take place. The focus is on discovery and understanding. Qualitative research has been called a "human science approach" and the focus is on understanding the human experience. It is an especially good approach for discovering the essential structure of a human experience or phenomenon. Indeed, it is the only approach available to you until you begin to understand the dynamics of a series of phenomena. Once you begin to know the nature of the phenomena, you can begin to measure and quantify things.

For example, it a good approach to take when we want to ask questions such as, what is the essential experience of being a person who stutters? Or, what is the essential experience of being an especially good (or poor) clinician? These are not easy questions to answer. Being a good clinician is not likely to be strongly associated with things that are easy to quantify, such as how many CEUs one accumulates or how many degrees you have. Or even whether or not you have achieved specialty recognition. But once we know what some of these characteristics are, we can begin to promote and quantify them.

Re-storying with narrative therapy

My students and I have been taking courses and reading about topics such as personal construct theory, phenomenology, content analysis, and narrative therapy during the past few years. I can truly say that I have learned more from my students than they have from me—a good metaphor from a constructivist or narrative point of view. That is, we learn a lot from the people we are trying to help. There are many things that are appealing about a constructivist approach to therapy and I will finish by commenting on a few. It may be that these concepts will inform our choices about treatment in the future.

In a wonderful investigation concerning the essential nature of caring and noncaring nurses, Reimen (1986) stated that, "It is logical to assume that the best source of information about the client is the client" (p. 290). As clinicians taking this position, we are able to relinquish our role as the "experts." We are no longer in the role of the "unquestioned authority" and no longer forced to demonstrate our "immaculate perception." It seems to me that some forms of therapy are likely to have the opposite effect. That is, the treatment strategy can enhance the importance of the clinician and promote the clinician as an "expert" or even "the" expert. It may also foster egocentricity and a self-absorption that may have been there already.

I find the narrative approach appealing because it is optimistic and truly client-centered. This approach to therapy places the client in the position of authority. Although, as clinicians, we (hopefully) are experts about the stuttering experience, it is the clients who are in the position of authority concerning their life. Our acknowledgement of their authority facilitates the client's rewriting of "their story." Our basic tasks are to understand their story and to assist them in re-authoring it. We are in the role of co-author or perhaps editor. But it is the clients who are in the lead and that is where they should be. We cannot force people (at least most adolescents and adults) to do what we suggest. As with qualitative research, a narrative approach to therapy fosters discovery, ambiguity, and experimentation. Just as not everyone is going to be happy with releasing the mantle of the authority, not everyone is happy with the ambiguity of the change process.

When using a narrative therapy approach for diagnosis, the emphasis is not so much about test results, especially if the tests tell you only about the surface features of the phenomena. It will take several meetings to begin knowing the person and become calibrated to them. It usually takes time to begin to understand a person's story and to communicate that understanding back to the client. We are talking here about understanding or "knowing" this person's experience in a deeper way, something constructivists call a "thick" description. For many reasons, often because of time and associated expense, most clinicians distinguish only a "thin" description.

Michael Mahoney (2000) has recently written about this type of knowing. He points out that there is a wide gap between thinking about something and experiencing it. It takes time and it takes some work to begin to know "an other"—at least as much as we ever can. But we need to know enough to be calibrated to them and to help them grow in directions they (not necessarily we) need to go. And as Mahoney pointed out, it also helps us to understand that it is the client, more than the therapist, who must live out the consequences of the choices that are made.

One example of a narrative approach is the externalization of the problem—the separation of the problem from the person. That is, the person is not the problem. The problem is the problem. As this separation occurs, the client finds greater flexibility in problem solving. A narrative approach allows the person to begin understanding and revising their old story, a story likely to be dominated by the major theme of stuttering. The person begins to re-author a broader story that includes themes that run counter to the old story. Narrative therapists sometimes call these "unique outcomes" or "sparking moments" where one or more of the person's talents show themselves in spite of the overriding influence of the problem. Because of the success of these techniques in promoting change with other complex problems (Monk et al., 1997), we suspect that a narrative approach to therapy may foster successful (particularly long term) change for many people who stutter.

Mahoney's (2000) suggestions for training therapists parallel my own views about the many problems inherent in a dogmatic, manual, technique-driven approach to helping. It has been suggested that such an approach may well be effective for those clients who are well-motivated and independent in taking advantage of a prescribed regimen (see Strupp, 1982). This is likely to be the situation, for example, with intensive therapy programs where clients must allocate significant time and money in order to enroll. But many clients cannot or do not meet these requirements. No client is the same as another, and once we know them, we will see that, as Mahoney suggested, some people respond better to more structured guidance; some need support; some need to be challenged; some need both a challenge and support; and some need more reassurance. The clinician must have enough experience and sensitivity to understand this. Mahoney suggests that along with "knowing how," we also need to know that a response might be best for this person or when might be the right moment to experiment with a technique or idea. The clinician must have street smarts. But, because we are not really experts about this person, we do not know for sure. We need to be comfortable with ambiguity.

Mahoney (2000) also described some preliminary findings that he and his colleagues have gathered on psychotherapy practitioners and their tolerance for ambiguity. They found that psychotherapy trainees, like the clients they serve, often are impatient for simple answers to complex questions. He suggests, therefore, that important themes in their development are likely to include patience and a respectful tolerance of ambiguity and complexity. Many of the therapists in their investigations report substantially increased tolerance for ambiguity as they gain career experience. Furthermore, they found that the therapists whose conceptual understanding of their work more readily accommodates ambiguity are the therapists who are happier and generally satisfied with their work. Accordingly, therapists who maintain an open and flexible orientation toward their work appear to be less at risk for quitting their profession than those who are more closed and rigid.

I will finish with comments from two current clients. One of the narrative techniques of externalizing that we employ is to ask the person to create a metaphor for what it is like to stutter. After thinking about it for a moment, a 14-year-old boy who had recently begun therapy said, "It is like I am a butterfly trying to fly, but I am constantly buffeted by strong winds. I cannot move forward like I want and it is frustrating." I believe such a description tells us volumes about his experience with stuttering and provides some clues about what he will consider to be important as we proceed with therapy.

Another person, a 24-year-old college student, said, "When I stutter, I feel like a deer in the headlights." In fact, he often looked remarkably like that when he was experiencing a particularly difficult stuttering moment. When I asked him how he might rewrite that metaphor into what he would like to become, he said, "A performer in the spotlight!" Based on his current success, I believe that he is well on the way.

References

Ainsworth, S. (1974). The specialist in the treatment for stuttering. *Journal of Fluency Disorders, 1,* 48–53.

Allard, F. & Starkes, J. T. (1994). Motor-skill experts in sports, dance, and other domains. In A. K. Ericsson & J. Smith (Eds.) *Toward a general theory of expertise: Prospects and limits* (pp. 126–152). Cambridge: Cambridge University Press.

American Speech-Language-Hearing Association (1995, March). Guidelines for practice in stuttering treatment. *ASHA, 37*(14), 26–35.

Berliner, D. C. (1994). Expertise–The wonder of exemplary performances. In J. N. Mangieri & C. C. Block (Eds.), *Creating powerful thinking in teachers and students* (pp. 161–186). Fort Worth, TX: Holt, Rinehart & Winston.

Braithwaite, J. (2002). Rules and principles: A theory of legal certainty. *Australian Journal of Legal Philosophy, 27,* 47–82.

Blood, G., Blood, I., Tellis, G., Gabel, R., Mapp, C., Wertz, H., & Wade, J. (1998). Coping with stuttering during adolescence. In C. Healey & H. Peters (Eds.), *Proceedings of the Second World Congress on Fluency Disorders* (pp. 319–324). Nijmegen University Press.

Blood, G. W., Blood, I. M., Tellis, G. M., & Gabel, R. M. (2003). A preliminary study of self-esteem, stigma, and disclosure in adolescents who stutter. *Journal of Fluency Disorders, 28*(2), 143–159.

Bloodstein, O. (1949). Conditions under which stuttering is reduced or absent: A review of literature. *Journal of Speech and Hearing Disorders, 14,* 295–302.

Brisk, D. J., Healey, E. C., & Hux, K. A. (1997). Clinicians' training and confidence associated with treating school-age children who stutter: A national survey. *Language, Speech, and Hearing Services in Schools, 28,* 164–176.

Boberg, E. (1981). *The maintenance of fluency.* New York: Elsevier.

Conture, E. G. (2001). *Stuttering: Its nature, diagnosis, and treatment.* Boston: Allyn & Bacon.

Cooper, E. B. (1985). *Cooper personalized fluency control therapy—revised.* Allen, TX: DLM.

Cooper, E. B. & Cooper, C. S. (1992, November). *Clinician attitudes toward stuttering: Two decades of changes.* Paper presented to the annual meeting of the American Speech-Language-Hearing Association, San Antonio, TX.

Craig, A. (1998). Relapse following treatment for stuttering: A critical review and correlative data. *Journal of Fluency Disorders, 23,* 1–30.

Craig, A. & Calver, P. (1991). Following up on treated stutterers: Studies of perceptions of fluency and job status. *Journal of Speech and Hearing Research, 34,* 279–284.

Craig, A. & Hancock, K. (1995). Self-reported factors related to relapse following treatment for stuttering. *Australian Journal of Human Communication Disorders, 23,* 48–60.

Culatta, R. & Goldberg, S. A. (1995). *Stuttering therapy: An integrated approach to theory and practice.* Needham Heights, MA: Allyn & Bacon.

Dreyfus, H. L. & Dreyfus, S. E. (1986). *Mind over machine.* New York: Free Press.

De Nil, L. F. (1999). Stuttering: A neurophysiooogical perspective. In N. Bernstein Ratner & E. C. Healey (Eds.), *Stuttering research and practice: Bridging the gap* (pp. 85–102). Mahwah, NJ: Lawrence Erlbaum Associates.

De Nil, L. & Kroll, R. (2001) Searching for the neural basis of stuttering treatment outcome: recent neuroimaging studies. *Clinical Linguistics and Phonetics, 15,* 163–168.

DiLollo, A., Neimeyer, R., & Manning, W. (2002). A personal construct psychology view of relapse: Indications for a narrative therapy component to stuttering treatment. *Journal of Fluency Disorders, 27*(1), 19–42.

Eisenson, J. & Ogilvie, M. (1963). *Speech correction in the schools* (2nd ed.). New York: Macmillan.

Ericsson, A. K. & Smith, J. (1991). Prospects and limits of the empirical study of expertise: An introduction. In A. K. Ericsson & J. Smith (Eds.), *Toward a general theory of expertise: Prospects and limits* (pp. 1–39). Cambridge: Cambridge University Press.

Fransella, F. (2003). From theory to research to change. In F. Fransella (Ed.), *International handbook of personal construct psychology* (pp. 211–222). West Sussex: Wiley.

Goldman-Eisler, F. (1961). The continuity of speech utterance: Its determinants and its significance. *Language and Speech, 4,* 220–231.

Guitar, B. (1998). *Stuttering: An integrated approach to its nature and treatment.* Baltimore: Williams & Wilkins.

Guitar, B. (2003). The Lidcombe program in historical context. In M. Onslow, A. Packman, & E. Harrison (Eds.), *The Lidcombe program of early stuttering intervention* (pp. 27–40). Austin, TX: Pro Ed.

Held, B. (1995). *Back to reality: A critique of postmodern theory in psychotherapy.* New York; Norton.

Herbert, J. D., Lilienfeld, S. O., Lohr, J. M., Montgomery, R. W., O'Donohue, T. O., Rosen, G. M., & Tolin, D. F. (2000). Science and pseudoscience in the development of eye movement desensitization and reprocessing: Implications for clinical psychology. *Clinical Psychology Review, 20*(8), 945–971.

Hillis, J. W. (1993). Ongoing assessment in the management of stuttering: A clinical perspective. *American Journal of Speech-Language Pathology, 2*(1), 24–37.

Hillis J. & Manning, W. (1996, November). *Extraclinical generalization of speech fluency: A social cognitive approach.* Presentation to the annual meeting of the American Speech-Language-Hearing Association, Seattle.

Ingham, R. J. & Bothe, A. (1997). Self-measurement and evaluating stuttering treatment efficacy. In R. F. Curlee & G. M. Siegel (Eds.), *Nature and Treatment of Stuttering: New directions* (pp. 413–437). Boston: Allyn & Bacon.

Ingham, R. J. & Cordes, A. K. (1999). On watching a discipline shoot itself in the foot: Some observations on current trends in stuttering treatment research. In N. Bernstein Ratner & E. C. Healey (Eds.), *Stuttering research and practice: Bridging the gap* (pp. 211–230). Mahwah, NJ: Lawrence Erlbaum Associates.

Johnson, W. (1962). *An open letter to the mother of a "stuttering" child*. Danville, IL: Interstate Printers and Publishers.

Kelly, G. A. (1963). *A theory of personality*. New York: Norton.

Kubler-Ross, E. (1969). *On death and dying*. New York: Simon and Schuster.

Levitt, H. M., Neimeyer, R. A., & Williams, D. (2004). Rules vs. principles in psychotherapy: Implications of the quest for universal guidelines in the movement for empirically supported treatments. *Journal of Contemporary Psychotherapy, 35*, 117–129.

Luterman, D. (2001). *Counseling persons with communication disorders and their families*. Austin, TX:Pro-Ed.

Luterman, D. (2003). Helping the helper. *Perspectives on Fluency and Fluency Disorders, Division 4, 13*(2), 19–20.

Mahoney, M. J. (2000) Training future psychotherapists. In C. R. Snyder & R. E. Ingram (Eds.), *Handbook of psychological change* (pp. 727–735). New York: Wiley.

Manning, W. H. (1994, November). *The SEA-Scale: Self-efficacy scaling for adolescents who stutter*. Paper presented to the annual meeting of the American Speech-Language-Hearing Association, New Orleans.

Manning, W. H. (1999). Progress under the surface and over time. In N. Bernstein Ratner & E. C. Healey (Eds.), *Stuttering research and practice: Bridging the gap* (pp. 123–129). Mahwah, NJ: Lawrence Erlbaum Associates.

Manning, W. (2001) *Clinical decision making in fluency disorders, second edition*. San Diego, CA: Singular.

Manning, W. H. (2004). "How can you understand? You don't stutter!" *Contemporary Issues in Communicative Disorders and Sciences, 31*, 58–68.

McGuire, D. (2000). *Freedom's road: Manual for the use of the McGuire method for recovery from stammering*. Hoofddorp, The Netherlands: The McGuire Institute.

Monk, G., Winslade, J., Crocket, K., & Epston, D. (1997). *Narrative therapy in practice: The archaeology of hope*. San Francisco: Jossey-Bass Publishers.

Murphy, B. (1999). A preliminary look at shame, guilt, and stuttering. In N. Bernstein Ratner & E. C. Healey (Eds.), *Stuttering research and practice: Bridging the gap*. Mahwah, NJ: Lawrence Erlbaum Associates.

Neimeyer, R. A. & Raskin, J. (2000). *Constructions of disorder*. Washington: American Psychological Association.

O'Brian, S., Onslow, M., Cream, A., & Packman, A. (2003). The Camperdown Program: Outcomes of a new prolonged-speech treatment model. *Journal of Speech, Language, and Hearing Research, 46*, 933–946.

Onslow, M., Packman, A., & Harrison, E. (2003a). *The Lidcombe program of early stuttering intervention*. Austin, TX: Pro Ed.

Onslow, M., Packman, A., & Harrison, E. (2003b). *The Lidcombe program of early stuttering intervention: A clinician's guide*. Austin, TX: Pro-Ed.

Ornstein, A. & Manning, W. (1985). Self-efficacy scaling by adult stutterers. *Journal of Communication Disorders, 18*, 313–320.

Perkins, W. H. (1983). Learning from negative outcomes in stuttering therapy: II An epiphany of failure. *Journal of Fluency Disorders, 8*, 155–160.

Population Reference Bureau Report, August 17, 2004. Population Reference Bureau, 1875 Connecticut Ave., NW, Suite 520, Washington, DC 20009 (website: prb.org)

Prochaska, J. O. & DiClemente, C. C. (1992). Stages of change in the modification of problem behaviors. In M. Herson, P. Eisler & P. Miller (Eds.), *Progress in behavior modification* (pp. 184–218). Sycamore, IL: Sycamore Publishing Company.

Prochaska, J. O., DiClemente, C. C., & Norcross, J. C. (1992). In search of how people change: Applications to addictive behaviors. *American Psychologist, 47*(9), 1102–1114.

Quesal, R. (2002, October) *Some people just don't get it*. Presentation to the Fifth International Stuttering Awareness Day Online Conference.

Quesal, R. (2003). Evidenced-based practice in stuttering: Current controversies and considerations. *Ishail.cor: The Newsletter of the Illinois Speech-Language-Hearing Association, 29*(2), 10–11.

Reimen, D. J. (1986). The essential structure of a caring interaction: Doing Phenomenology. In P. M.

Munhall & C. J. Oiler (Eds.), *Nursing research: A qualitative perspective* (pp. 85–105). Norwalk, CT: Appleton-Century-Crofts.

Riley, G. & Riley, J. (2000). A revised component model for diagnosing and treating children who stutter. *Contemporary Issues in Communication Sciences and Disorders, 27*(2), 188–199.

Ryan, B. P. (2001). *Programmed therapy for stuttering in children and adults.* Spring, IL: Charles C. Thomas.

Shaw, B. F., Elkin, I., Yamaguchi, J., Olmsted, M., Vallis, T. M., Dobson, K. S., Lowery, A., Sotsky, S. M., Watkins, J. T., & Imber, S. D. (1999). Therapist ratings in relation to clinical outcome in cognitive therapy of depression. *Journal of Consulting and Clinical Psychology, 67,* 837–846.

Silverman, F. H. (1992). *Stuttering and other fluency disorders.* Englewood Cliffs, NJ: Prentice-Hall.

Simon, H. A. & Chase, W. G. (1973). Skill in chess. *American Scientist, 61,* 394–403.

Smith, A. & Kelly, E. (1997). Stuttering: A dynamic, multifactorial model. In R. F. Curlee & G. M. Siegel (Eds.), *Nature and treatment of stuttering: New Directions* (2nd ed.; pp. 204–217). Needham Heights, MD: Allyn & Bacon.

Smith, A. (1999). Stuttering: A unified approach to a multifactorial, dynamic disorder. In N. Bernstein Ratner & E. C. Healey (Eds.), *Stuttering research and practice: Bridging the gap* (pp. 27–44). Mahwah, NJ: Lawrence Erlbaum Associates.

St. Louis, K. O., Yaruss, J. S., Lubker, B. B., Pill, J., & Diggs, C. C. (2001). An international public opinion survey of stuttering: Pilot results. In H-G. Bosshardt, J. S. Yaruss, & H. F. M. Peters (Eds.), *Fluency disorders: Theory, research, treatment and self-help. Proceedings of the Third World Congress on Fluency Disorders in Nyborg, Denmark* (pp. 581–587). Nijmegen: International Fluency Association.

Strupp, H. H. (1982). The outcome problem in psychotherapy: Contemporary perspectives. In J. H. Harvey & M. M. Parks (Eds.), *Psychotherapy research and behavior change* (pp. 43–71). Washington, DC: American Psychological Association.

Van Riper, C. (1939). *Speech correction: Principles and methods* (1st ed.). Englewood Cliffs, NJ: Prentice-Hall.

Wampold, B. E. (2001). *The great psychotherapy debate: Models, methods, and findings.* Mahwah, NJ: Lawrence Erlbaum Associates.

Westen, D. & Morrison, K. (2001). A multidimensional meta-analysis of treatments for depression, panic, and generalized anxiety disorder: An empirical examination of the status of empirically supported therapies. *Journal of Consulting Clinical Psychology, 69,* 875–899.

Wingate, M. (1971). The fear of stuttering. *Journal of the American Speech-Language-Hearing Association, 13,* 3–5.

Yairi, E. (2004). The formative years of stuttering: A changing portrait. *Contemporary Issues in Communication Science and Disorders, 31,* 92–104.

Yairi, E. & Ambrose, N. G. (1992a). A longitudinal study of stuttering in children: A preliminary report. *Journal of Speech and Hearing Research, 35,* 755–760.

Yairi, E. & Ambrose, N. G. (1992b). Onset of stuttering in preschool children: Selected factors. *Journal of Speech and Hearing Research, 35,* 782–788.

Yairi, E. & Ambrose, N. G. (1999). Early childhood stuttering I: Persistency and recovery rates. *Journal of Speech, Language, and Hearing Research, 42,* 1097–1112.

Yairi, E., Ambrose, N. G., & Niermann, R. (1993). The early months of stuttering: A developmental study. *Journal of Speech and Hearing Research, 36,* 521–528.

Yaruss, J. S. & Quesal, R. (2002). Academic and clinical education in fluency disorders: An update. *Journal of Fluency Disorders, 27,* 43–63.

— 8 —

The Treatment of Stuttering:
From the Hub to the Spoke

Description and evaluation of an
integrated therapy program

Catherine S. Montgomery

The American Institute for
Stuttering Treatment and Professional Training

A few years ago at the International Fluency Association's Third World Congress in Denmark, Paul Cooke began his presentation by rolling a bicycle into the room. He used it to make the point that our main role as clinicians is to help our clients move from allowing their stuttering to be the *hub* of their lives to it simply being a *spoke* on the wheel (Cooke, 2000). I thank Paul for that very powerful metaphor that has remained with me as a theme that represents what I too believe to be the overarching intention of our treatment with those who stutter.

This chapter reflects learning from 25 years of focused work in the treatment and study of stuttering and exposure to approximately 3,000 individuals who stutter, primarily adults and teens. Broadly, what I've experienced personally and observed in many of my colleagues over these many years in regard to treatment for school-aged children, teens, and adults can best be described as a movement of melding, flexibility, of holism, a movement away from polarization and dogma, as well as a regard for the whole person affected by stuttering.

The current generation of clinicians is fortunate to have a smorgasbord of models from which we can choose, given to us by our esteemed predecessors and colleagues. To these, we can mix and match and add our own elements based on the individual's needs. I find it interesting that after decades, many of us have been returning to the ideas of those who came even earlier. Clearly a holistic thinker, in 1926, Dr. Frederick Martin, the director of a residential treatment program for stuttering, wrote in *The Manual for Speech Training* (1926):

> *It is not by the laying of a cornerstone that a building is completed, but by the careful placing and amalgamating of one stone upon the another. So, must constant, sufficient, physical and mental exercises by a speech case until the necessary organs habitually function properly and the correct visual, auditory and kinesthetic images have become fully developed and fixed. Speaking without difficulty, at any one time, does not necessarily correct the disorder. Unless that central nervous system is well fortified, it may revert to its old behaviorism under the strain of emotional or exciting conditions of the class room, business or society. ... As Curry of Boston once said, "He must learn to harmonize and vitalize the mind, body and voice."* (p. 14)

Observations about the dimensions of stuttering

I'd like to begin in the present and offer my own observations and philosophical perspectives on the nature of stuttering, which provide the context for my treatment approach. Fundamentally, I believe that stuttering treatment is a healing process, a recovery from pain, a process of self-acceptance, and a building of self-esteem. A client of mine recently commented, "until my treatment [at age 46], not only was my speech blocked, but my entire life was blocked, and this program has been a discovery of who I am as a person. I'm no longer just a guy who stutters." Another young client in his 20s described this program as "a course in life, and oh yeah, I also learned how to manage my speech." Treatment can be a wonderful unfolding and discovery of self as one works his way through the physical and psychological labyrinth.

This healing process begins during the client's first consultation visit during which time he[1] is educated about what is currently known about the nature of stuttering. Information is shared from my learning and experience as well as current research findings. Simply knowing some facts about stuttering can bring great relief. I'd like to share with you my view of stuttering and how I describe it to my clients and their families.

---

[1]Please note that masculine pronouns are used in reference to the clients, reflecting the majority of those who stutter, as well as to provide ease in reading.

Answering the client's question:
"What causes my stuttering?"

First, I think we have come to a fair consensus that stuttering has neurological and genetic underpinnings (De Nil, 1999; Drayna, Kilshaw, & Kelly, 1999; Foundas, Bollich, Corey, Hurley, & Heilman, 2001; Ingham, 2001; Sandak & Fiez, 2000; Shugart, Mondorff, Kilshaw, Doheny, Doan, Wanyee, Green, & Drayna, 2004; Sommer, Koch, Paulus, Weiller, & Buchel, 2002; Yairi, 1998). Recently, De Nil (2003) noted that, of everything we have learned about stuttering in the last 30 years, one the few findings that can be stated as fact is that stuttering has a strong genetic component. Findings show that genetic factors play an important role not only in the cause of stuttering but also in its recovery and persistency pathways (Ambrose, Yairi, & Cox, 1993; Andrews & Harris, 1964; Howie, 1981; Kidd, 1984).

The implications of these findings are important for counseling parents of young children who may be showing signs of dysfluency. This information can be helpful in removing any guilt the parents may be feeling. In addition, for those parents who know of family history, they may be guided to early intervention for their child. For teens and adults, this knowledge can ameliorate any latent and misinformed hypotheses they may have regarding the origins of their own stuttering.

That stuttering has neurological origins was the only thing that made complete sense to me from my earliest encounters with those who stutter, although we have much yet to learn about what occurs neurologically on motor and linguistic levels. My clinical observations have created a personal belief that the laryngeal block is the physical core manifestation of stuttered dysfluency and that all other stuttering phenomena are byproducts of or a compensation for the physical struggle in the larynx.

When asked to describe their physical experience of stuttering, most clients describe it as a tightness in the throat and/or vocal tract or chest, with descriptors such as "stuck," "paralyzed," "a stoppage," or "I *know* the word, it just won't come out." They often point to their throat as the primary place they feel blockage the most. This is by far the most common description that I have received from the approximately 3,000 teens and adults who stutter that I have worked with over the years.

Thus, I view the physical characteristics of dysfluent speech in the following way: Because the vocal folds are not operating properly, the body compensates for the speech attempt by working the articulators harder, thus creating the muscle distortions we traditionally describe as "repetitions" and "prolongations," as well as the other "secondaries" such as eye blinking, facial contortion, clenching fists, and so forth. These all appear to be natural, instinctive, physical struggle behaviors that occur in the effort to open the airway as well as to speak.

These observations are supported by the basic research literature. Historically, the larynx has been singled out as the organ that plays the central role in stuttering, even as early as Yates in 1800 (and in the work of other early researchers reviewed by Adams, Conture, & Freeman, 1984). Other studies summarized by Adams, Conture, and Freeman (1984) have indicated that the larynx is often (1) inappropriately, nonpredictably open, or (2) inappropriately closed during instances of stuttering. Other research has found both inappropriate glottal openings as well as tightly adducted true/false vocal folds during different instances of stuttering. In addition, Freeman and Ushijima (1978) found abnormal muscle activity during *perceptually fluent* utterances of stutterers, which indicates that the larynx appears to function in an abnormal manner even while "fluent." Webster (1978) was convinced that the central features of stuttering are found directly and only in the motor events which occur at the level of the larynx and vocal tract. Guitar (1998), viewing the physiological underpinnings of the stuttered moment more broadly, believed that blocks can occur at the respiratory, laryngeal, or articulatory level.

Describing the breathing patterns of people who stutter (PWS), Runyan and Runyan (1999) found that prior to treatment, their clients expanded or pushed their thoracic/diaphragmatic area outward prior to production of speech. Woods, Twohig, Fuqua, and Hanley (2000) characterized stuttering as including a series of breathing abnormalities, including irregularity of the respiratory cycle, prolonged exhalation, and even complete cessation of breathing. To me, this is consistent with a belief that the laryngeal tightening naturally causes a physical struggle in order to open up one's airway.

Therefore, the physical component of stuttering might be accurately described as miscoordination of an otherwise normal respiratory, vocal, and articulatory system. Dysfluency is the byproduct of that miscoordination. Fluent speech is the natural byproduct of a coordinated motor system, which is a goal of stuttering therapy.

Variability of symptoms

Although no one would ever conceive of suggesting that a blind person should just "focus in" or suggest that a deaf person just "concentrate and listen harder," those who stutter deal with this kind of remark all the time. Why? Not only are we better educated about blindness and deafness and regard them as purely physical disorders, but both conditions are static, without variability in their symptoms.

What confounds people so much about stuttering is its variability, which just adds to its "mystery." "He was just talking fine over there. Why is he stuttering now? Well, it *must* be something psychological or it *must* be due to nerves. Just slow down, just breathe! It must be something that he can control." We all know the common misconceptions. I believe that this variability has significantly contributed to centuries of myth and misunderstanding about the disorder of stuttering.

PUBLIC PERCEPTION

I would venture to say that most, if not all people, who deal with *any* disorder, disease, or disability (a deviation from the norm) experience mental and emotional suffering. To a large extent, their suffering depends on public perception of their disorder. Certain diseases and disorders engendered secrecy and shame, such as AIDS and alcoholism. Now, with public education, those who were suffering and closeted are not only out and getting the help they need, it's even become "fashionable" to go to AA meetings.

Unfortunately, even with the dawn of a new century, the stigma surrounding stuttering significantly contributes to the "handicap" it creates for those affected and their families. Public ignorance thus becomes a major contributing factor to the mental and emotional complexities of stuttering which can then affect the physical manifestation of the dysfluency (Blood, 2000). People who stutter are blamed for their disability as no other handicapped persons are, and stuttering remains one of the few disabilities that people still laugh at. A blind client of mine once remarked that it was *worse* to deal with stuttering than blindness because of public ignorance.

Thus, those who suffer not only bear the burden of the often painful physical struggle to speak but they bear the *added* burden of humiliation, shame, and guilt; a shame that can reach to one's core. Because parents are often uninformed, it has been my observation that they often suffer the same shame and guilt. For those who stutter, mental, attitudinal, and emotional responses are *learned* and develop as a result of ignorance to the true nature of the disorder. The stressful emotions of embarrassment, fear, frustration, and anger all come as a result of this physical difference and others' reactions to it. It is the person who stutter's *perception* of continued negative responses and, as a result, avoidance becomes a natural byproduct.

Stress and conditioned learning

PWS usually report large degrees of stress about speaking and stuttering. My interpretation of stress is that it stems largely from learned attitude: it is a response to a self-created judgment that this situation is "bad" for me. Kaufman (1977, 1991) noted that "We walk through life constantly judging; judging life's situations to be either good for us or bad for us and our entire experience of the situation flows from that judgment." It is not a person or situation that creates our stress, it is our own *beliefs* about that person or situation that does. We can consider stress to be a by-product of additude.

There is a very strong *learned component* in stuttering that we've come to call "expectancy." Quite normally, certain cognitions and emotions result from an experience of stuttering on a certain word, in a certain situation, or with a certain person. Saying one's name is a classic example. A client is likely to remember the "bad" experience of stuttering while trying to say his name. The next time someone asks his name, the memories come flooding back, creating an instant fear, just as Pavlov's dog learned to attach the ringing bell to the anticipation of the steak (salivation). In anticipation of the impending "battle," the body physically responds in "fight or flight" mode with rapid breathing and increased tension that help to recreate the block. Because of the repeated experiences, it is easy to develop the belief or expectation that saying one's name will cause blocking. This belief becomes the speaker's own personal "fact." This belief may then extend to all or most words that begin with the initial sound of the name or to an expectation of stuttering with certain addressees that may grow with time and experience.

If my client is now 35 years old, he has blocked on his name hundreds of thousands of times and he's likely had many experiences of negative reactions to his stutter. The block on his name therefore becomes reflexive. His expectation, belief, and behavior has been reinforced over and over to the point where he simply "knows" it's going to happen.

CONDITIONED LEARNING PLAYS A MAJOR ROLE IN THE VARIABILITY OF STUTTERING

The "fight or flight" response

The acute stress response, or the "flight or fight" response, was first described by Cannon (1929, 1939) when describing how animals react to threats with a general discharge of the sympathetic nervous system. It is a general adaptation syndrome that regulates stress responses among vertebrates and other organisms. The fundamental purpose of the fight or flight response is physical strength and self-preservation. In humans, with the recognition of a threat (fear), the release of adrenaline causes increased heart rate, shallower and more rapid breathing, blood flow diversion to support the larger muscles, digestion slowing in order to conserve energy to be used toward physical strength (this is what creates the "butterflies in the stomach" feeling), and tightening of muscles throughout the body. All of this creates physical strength so that we can either "flee" the situation or "fight" the threat (Handly, 1995).

Unlike animals, humans more commonly face a different type of threat: an emotional threat, a threat to our ego or positive sense of self. It is human nature to want to "flee" from negative judgments or any sort of perception of being "less than." The brain, as well developed as it is, does not differentiate between physical and emotional threat. If a stimulus is perceived as a threat, a more intense and prolonged discharge of the locus ceruleus activates the sympathetic division of the autonomic nervous system (Thase & Howland, 1995). One can extrapolate from this that because of the learned expectancy (fear) of stuttering moments, this natural physiological response kicks in and helps to create the block or exacerbate it. No wonder people think stuttering is "caused by nerves." It certainly can appear that way.

Avoidance

A few years ago, Walt Manning (1999) made a simple yet quite profound statement that I've grown to appreciate as being one of the most important messages we can give to our clients: "Your emotions and avoidances are all normal human reactions to an abnormal physical condition." Bloom and Cooperman (2003) noted that Luterman (2001) expanded on this concept and felt that the vast majority of our clients are simply experiencing a normal reaction to a communication disorder, which can create genuine stress and anxiety. Any one of us would react the same way given the same circumstances and experiences.

Because of the perpetuated cultural myths about stuttering, those who stutter continue to work very hard to hide or minimize their stuttering. The clients' understanding of the fact that they are reacting in a normal, human way can be enormously healing for them; that it is human nature to protect ourselves from the pain of potential negative judgment. Once they understand this, many tell me that they have been able let go of the burden of guilt for avoiding speaking and trying to avoid stuttering.

Principles of assessment

One of the measurement tools that I use is the *Perceptions of Stuttering Inventory* (*PSI*; Woolf, 1967). When speaking with clients and their families about the layers of stuttering, I find its breakdown of descriptors of behavior into the three categories of "struggle," "expectancy," and "avoidance" to be quite useful to tie the layers together: that this genetically predisposed neurologically-based condition begins with the physical "struggle." What then develops is the "expectancy" of that physical struggle, and then, as a result of both, "avoidance" strategies are developed.

What the PSI doesn't ask about are attitudes and emotions which the more current self-assessment measurement tools emphasize, as well as assessing the client's perspective on the handicapping impact of stuttering on his life. For example, the *Wright & Ayre Stuttering Self-Rating Profile* (*WASSP*; Wright & Ayre, 2000) asks the client to rate not only his stuttering behaviors but also his feelings of frustration, embarrassment, fear, anger, and helplessness, as well as how "disadvantageous" his stuttering is at home, socially, educationally, or at work. The *Overall Assessment of the Speaker's Experience of Stuttering* (*OASES*; Yaruss & Quesal, 2004, in press) is a more recent measurement instrument for assessing several aspects of the speaker's experience of stuttering, including fluency, personal and environmental reactions, difficulties with functional communication, and the impact of stuttering on the speaker's quality of life.

In my clinic, the first formal assessment consists of a history form, *PSI,* and *WASSP*. Because there is no formal measure of fluency at this point, I share with the client that I am truly more interested in how the dysfluency is affecting his life, much more than stutter frequency, but I do ask if what I'm seeing and hearing that day is typical or not.

A collection of speech samples during conversation and reading, as well as the *OASES* are done once the client has enrolled in treatment.

The first day of treatment involves obtaining videotaped samples which are scored as a percentage of dysfluent words. These data are then added to the self-report inventories to round out the pretreatment measurements.

SETTING MUTUAL GOALS

During the evaluation, I always ask why one is seeking treatment. Most say the obvious: fluency. I always question further to ask what the client believes greater fluency will do for him in his life. Typical answers include getting a better job, being able to be more social, feel more confident, participate more in school, for example. Again, we return to basic human nature. What clients are really seeking is to get out of pain and to move toward comfort, although most certainly don't verbalize it that way. Our clients want to become more lovable and acceptable, believing that their stuttering has rendered them either unlovable or unacceptable or both. They want to feel good about themselves. They want to be heard. They want freedom from restriction and hindrance. They want to move from being "disabled" to "able." The bottom line is that they want to be able to say what they want, whenever they want, with whomever they want. It's about freedom, choice, and self-esteem.

Thus, we begin by emanating a sense of genuine respect and an unconditional acceptance. We begin by really listening to the client. We don't presuppose that we know what is best for him. We are there to provide information so that he can make the decision that is best for him.

In a similar vein, when I meet with a teen and his parents, I am there first as the teen's advocate. I always meet with him privately to ask if he has been "dragged in" by his parents or if this was truly his idea. I let him know that I am on his side, that this is going to be *his* decision and his decision only. I let him know that it's perfectly okay to do absolutely nothing and that if he's not ready or willing, I will assist him in conveying that to his parents.

Doing nothing may be in the teen's (or adult's) best interest at a particular juncture in his life, and parents (and spouses) need to know that it is really okay to do nothing, which can often be difficult for them. They can know that doing nothing is truly doing something and that it may be the best way to support their loved one at this time. Conveying our advocacy and respect right from the start is a powerful way to develop rapport and trust with the client.

CONVEYING INFORMATION

After prompting the client to describe the physical sensation of stuttering, I explore the complexity of speech production with him, a coordination of over 100 different muscles. We explore the physiology of the laryngeal block, by asking the client to hold his breath while keeping his mouth open so that he can isolate the feeling of the closure of the folds. We explore opening and closing the vocal folds and then ask him to close them and push, feeling the pressures build up in the body. I ask the client if this is a familiar feeling and most agree that it is, that it feels like blocking. More often than not, clients tell me that no one has ever explained it in this way to them and even fewer parents or spouses have been given the opportunity to get a glimpse into the physical experience of stuttering.

Once we have educated each other, I then continue on with an in-depth orientation about treatment, giving rationale for each feature of our therapy approach and discuss follow-up as well. Of course, "success rate" questions are inevitable; our outcome results are provided later in this chapter and are shared with the client. The initial meeting is a time for assessing and informing. I do not ask for a decision and encourage the client to "shop around" and investigate all options for treatment if they so choose.

The treatment process

Although most of my practice has centered around an "intensive model" (lengthy daily sessions compressed into a short time frame), my preferred therapy components are applicable to nonintensive treatment as well. We employ an integrated treatment approach. By "integrated treatment" I mean not only a combination of approaches such as stuttering modification and fluency shaping, but also inclusion of work on the emotional, physical, and mental aspects of stuttering or, as Gene Cooper put it, the ABC's of stuttering: the affective, behavioral, and cognitive aspects (Cooper & Cooper, 2003).

In my judgment, this means moving beyond the field of speech pathology and into cognitive and sports psychology, human growth and potential, the study of meditation, understanding the process of change and motivation, for example. Being a student of human nature has been a fascinating and rich experience and has enabled me to grow personally as well as better serve my clients. When I engage in a therapeutic relationship with someone who stutters, it is just that: a relationship. It is a cooperative venture between people. That is why we explore desired outcomes together.

Based on client feedback, the following is a typical list of desired treatment outcomes:

To leave treatment:

- with the understanding and ability to use tools for speech management that will aid in speaking with less struggle and more fluently in most, if not all, speaking situations;
- with a knowledge of the current professional knowledge regarding the nature and possible cause(s) of stuttering;
- having educated family and friends about stuttering and his treatment experience;
- feeling at peace with stuttering and having reached a new level of acceptance and understanding;
- with the freedom, comfort, and ability to say what one chooses in speaking situations and to enter into chosen speaking situations freely and without hesitation;
- being comfortable with stuttering and being comfortable advertising the fact that one stutters with friends, family, peers, and coworkers as well as strangers; and
- with a strengthened self-image and confidence.

In summary, because so many struggle to speak we must include the goal of enhanced speech fluency. Because so many feel victimized, we must include the goal of empowerment. Because so many feel bound, we must address the goal of freedom. Because so many feel limited, we must enable the goal of choice.

Integrating treatment

We begin treatment with inspirations from Sheehan (1970), Van Riper (1973), Bloodstein (1993), and Breitenfeldt and Lorenz (1999), who all valued the therapeutic components of acceptance, desensitization, and avoidance and anxiety reduction. Guitar (1998) stated: "... the more [the person who stutters] is able to reduce his fear and avoidance, the more easily he can reduce his moments of stuttering" (p. 214). He continued by saying that "... these stutterers need to become less emotional about their stuttering. If this does not occur, Van Riper felt that advanced stutterers will not be able to modify their stuttering successfully ... that, like most people, [they] cannot adequately control fine motor acts such as modifying a moment of stuttering when they are wrought up emotionally" (p. 215). My own experience has affirmed this thinking. As one of my adult clients recently commented, "these skills are really great but I know I'd really have a hard time doing them if I still worried about stuttering."

Our direct management of speech incorporates features inspired by Van Riper (1973) and Webster (1977); we first use stuttering modification strategies to reduce the severity of stuttering moments or to "stutter more easily" and then we move into more of a "speak more fluently" or fluency-shaping approach. Clients can ultimately choose to manage their speech using one approach or to combine aspects of both approaches, which moves us away from the notion that these approaches are incompatible. They are not.

Although this is our general approach, one formula certainly does not apply to everyone. Integration also means flexibility and individualization. Although in an intensive program, we guide our clients through essentially the same experiences, ultimately they are exposed to a variety of skills and tools so that they can then customize their management as they become their own clinicians. We encourage them to participate fully and to not filter out certain experiences by feeling that they might not apply to them. More often than not, the one aspect of treatment that they felt was the least useful at first becomes the most important later in therapy. Finally, we believe that one can only make informed decisions about what will work best if one has tried it.

In our view, an integrated approach includes the following concepts:

- Acceptance of stuttering.
- Liberation from avoidance.
- Changing attitudes and emotions.
- Techniques for stuttering more easily (stuttering modification).
- Generating more fluency through speech muscle retraining (fluency shaping).
- Provision of choices and options for speech management.

Although these components are presented in sequential form, we believe that there is a synergy and an interaction among them and that these activities can facilitate change on many levels. For example, being educated about stuttering can impact one's feelings and attitudes as well as effect the attainment of physical skills.

Treatment component I: Education

SHARING CLIENT AND THERAPIST VIEWS

On the first day of an intensive session, up to eight clients come together; for many of them, this is their first time ever encountering another person who stutters. This time is also used to gather individual baseline information in the form of the *OASES* and to collect the pretreatment video sample. In a group orientation session, desensitization begins as I ask each person to share his or her own "theory of stuttering." What do they believe causes stuttering? My hope is that early on, the client develops a sense that this is a safe place for talking and that it's okay to stutter. Moreover, his opinions will not be judged. Each theory is accepted as possible given the information one possesses.

I then share my theory, and emphasize that it is based on my experience as well as a body of research. The AIS treatment components and expectations are reviewed and explained in reference to my beliefs about stuttering. I believe it is critical that the client be thoroughly educated. This is true even for our younger kids. Information is empowerment, no matter what the age. It is important that a context for treatment be provided and that everything makes sense to the client. Often a graduate intern or visiting clinician will remark that our clients seem to "know a lot more about speech than I do!"

Treatment component II: Identification and desensitization to moments of stuttering

Barry Guitar (1998) presented a concise rationale for identification work in stuttering treatment: "If the stutterer is to change, he must become aware of what to change" (p. 216). This is a common sense concept that applies to many other aspects of behavior, including sports training. Identification involves activities such as viewing onself on video and freezing and/or tallying moments of dysfluencies to help heighten awareness of the physical behaviors and tensions as well as the mental expectations, fears, and avoidances that accompany stuttering. Identification goes hand-in-hand with desensitization.

Along with the client's newly enlightened sense of the neurological and physical aspects of stuttering, we suggest adopting an attitude of healthy curiosity: approach rather than avoid to see what you can learn.

The more one becomes aware of his behaviors, the more everything makes sense as changes are made.

LETTING THE STUTTERING OUT:
AVOIDANCE REDUCTION/ELIMINATION

As discussed earlier, avoidance is a natural by-product of the desire to conceal something shameful. We help our clients to understand that most of their avoidance has developed as a result of unfortunate past experiences and help them to become more open with others in regard to their stuttering, to talk about it with friends, family, co-workers, schoolmates, and even strangers.

We carefully guide our clients through experiences that develop more accepting, self-respectful attitudes about oneself and help to develop the realization that most people, although they don't understand stuttering as we would prefer them to, do *not* judge stuttering as negatively as our clients might think. We acknowledge with them that avoidance provides comfort in some way, at least for the short term. The problem, in the long run, is that it complicates the problem of stuttering, and that avoidance can end up ruling one's life.

In discussing these issues, I challenge clients with a "what if" notion. What if there were no means to improve fluency? What if they would always stutter to the same degree that they currently stutter? Would their greatest desire be to live a full life in spite of the dysfluency? Would they desire to no longer allow their stuttering to rule? We begin working with the notion that they can choose to transform their life by liberating themselves—by refusing to avoid situations, by refusing to switch words, by saying what they want, when they want, in spite of dysfluency. In keeping with "approach rather than avoid," we challenge them to "do their *best* stuttering," that not only is it okay to stutter, but we actually *want* them to stutter and ask that they adopt the same attitude. In doing so, they can begin to understand what they do when they stutter and to understand all of the strategies that they've employed to help themselves, as well as to understand how many of their strategies actually contribute to greater dysfluency.

Although most of my clients initially balk at desensitization experiences early in treatment, they most often report that this was the most important and meaningful work they did in treatment. Many have said that they could be quite satisfied leaving the intensive even before we have begun any work on speech management because they had found their freedom. The actual management of the speech becomes the frosting on the cake.

The benefit of addressing fear and avoidance in the early phase of treatment is that the client becomes much more emotionally available to work on speech management skills when they are introduced next. The management skills are so much easier to apply if the fear of stuttering and listener reaction is no longer there or, at the very least, minimized.

VIEWING THE VIDEO:
MAKING STUTTERING THE OBJECT OF STUDY

Before the video is viewed, the clients write down descriptions of their stuttering and physical behaviors as well as thoughts and avoidances. We then sit as a group, view each video and discuss our observations. These often include:

- Their apparent approach to speech, quality of stuttering (e.g., tense vs. "easy"), and patterns of eye contact and voice quality.
- Avoidance behaviors (verbal and nonverbal, such as circumlocutions and loss of eye contact).
- The presence of postponements, timing tricks, or starters, such as throat clearing or saying "um."
- Characteristic dysfluency types in the speaker's stuttering pattern.
- Evident loci of physical tension.
- Struggle and escape behaviors.
- The speaker's reports of thoughts and feelings before/during/following speaking situations.

Following the viewing of the video, the clients begin to tally these behaviors. In our intensive model, tallying begins in day one and is phased out by day four. Clients are given a steno book on which they create two columns marked to record stuttering and avoidances. As they engage in conversation with one another, friends, or family members over the first few days of treatment, a slash mark is drawn for each moment of dysfluency as well as use of any form of avoidance. It is actually the act of stopping and catching oneself that is so very useful here. Not only does this activity help to heighten overall awareness of behaviors, but the act of stopping the moment of the block is the precursor for management of the blocks.

Principles used in tallying reinforce its role in desensitization. Thus, we teach the clients strategies suggested by Brietenfeldt and Lorenz (1989):

- To maintain eye contact while speaking;
- To maintain eye contact until a stuttered word is completed;
- To stop after a stutter, disengage eye contact, and tally the moment of stuttering or avoidance; and
- To resume eye contact and then resume conversation.

MIRROR WORK AND FREEZING

As Van Riper (1973) noted, examining the moment of a block can be a powerful exercise that educates as well as desensitizes, enabling the client to increase his tolerance for stuttering and to lose the fear of stuttered moments. Again, we teach the client to "approach rather than avoid." The purpose of mirror work is also to identify the locus and nature of tension in the moment of stuttering and to observe one's own role in the maintenance of tension.

We do this type of work first using the mirror and then without the mirror in conversation as each client takes turns being the "clinician" for another. The "clinican" stops his "client" in the moment of stuttering by instructing the speaker to "freeze" while he clenches his fist as demonstrated by Barry Guitar on the video, *Therapy in Action: The School-Age Child Who Stutters* (SFA, 1997). The client is to hold the moment until the "clinician" releases his fist, slowly. If the stutter is a repetition, the client continues to repeat until signaled to transition to the next sound; if the stutter is a prolongation, he continues to prolong until signaled; or if the stutter is a block, he freezes the block. The client then describes where he felt the block by identifying parts of his body that were affected and how they were affected.

Treatment component III:
Desensitization to listener reactions

VOLUNTARY STUTTERING

Although at first most of our clients abhor the idea of stuttering on purpose, they eventually find it very helpful. We particularly encourage stuttering on purpose with our most "closeted" clients: those who have gone to great lengths to hide and camouflage their stuttering and who, to many, appear quite fluent. Although the physical management of stuttering is quite possible, it remains imperfect and is certainly not a "cure." Thus, it is very important that our clients learn to tolerate and accept dysfluency in order to reduce the negative emotions associated with stuttering, and to confront the fear by doing what is feared.

For example, many fear introducing themselves because of so many experiences stuttering on their names. We suggest that they stutter purposefully while saying their name to get it out into the open. This then provides the opportunity to acknowledge their stuttering by making a casual comment about it such as, "whoa, let me do that again. I stutter sometimes, so hang on a second!"

SELF-ADVERTISING ON THE PHONE AND IN STORES, WITH FAMILY AND FRIENDS

Self-advertising, or self-disclosure, is potentially the most powerful tool for overcoming shame and embarrassment. It can create a "stutter-friendly" environment, eliminate the fear of assumed listener reaction to stuttering and/or speech management, and communicate an attitude of confidence, comfort, and ease to the listener. We encourage our clients to view self-advertising not as an apology, but rather as a statement of fact. It provides an opportunity to educate family, friends, peers, and coworkers. Also, self-advertising can be viewed as a *responsibility* of the person who stutters, as is discussed in greater detail later in this chapter.

In our intensive program, our clients begin work on the telephone on the *very first day* of treatment and, by the end of three weeks, will have hundreds of experiences on the phone practicing self-advertising or self-disclosure as well as management skills. Early in treatment, we travel outside to stores and practice self-advertising with store clerks. The most challenging activity for most of our clients is the practice of doing surveys about stuttering in a nearby park, which requires them to go up to strangers, introduce themselves, and ask some questions about stuttering, while allowing their stuttering to be evident (another activity developed by Breitenfeldt & Lorenz, 1999). Among the questions they typically ask are:

"Excuse me, my name is _____ and I'm a stutterer working on my speech. Would you mind taking a couple of minutes to answer a few questions about stuttering?"

1. "What do you think causes stuttering?"
2. "What would you do if your child stuttered?"

3. "What do you think a stutterer should do to overcome his or her stuttering?"

4. "Do you know anyone else who stutters? Who?"

5. "Do you have any questions about stuttering?"

A worksheet is provided to keep track of emotional reactions before and after each activity as well as listener reaction. Although each client ultimately customizes his self-advertising style, in the beginning we include a few requirements. Because most who stutter have difficulty saying their names as well as the word "stutter," we ask that they say at least their first name and use the "s" word in some form. For example: "I'm John and oh, by the way, sometimes I stutter, so just hang in there with me! When do you close tonight?"

Obviously, most of our clients initially react with fear. Understandably, most of them expect listeners to hang up, be impatient, or be rude. Most have a history of avoiding phone calls. They are often surprised to find that most people do not respond negatively; that, at the very least, they get a neutral reaction, and in fact, quite often a positive, supportive reaction from the listener. However, the reality is that there *are* rude (or uninformed) people out there and our clients need to be prepared for this. The point is made that it's probably because of the few rude responses they may have gotten in the past that they have shut down and gone into hiding. We challenge our clients with the question, "are you still willing to let one rude (uninformed) person dictate your life's activities?"

Working in peer pairs is very important on the early phone activities. Many have commented to me that they probably would not have even gotten on the phone had it not been for their partner's encouragement (and pressure). Although my staff and I always do the first call to demonstrate while doing our "best stuttering," it's just not the same. Peer pressure and support is invaluable here.

It's also important that the advertising *not* be an apology. There is nothing to apologize for. Again, the feeling we seek is one of self-respect, dignity, and even a sense of humor. Advertising helps the listener to know how to respond and it also communicates to the listener a high level of comfort and confidence. I am often so moved watching our clients progress toward liberation when they reach the day that they ask if we're going to do more calls because "they're fun!"

The same worksheet is used as we make our way out into the world the next day by visiting local stores. Again, the clients work in pairs and are asked to approach store clerks, self-advertise while maintaining eye contact, and ask a question. I witness fear, courage, and ultimately, triumph. I have found that it's very important for each of our clients to advertise in ways that suit their own personalities. There are also many different ways of advertising that depend on the type of situation and the type of relationship. Self-advertising can range from a very casual acknowledgment of "hang on a second, let me say that again" to a more formal statement, for example, at the outset of a job interview or presentation.

One of our groups was discussing the fact that most who stutter fool themselves into believing that people don't really notice the stuttering and that is why they think they don't need to advertise. I noticed one client having what seemed to be a "light bulb" moment and I asked him what he was thinking. He said, with a huge grin on his face, "oh my gosh, it's just like a comb-over!" as he finally acquiesced to the idea of self-disclosure. What a great metaphor. Self-advertising can later be used to let people know that they are working on their speech, and thus it empowers people with the courage to utilize new skills and to make mistakes or "sound a bit different." The consequence of "failure" is no longer there. For example, "Boy, I'm having a tough time talking today. I really want to focus in on my skills." One of my clients coined the term *stuttery,* as in "I'm having a stuttery day today!"

Self-disclosure is not only a means to relief, liberation, and personal empowerment; we view it as a *responsibility* of the person who stutters. Understandably, many, if not most, of our clients complain about the fact that most people "just don't understand" and get angry when others try to be helpful or fill in words for them. I challenge them with the question, "well, have you ever asked anyone not to do that?" Of course not. Most are expecting (or hoping) listeners to be mind readers. I suggest that, as much as I can understand their frustration and anger that they, in fact, have a responsibility to their listeners to self-advertise. As we well know, the entire dynamic of the speaking situation is often negatively altered by concerns about the other person's perceptions and reactions. Advertising "cleans up the communicative space" and allows for clearer and more stress-free communication.

Originally named "The Bill of Rights for People Who Stutter," "The Bill of Rights and Responsibilities of People Who Stutter" was renamed as such when it was decided that people who stutter also have certain responsibilities. The brainchild of Michael Sugarman, and sponsored by the International Fluency Association and the International Stuttering Association, the Bill circulated internationally among the stuttering community a few years ago and is now available in brochure and poster form (see www.isa.org). Among "Responsibilities" are that the PWS:

- Understand that conversational partners may be uninformed about stuttering and its ramifications or that they may hold different views of stuttering;
- Advise listeners or conversation partners if one needs additional time to communicate;
- Be conscious that he or she has the power to promote awareness about stuttering and its ramifications.

Before I move on, I'd like to share a wonderful real-life application of self-advertising. Following his treatment here at the American Institute, one client, who is not an actor, auditioned for a national television commercial. Twice, he had to enter a very large room with about 40 or more people, including technicians, make-up people, the director, and cameras. He began each time by saying, "before we start here, I just want to let you all know that I have a stutter. I've got it pretty well managed but sometimes it shows up. So are we cool with this? Okay, great, let's go!" He said it with charm, strength, and confidence. Not only did he surpass 80 other people to get the commercial, but the crew gave him a standing ovation at the end of the filming, and as the director was hugging him he said, "what do you mean you stutter? You didn't stutter at all!" He later told me that the advertising made all the difference in the world. It took the pressure off so that he could much more easily access his physical management skills. He was chosen and was seen on national television as a spokesperson for a large personal computer company!

As we move into the next phase of treatment, our clients have "walked the coals"—letting their stuttering out, studying and identifying physical, mental and emotional responses, becoming more fearless, and building a sense of self-respect and acceptance. Developing the attitude that it is okay to stutter is liberating, but interestingly, some clients experience a fear of acceptance. They fear that if they *really believe* it's okay to stutter then they won't continue to be motivated to change it. Some people hold to a belief that becomes a "black or white" situation: that one either accepts the stuttering or they do something about it. That acceptance somehow renders one passive.

However, these need not be mutually exclusive. We can do both: accept *and* take action. Alcoholics Anonymous is famous for this stance. Once our clients embrace this thinking, they often find that the acceptance of the stuttering as a part of them is, in fact, what strengthens them to work on the speech; their new comfort level with themselves and moments of dysfluency actually allows them to access their new skills much more easily. We talk about an attitude of nonjudgmental acceptance. We encourage our clients to embrace their humanity which includes their very human imperfections. After all, there is no such thing as a perfect person! We decide that we can accept the stuttering and also work toward change.

Treatment component IV: Managing moments of stuttering

STUTTERING MODIFICATION

Direct speech management begins with the stuttering modification component. In employing the techniques I discuss next, my personal bias is to use as little of the classic speech therapy jargon as possible. Too many of our clients have been plied with "techniques," too often without any grounding in information about why and how the "techniques" work. Instead, we talk about the fact that what they are doing is managing and changing tension levels in the voice and speech muscle system and use that type of terminology.

In order to give our clients some useful tools that can be applied immediately to begin to minimize the severity of blocks, we start with the "stutter more easily" approach by working with tension levels of the articulators. We use many of the exercises developed by Breitenfeldt and Lorenz (1999) to teach the concept of tension-free articulation. Through the earlier activities of freezing and mirror work, our clients have begun to develop awareness of the loci of tension and some ability to modify and "pull out" of tension. We next begin the process of understanding more specifically how speech sounds are made; literally, we provide a simple phonetics tutorial. They are shown diagrams of the vocal tract and we point out that all of their "pieces and parts" are intact and that they can learn how to manage their muscles "manually."

The differing sound characteristics are introduced and categorized. Because the locus of tension for vowels is primarily the vocal folds, we focus first on the consonants in terms of modifying tension at the place of articulation. We then introduce the classes of consonants, from continuants to fricatives and then to plosives. To address the management of vowels in the short term, simply prolonging a vowel helps some of our clients move through a vocal block more easily. We focus more on the management of vowels and the vocal folds during the fluency shaping component.

We manipulate tension levels by experimenting with a word on which our client typically stutters. Each one chooses a word (often their name) that begins with a consonant. We identify where that sound is articulated: what is touching what in the mouth? I ask the client to put as much pressure and tension as he can muster on that articulatory position and push out the word. This is identified as "100% tension." Then I ask him to reduce it to 50%, then 20%, then 10%, 5%, and 0%, with 0% being normal articulation or even under-articulation.

Next, we review all of the consonants in terms of place of articulation as they learn to create and feel a "light contact," or 0% tension, in initial consonants. An exaggerated form of practice is done in the form of "stretching" or "prolongation." Our goal is that the sound be prolonged or stretched in order to provide enough time to actually feel the placement; "prolongation" is *not* the skill. Holding the position of the articulators is the means to learning and feeling 0% tension and, ultimately, normal articulation.

Next, we teach that there can be three different opportunities for modifying one's speech: before, during, or after a stuttering moment, therefore either preventing the block or reducing the severity of the block. Specifically,

Before: If a stutter is expected, before the block occurs, we ask the client to modify going *into* the word by applying 0% tension (with differing levels of prolongation depending on the challenge);

During: If caught in a stuttering moment, we teach that tension can be reduced while holding the position, then slowly and smoothly transitioned into the next sound (called a "pull out" by Van Riper);

After: Van Riper called poststutter corrections "cancellations." We call it a "do-over" and ask the client to say the whole word over again with 0% tension.

Therapy employs individual practice using a tape that addresses all consonant sounds in words and sentences. This is followed by a session of reading aloud practicing the exaggerated prolongations and 0% tension on the first three words of each sentence as well as when needed. Next, we do some conversational practice in pairs, thus preparing clients to go out that evening to experiment with their new awareness and ability. After the challenges of desensitization work, this usually comes as welcome relief from at least some of the physical struggle of stuttering, and clients seem quite grateful to have something to begin to use to make speaking less effortful.

Treatment component V: Motor training

FLUENCY SHAPING

As most of us are aware, the classic Precision Fluency Shaping Program (PFSP) (Webster, 1977) endeavored to shift thinking about the treatment of stuttering and presented a highly structured process that results in the generation of fluent speech, a significant step beyond modifying moments of stuttering. Webster took a primarily physiological approach and devised a system for training speech muscle coordination, the byproduct of which is speech fluency.

My interpretation of this aspect of treatment has been to simplify and streamline as much as possible, allowing for greater ease in the learning of the skills and most importantly, easier access to those skills during speaking situations. Rather than use the term *targets,* I prefer the use of more physical/muscular descriptors, so I call this *vocal fold management.*

The basic goal of management of the vocal folds is to achieve normal, natural breathing and voice production. A critical element is the development of kinesthetic/proprioceptive sensory awareness, a physical/muscular orientation that gives the client a tangible sense of manipulating the voice mechanism. Van Riper (1973) stressed this in his writings as well. Training of motor skills is typically accomplished by breaking the motor activity down into components.

In the intensive model, the following steps to establish diaphragmatic breathing awareness are accomplished in blocks of time throughout a 7-hour day. We meet as a group for instructional purposes; these groups alternate with individual work in 15- to 20-minute "formal" practice sessions that are presented in our Client Manual (Montgomery, 2002).

Breathing for Speaking. Our activities in this unit include:

- Breathing awareness exercises
- Education regarding the diaphragm and how normal breathing works
- Education regarding the "fight or flight" response
- Awareness of diaphragm and rib cage function
- Introduction of a "4 Step Breathing Sequence"
- Discussion of rationale for each step.

As does anyone who works with the voice, whether it be for treatment or performance, we spend some time working with diaphragmatic breathing in order to support management and control of the vocal folds. The literature also supports direct work on breathing as part of treatment for stuttering. Therapy that included regulated breathing produced a 68% decrease in stuttering 10 months posttreatment (Woods et al., 2000). Similarly, Runyan and Runyan (1999) included a breath management component in their therapy. Deeper, more diaphragmatic breathing helps to keep our throat muscles more relaxed, relaxes the whole body, keeps our minds clearer, reduces the effects of adrenaline (the "fight or flight" response), and allows us to take in more air volume which is the fuel for "running" the voice (Rama, Ballentine & Hymes, 1979).

We first guide our client in a "closed-eye" awareness activity to discover what movement he feels in his body as he inhales and exhales normally. Next, we introduce some anatomical drawings to educate about the breathing process and particularly the movement of the diaphragm. Where is it located? How is it shaped? How does it work? It's important that the client understands that he already "knows" how to breathe and that all we are suggesting is that he simply bring certain awarenesses to it and that he will be aiming for an optimal, fuller form of breathing for speech purposes.

With greater understanding of the mechanism, we introduce the idea of a sequence that begins with an exhalation: that one releases leftover air before the inhalation takes place. Too often clinicians will instruct their clients to "breathe before you speak." However, we have discovered that this can actually contribute to more tension in the vocal tract by inhaling "on top of" air already in the lungs. We refer to this as "packing" the air.

Once excess air has been naturally and easily released (not pushed), the inhalation can then begin in a more comfortable, relaxed way. The anticipation of difficulty in speaking can create what many call "pre-blocking," and many who stutter create tension in the vocal tract prior to speaking. This is counteracted by maintaining a relaxation of the articulators at the beginning on the inhalation. As the inhalation continues, we suggest that one can simply "follow the air stream" as the diaphragm descends and the ribs expand. We ask our client not to focus on the front of the diaphragm, as most who teach breathing do, but rather on the sides of the ribs or even the lower back, as this avoids pushing with abdominal muscles in the effort to "expand the diaphragm." This allows for a much more natural and tension-free inhalation, or as one of our clients called it, "360 degree breathing." The front part of the diaphragm will still move out, but it does so naturally and without tension. As much air is taken in as can be done comfortably. Once the inhalation is taken, the next physical focus is on maintaining the openness of the vocal folds. Prior to the introduction of voicing, this feeling is purely an openness. It feels like nothing is going on in the throat, only air passing out.

It's useful to think of the parts of the breathing process in a sequence and it's very important to *feel* the physical reference points. This is how we approach the process in a manner similar to Webster's (1977) "Full Breath Target." Before we begin to move into learning how to start the voice without tension and closure, we do some contrasting, noticing the feeling of openness versus the purposeful closure of the folds by closing the folds and holding the breath while keeping the mouth open in order to isolate the closure to the folds instead of the mouth. This step is vital.

VOICING

We next move into starting the voice without tension and closure. Normal voice production occurs with simultaneous exhalation and voicing that begins without hesitation. Any hesitation can cause the folds to close. Inversely, allowing air to escape before voicing is abnormal and too much air can escape.

So, clients are instructed to simply allow the voice to begin on the immediate outflow of air with open, relaxed folds, without *any* closure of the folds, even the slightest. Again, the contrast exercise is very important here so that they can really feel the difference in the throat between closed and open folds. We then progress from maintaining open, relaxed vocal folds on initiation and continuation of voicing first on a schwa or "neutral" vowel sound (no activation of the articulators) and then on all vowels, as Dahm (1997) suggested. It's about the interaction of the breath stream and vocal folds and we ask them to sustain each sound with a constant air pressure. It's important at this point that there is no pitch or loudness change.

Once the ability to coordinate the breathing pattern with voicing has been established, this then is shaped into the normal intensity change in the voice that occurs on each syllable: the low amplitude vibration that increases in intensity (loudness) and then returns to low amplitude. So, each syllable is produced in a "soft-loud-soft" pattern. Kinesthetically, it is described as a "gentle-strong-gentle" intensity change, known as the original "Gentle Onset Target" (Webster, 1977). A full 7-hour day is devoted to the establishment of voicing and proceeds as above, group instruction alternating with individual practice sessions. (A total of approximately 10 to 12 hours is devoted to single syllable practice.) In essence, this is about training in the normal sine wave pattern of vibration that naturally occurs in fluent speakers, understanding that our vocal folds normally "pulse" on each and every syllable; that there is an increase in air pressure on *every* syllable. Research has shown us that the sine wave is essentially absent in the vocal pattern of the PWS; that the vibration pattern tends to be irregular and overall stronger, even while speaking fluently (Freeman & Ushijima, 1978).

The very end of the first week and beginning of the second week in the intensive marks the time to reconnect syllables to begin to create more of a flow. Webster calls it "Amplitude Contour." I retain the word "contour" because to me, it implies a connectedness of the vibration pattern. Some call this "continuous phonation," although it is important to retain the notion of kinesthetic feedback of the "pulsing" or intensity change from one syllable to the next. In this phase, we shorten syllable duration by half (approximately 2 seconds to 1 second per syllable), connecting no more than three syllables per breath. We move to practice on two- and three-syllable words, then phrases, and then sentences, using a loudness or intensity "pulse" on each syllable.

Following practice the same way in conversation, prepared speeches are presented at this level, augmented by a "toughening exercise" for practice in being interrupted (approximately 15 to 20 hours at the three-syllable level of practice).

As the skill is practiced and developed, the syllables can be systematically decreased by adding more syllables to the breath to no more than six per breath (e.g. *Themarathonisrun / inNovember*). Then, inflection is added with a much slighter pulsing of intensity on each syllable. Practice on multisyllablic words, phrases, sentences, etc. is followed by practice in conversation, speeches, toughening, and word games such as "Taboo" that require focus under time pressure. Outside practice (including the phone) is combined with self-advertising.

During the second weekend, clients take the management skills out into the world even more by practicing with friends and family. As clients return for week three, because of this practice, speaking rates have naturally become more rapid (approximately 20 to 30 hours at the six syllable level of practice).

GENERALIZATION (THIRD WEEK OF INTENSIVE)

During the generalization phase of our therapy, we emphasize continued practice in all contexts in and out of clinic, including prepared speeches for family and friends. We encourage practice using differing levels of exaggeration for the techniques that have been taught. With greater flexibility comes greater management. Regardless of which approach is taken, the client's ability to manipulate and exaggerate behaviors demonstrates true ability and the potential for greater mastery. Although it may simply sound like one is "slowing down," exaggeration of behaviors is increased in order to gain greater kinesthetic feedback and thus greater muscle management ability. We encourage our clients to experiment with increasing rate as well to "push the envelope" and test the system. Understanding that many factors, both internal and external, can affect one's ability to manage speech is important. Reduced exaggeration can be chosen in low stress situations, an average level of feeling and awareness can be applied in many situations, or exaggeration may need to be increased in more stressful circumstances. Also, our clients need to know that it's completely OK to abandon any type of management, without guilt!

Finally, we assist the client in combining all management tools: advertising, pull-outs, voluntary stuttering, mental imagery, self-talk, use of vocal fold management, choosing to use skills or not, becoming one's own clinician, and so on. We also counsel the client about factors that can influence ability to manage speech (approximately 30 to 40 hours at the "normal" level of practice during the course of the intensive program).

Some internal states that can affect our client's speech management can be physical, such as illness, fatigue, or tension, cognitive such as negative self-talk, negative belief, perceptions or emotions such as anxiety, fear, shame, or anger. External factors can include the speaking situation, the content of the message, the dialogue partner, or fluency-disrupting triggers.

KEY POINTS FOR BREATHING AND VOCAL FOLD TRAINING

The vocal vibration pattern is created consciously and articulation can become automatic. In meeting this goal, it is useful for the client to understand the difference between voiced and voiceless sounds for troubleshooting purposes. It's important to know when and on what sounds the vocal folds should be vibrating. The intention is to create a coordination of the speech musculature with the byproduct of the coordination being fluency. Therefore, the focus is on *feeling* the coordination, not on simply "speaking fluently." We also emphasize that what is being taught is normal, natural speech and voice production, rather than a strategy to avoid stuttering. Finally, should the client so choose, the stuttering modification skills can become secondary and be added as an adjunct if needed.

Treatment component VI:
Affective and cognitive change

SELF-TALK AND MENTAL IMAGERY

Prior to an intensive program, I ask that my clients read some books to prepare them for some of the aspects of treatment. *What To Say When You Talk to Yourself* by Shad Helmstetter (1982) and *Happiness Is a Choice* by Barry Neil Kaufman (1991) both focus on our ability to change beliefs and attitudes and describe a very basic cognitive psychology in nontechnical terms. I typically begin to bring this information into treatment during the early desensitization experiences. For example, Nutt-Williams and Hill (1996) reviewed studies suggesting that what we say to ourselves affects our behavior. For this reason, many psychologists believe that our self-talk can help us attain the goals we set and maintain the standards we have adopted, but these same processes can also negatively alter our perceptions of ourselves and the world around us. Effective positive self-talk is the starting point and the foundation for acquiring the positive constructive attitudes and thoughts necessary for achieving a positive self-image and thus greater management of speech (Cauchon, 1994).

Our observations and experiences with those who stutter clearly indicate that most, if not all, of our clients can benefit from direct cognitive work. Cognition can be changed in a few ways. The way we think can be changed through experience. For example, through the experiences of the desensitization work, thinking can change from "There's no way I'm going to tell someone that I stutter" to "Wow, this isn't so bad" or "I actually feel better because of this" or "It really helps to advertise!" The experiences of making skills work in real life situations can change the thinking to "Maybe I *can* do this!" or "Wow, this really works!"

Cognition can also be changed more directly by raising awareness of current thinking patterns and by consciously changing one's thoughts and mental pictures. It's the way our minds naturally work: We mostly unknowingly give ourselves messages and create pictures. The good news is that these messages and pictures can be changed to create an internal support system that can then support the efforts in speech management. Mental imagery can be a psychological/mental tool for positive self-support as the client creates a new "image of self." Visualization or mental imagery is similar to self-talk, but uses pictures instead of words and is using one's ability to "image" or "imagine." Visual imagery is something we all do every day and can be used to overcome ingrained attitudes and thinking patterns that can sabotage the use of speech management (Bond, 1993).

These ideas have been around for centuries and have found their way into modern sports training and sports psychology. Feltz and Landers (1983) contend that visualization has repeatedly been demonstrated to enhance the performance of athletes and others. Some studies have been done that demonstrate the effects of mental imagery as well as give us an explanation of why it works. According to Porter (1990),

> *The reason visual imagery works lies in the fact that when you imagine yourself perform to perfection and doing precisely what you want, you are in turn physiologically creating neural patterns in your brain, just as if you had physical performed the action. These patterns are similar to small tracks engraved in the brain cells which can ultimately enable an athlete to perform physical feats by simply mentally practicing the move. Hence, mental imagery is intended to train our minds and create the neural patterns in our brain to teach our muscles to do exactly what we want them to do.* (p. 17)

Hutchison (1984) refers to two remarkable studies. Richardson (1969) divided his subjects into three groups after testing their skills at sinking a basketball from the free-throw line. One group was to practice on the court every day. Members in the second group were told to simply visualize themselves practicing each day. And the third group did nothing. At the end of 20 days, the groups were retested. The group that did nothing predictably showed no improvement. With an improvement of 23%, the group that practiced *only* in their mind's eye showed almost the same degree of improvement (24%) as the group that practiced physically every day. Imagine the potential achievements of a fourth group who both visualizes *and* physically practices.

Jacobson (1938), a developer of Progressive Relaxation, studied this link between mental image and body by having people visualize themselves running. Their minute muscle contractions were measured and were found to be of the type the subjects would have produced if they had actually been running. When the mind perceives something as happening, it tends to generate organic changes. It is therefore not surprising that Ingham, Fox, Costello, Ingham, and Zamarripa (2000) reported that imagining motor behavior in general—and speech in particular—has often been reported to produce similar [brain] activations to those reported for the overt behavior in both fluent speakers and those who stutter. Imagery may help to develop the kind of neural patterning for the creation of fluent speech production.

I introduce these concepts to my clients with an experiential exercise. I ask them to hold out what they believe to be their strongest arm and tell them to resist my pull as I pull down on that arm with both hands to "test" their strength. They lower the arm back down, close their eyes and for one minute repeat to themselves silently over and over, "I'm very, very weak." Once the minute has passed, I ask them to open their eyes and lift the same arm as I go from one to the next, and with most of my clients, I need only one hand to quite easily push the arm down. They have, in effect, become "weak," just as they told themselves! This is a powerful experience that launches us into a great discussion about self-talk and visualization as they begin to discover the impact of thoughts and words on behavior and attitude.

It's important that we acknowledge with clients that any negative self-talk relating to stuttering has served a very important function and that they shouldn't judge themselves negatively for having done it. The thoughts have been there to protect them and to prepare them to handle a situation. The problem is that these warnings actually *help* to create the dysfluency.

MEDITATION

Another book I assign my clients to read is *Anxiety and Panic Attacks: Their Cause and Cure* by Robert Handly (1985). Handly recovered from severe anxiety attacks and shares his process of recovery with the reader. In addition to providing a nice treatise on the "fight or flight" response, he offers a good deal of information about "going into alpha" or meditation. The process of meditating is quite simply bringing ourselves to a natural, slower brain wave state. For our clients, meditation can facilitate one's ability to stay focused on speech muscles and enhance a sense of well-being and confidence. Meditation can enable one to create greater mental clarity and focus, heightened awareness of body tensions and the ability to release them, increased energy and vitality, a greater overall sense of relaxation, the means to deepening cognitive changes and helping them to become more permanent and, as research has shown, a stronger immune system, an increase in endorphin production, and lower blood pressure (Luks & Barbato, 1989). All these benefits and it doesn't cost a dime.

OTHER ATTITUDINAL STRATEGIES

Reframing assumptions about listener reactions

There are important lessons to be learned about assuming that we know what another person is thinking or how they are feeling. A facial expression, gesture, or body posture might not mean what we think it does, and those who stutter, having lived a lifetime of dealing with reactions, are likely to be overly sensitive and to interpret many normal signs as a negative response to their speech. A normal speaker might perceive a frown as confusion whereas a person who stutters might perceive it as some form of disapproval. Thus, we talk about reframing assumptions, or, as the politicians put it, putting a different spin on it. A client, an attorney, shared that his most challenging speaking situation remained speaking with his boss. I asked him what he typically thought about as he went into the boss' office. "I'm worried that I might stutter and what he'll think if I do, especially in light of the fact that the company paid for my therapy program and all." "Do those thoughts support your speech management?" "Well, no. It just makes it harder because I'm putting a lot of pressure on myself."

I challenged some of these assumptions. "From what you've told me

about him, I get that he really respects you. Has he ever made any negative reference to your speech? Maybe he's just really interested in what
you have to say about this project. The reality is that you don't know
what he's thinking. So, as long as you're making it up, why don't you
choose to believe that he has a lot of respect for you and that he's looking
forward to the conversation?" In the end, we both agreed that this
assumption would make speaking easier rather than harder: *as long as
you're making it up, why not make it positive?*

TAKING ON RISKS AND CHALLENGES

Accepting the adrenaline

Taking risks can be a big part of the overall process of minimizing the
impact of stuttering on one's life. I have witnessed so many courageous
clients who, with our encouragement and support, do those things they
have feared the most, and triumph. A fearless attitude is one that we foster
with the thinking that there is no such thing as failure, only *feedback*, and to
look at everything as an opportunity for greater learning. We can learn from
the times when we do well and we can learn from the times when we don't.
By challenging oneself, situations that were once stressful are no longer
stressful, or at the very least, not as stressful. What a confidence builder!

We encourage our clients to challenge themselves in many ways. For
example, to ask directions when they don't really need them. Call miscel-
laneous numbers and ask for yourself to practice managing your own
name. Go to the mall, just to practice. Volunteer in class. Volunteer to
read Bingo numbers! Join Toastmasters or take a public speaking class.
Do all the talking you never did before. One of my clients challenged
himself by self-advertising to all of the riders on the subway and we now
have the "Ben Challenge" that others can decide to take on!

Remember in driver education when the instructor told you to "go
with it" if your car started skidding on ice? Well, we suggest a similar
strategy when it comes to feeling nerves or anxiety or the fight/flight
reaction. Go with it. Don't fight a normal response. Tell yourself it's okay.
It can also be known as *Feel the Fear and Do It Anyway* (Jeffers, 1987),
another wonderful book that we use in our maintenance groups.

Clients have told me that they've had times when they thought they
"lost everything." And, although it wasn't particularly fun to go through,
they said they were able to figure out where they went off-track and to fix
it. It may have taken a few hours or days, but they regained after the "fall"

and they all tell us that it was the *best* thing that could have happened to them because they learned they need never fear a fall again. These experiences teach them that they are in charge and that they are empowered to make changes.

More strategies for support

Creating a supportive environment

A huge part of dealing with a stuttering problem is the ignorance that most people have about it. It's time for our clients to rechannel their anger and frustration and to start doing something that will help educate and inform people. It will help them and it will also help others who stutter. It's about creating a broader support system of individuals who are knowledgeable and understanding as well. Because we have educated them, they now know how to react to the next person that they might encounter. One more informed person is one less ignorant one.

Our clients learn to educate by doing surveys with friends, families, and coworkers, which opens up those lines of communication. Beyond that, family and friends are invited in to witness the presentations given by our clients at the end of the intensive, during which time they talk about what they learned in treatment. They'll need to take this out into life by talking with colleagues, teachers, employers, etc. We encourage our clients to let those around them know what it is they're working toward and to let them know how they can be supportive. Support can come simply from knowing that they "get it." In this way, there are no questions, no mysteries. People will understand that they are a "work in progress," that they will still stutter and if they do, they know how to change it if they want to. There will be an understanding that they may have "off" days once in a while and why they might need to "slow down" occasionally. This newly educated support system will also be there to applaud and appreciate their successes with them.

Clearing out potential roadblocks to recovery and creating a vision for change

I believe that this last piece of cognitive work is the closest thing we have to a crystal ball for predicting potential relapse. It was developed after many years of my trying to understand what forces are at play when one relapses. First, let me say that I don't view relapse as a negative phenomenon. Since therapy is not a linear process or a "cure" and because our clients are going through many layers of change, there will inevitably be times of challenge and inconsistency. One of the greatest gifts we can give our clients is to teach them to accept that these challenges are a normal part of the process and that much can be learned from them. In keeping with our attitude that "everything is opportunity," we view these times the same way. It's not "bad," it's simply feedback.

There can also be other factors at play that Van Riper (1973) and others have called "secondary gains." Thus, we developed an exercise to enable the client to begin to be aware of any benefits that he may have unknowingly derived from stuttering. These factors can seriously influence a client's concentration, motivation, and eventual outcome. Is the landscape clear to make this change? Is it okay, or will there be consequences?

The intention of this process is:

- To validate the client's feelings and attitudes about how stuttering has affected his life in a negative way;
- To enable the client to become aware of how his stuttering has been beneficial;
- To find alternatives to providing those same benefits;
- To enable the client to be clear about the potentially negative consequences of becoming a more fluent speaker, and ask himself: Is it okay to make this change?
- To enable the client to be clear about his reasons and motivation for change;
- To create a vision for change.

I have found that this exercise is best done toward the end of an intensive therapy program or longer term therapy process, when trust has been developed between the client and clinician and when the client has begun to develop some trust in his ability to speak more fluently. This can also be done earlier in treatment if a client seems to be having some learning conflicts or motivational issues. In the intensive, we gather as a group to process this. It is to be done in a nonjudgmental atmosphere while allowing the client to find most of his own answers. There is great benefit in doing this exercise in a group if possible.

Specifically, we ask the client to take some time at home and write out answers to four questions. Writing the activity out gives them time to think about it. We ask them to write anything they can think of in relation to these categories, even things they think might be minor or unimportant. Often, these things end up being the most important.

- What's "bad" about your stuttering?
- What have been or are currently the benefits of your stuttering?
- What might be the downside to greater fluency? Is there anything you might be giving up by being a more fluent speaker?
- What are the benefits of greater fluency?

PROCESSING THE LISTS

In order to validate and support feelings about the downside of stuttering, each client reads through this first list. This is later rewritten in the past tense. We spend a great deal more time processing the other lists. Regarding the benefits of stuttering, during group discussion we find that benefits tend to fall into three main categories:

- Past benefits such as "getting out of doing reports in school" or "dodging the military." These items tend to have no relevance to the client's present life, so we do not examine these in depth.

- Contribution to personality development such as "made me a better listener," "made me more compassionate," or "made me work harder." We can then ask, "With greater fluency, do you feel that you would lose your compassion (not be a good listener, or work less hard?)" In other words, are you risking losing any of these positive attributes because you've developed fluent speech? Is there a consequence to the fluency?

- Current benefits, such as "it's provided me with a handy reason for my failures," "makes me unique," "it's been an excuse not to do things," "it's been a way for me to know who's a good person and who's not, based on their response to my speech," or "it's protected me." These are the ones that can sabotage progress toward greater fluency. The clinician must then guide the client to find alternatives to the stuttering that would provide the same benefit. For example, "If you no longer stuttered, how would you judge people? How would you know who's a good guy and who's not?"

If stuttering has been used as an "excuse for getting out of doing things," I ask them to cite some specific examples and then come up with alternatives. (It isn't useful to generalize about these issues.) An "alternative" may end up being the realization of a newfound willingness to get involved in these things they had once avoided. Or, they may find other reasons for choosing *not* to do something, like those of us who don't stutter often do!

My clients tell me that they are often surprised by their answers and didn't realize how much they had gained from their stuttering. Generally, these issues can be resolved, attitudes modified, and beliefs changed with this exercise. However, on occasion, the issues are more complicated and require more processing time or a referral to a clinical psychologist. Answers to the potential downside of being a more fluent speaker often reflect fears about changing. For example, we hear "People will expect me to stay fluent." Again, I ask for specific examples: name someone. Who do you believe will expect this and why do you believe that this person would have that expectation? Typically, discussants encourage the client to educate people about their process of recovery: that they will not be perfect, that they will need to say, "Don't get concerned if I stutter once in a while. I know what to do about it," and so on. It's the process of creating a supportive environment.

Responses regarding the benefits of greater fluency tend to be positive and uplifting, as one might expect. However, I next ask them to rewrite this list in the form of affirmations. Affirmations are to be written in the present tense, with no negatives, and be stated with ownership. For example, "gives me more confidence" becomes "I am confident" or "I am a confident speaker." The benefit "it will allow me to say anything whenever I want" becomes "I say whatever I want whenever I want."

I ask each client to read the list of affirmations out loud in front of the group *with feeling*, to *believe* it as he speaks it. I next ask them to determine which item on the list is the most important and to close their eyes and visualize having this quality or reality in his life in at least two situations, perhaps one social and one at work. Once they have visualized it, they write down what was just visualized on the other side of the affirmation page. It is optional whether to ask the clients to share their vision with you or the group. I typically do not. I prefer for them to have a sense of privacy with this. It is just for them.

Our clients have now become clearer on why they came to treatment in the first place. This is the basis of motivation. The Olympic athlete's vision is seeing himself winning the gold medal and this vision serves as his basis for every decision he makes in his life: what to eat, when to get up, whom he socializes with, and so forth. The desire to have this reality causes him to make certain choices.

I encourage my clients to use these images as reminders to make the decisions and choices moment to moment in their lives that cause their behaviors to move in the direction of creating that vision. For example, making time to practice or choosing to have the courage to use speech skills in a new situation when it is tempting to go the "old" way and just get through the situation or advertising. As long as the desire is strong enough and the vision is clear, this will increase the odds of success in the long run. As one final step, I ask my clients to pair off and read each other's list of affirmations to one another: "*You* are a confident speaker," etc. This can be a very moving and powerful experience (Montgomery, 1999).

Treatment component VII: Integration

Most treatment components that have been described are accomplished by the end of week two in the intensive model. This allows for a full third week of integration of skills and attitude, and experimentation with various combinations of management strategies in-clinic and outside. It is also the time to begin to set some long-term goals and have clients make some decisions about the most ideal combination of strategies for themselves.

Becoming one's own clinician

After skills have been learned and practiced under supervision and with feedback, it's time for the client to take full responsibility for his own speech management: to step in and become his own clinician. Clients give themselves assignments to overcome remaining difficult speaking situations and new ones that crop up. If there is still avoidance or fear in certain situations, assignments need to be designed that challenge them in these situations. We provide a structure for a plan of maintenance over a 2-month period that asks them to assign themselves certain activities each day that incorporate the various strategies. This is designed with our guidance during the later stages of treatment.

Adjusting to fluency

At this point in treatment, clients are undoubtedly experiencing a lot of different emotions that run the gamut: from excitement to fear; from hopeful to skeptical; from feeling like they know what they're doing to feeling as if they don't know anything. All of this is normal and just about everyone goes through these feelings. Many report discomfort because they don't feel as if they "sound normal." They tell me that they think they sound slow, monotone, or just plain weird, and fear that people will respond to their speech in a negative way. All of these concerns are certainly valid. After all, they've spent a lifetime being concerned about people's reactions to their speech. One client even described his fluent speech as "beige"!

Even when everyone tells him he sounds great, the discomfort often remains. The primary reason is because the new speech production is simply *different*. The nervous system, the psyche, every aspect of oneself is used to being a certain way. With dysfluent speech there is a lot going on both physically and mentally. And now, most, if not all, of the physical struggle is gone or minimized and the new thinking is different. The speech is not monotone. It's just easier. This is what fluent speech *feels* like. There's much less effort going on and yes, it probably feels weird.

Although it is a normal human response to escape from discomfort, we encourage our clients to *embrace* the discomfort, that it's actually good for them because it's a sign that they are accomplishing what they came into treatment to do. Change can be uncomfortable, even disconcerting at times. But they came to change and they are!

Another important point to make is that for a while, they may find the need to sacrifice a bit of their usual spontaneity. It may feel as if it takes time to manage their speech and they may feel that they cannot respond as quickly as they would like. This is OK and will not always be the case. Again, as they become more masterful skill-wise, natural spontaneity does return. Self-advertising becomes an important tool to let people know that they may sound "weird," "slow," or different for a while and it's because they're working on managing their speech. They soon find that by advertising as their speech management becomes more normal, people's reactions are typically ones of positive support.

What I so appreciate and, as a clinician, enjoy about integrated treatment is the fact that our clients have options to accommodate their personalities, style, and goals. They can go for a combination of advertising along with acceptable stuttering, using skills occasionally including pull outs and/or light contacts and even some degree of vocal fold management. They can go full out with managed fluency and combine that with advertising to make it easier to use their skills without being self-conscious. Or, they can do nothing at all and accept that in spite of some amount of dysfluency in speech they are, after all, good communicators. We want them to be clear in their own minds that they are the ones making the choices and that they are satisfied with whatever they choose.

FRIENDS AND FAMILY DAY

At the end of the third week, family members and friends are invited for an afternoon to be further educated about treatment, to hear about what comes next, to understand realistic expectations, and to hear the clients' prepared speeches. I begin the afternoon with a reorientation about stuttering and the treatment experience. I always make it a point to tell them that I have such a high regard for their loved ones and that they are extremely courageous to have undertaken this challenge. The clients then share their own experiences and what it has all meant to them. Needless to say, there is not a "dry eye in the house." This is a very emotional and important time for them all. I talk about follow-up and then open up the floor for comments and questions. And finally, since invariably parents and spouses ask me how they can help, I turn that question over to the clients themselves, so that each client can gather with his family members to let them know how they can be supportive.

The intensive treatment model

As mentioned earlier, this treatment model can be done with individuals as well as groups, intensively or nonintensively. Let me explain the logistics of the intensive program model that we conduct at the American Institute for Stuttering.

It begins with a 3-week phase of intensive therapy, 5 days per week, 8 hours per day, Monday through Friday. A maximum of eight clients (age 12 through adult) are accepted. We also offer a children's 4-week intensive during the summer for ages 8 to 11 (4 days per week, 5 hours per day).

One of the misconceptions about intensives is that it is *all* group work. It is not. There is a variety of activities that goes on each day, which may include one-on-one sessions with the clinician, group sessions, client pairings for certain activities, or individual work sessions. Each client has a treatment manual and cubicle space that he or she calls "home" for the duration of the program in which they may do individual or paired sessions.

Treatment component VIII: Follow-up

Follow-up support is essential and is a continuation of treatment. The 3-week intensive is the beginning of a longer process of integrating all of the changes into one's life. Because this is an ongoing process of growing, we encourage a continuation by learning more about how to support one-self through this process of improving speech and communication as well as the process of living a more balanced, happy, and productive life. There are a number of ways to do this, including both continued involvement in programs at the Institute and/or seeking out other experiences such as Toastmasters; seminars such as those offered at the Option Institute; reading more books on attitude, change, motivation, and mind/body training; and certainly by joining a support group here at AIS or through the National Stuttering Association.

The initial intensive phase is followed with periodic follow-up sessions. The children return together for group sessions twice monthly for 6 months. As with the teens and adults, individual sessions are also available. Some of our children continue to attend individual sessions for 2 years postintensive. We do our best to stay in touch by phone with all of our clients as much as possible, especially those who are not local.

Although we offer individual weekly sessions for those who cannot attend an intensive, a combination of individual and group is ideal, as I have described above, and I feel it is essential in the treatment for most clients who stutter. Groups can provide the format for powerful peer learning experiences and support that otherwise would not occur in a one-on-one situation. So, when possible, we arrange for some group participation for our weekly individual session clients of all ages.

We offer a variety of ongoing support options to accommodate the differing needs of our clients in which they can become involved: A weekly practice/support group that is run by a rotation of peers, ongoing telephone and email contact with our staff, one hour individual sessions, full day "tune-up" sessions, and one week refresher programs.

Treatment component IX: Public education

To achieve any real progress, we must treat not only the physical condition and its psychological effects, but also the landscape of public acceptance and understanding about it. The lack of public understanding has created the necessity for us to spend a great deal of time on issues of shame and self-esteem with those in treatment. It is my belief that those of us who possess this knowledge must take more responsibility to seek out opportunities for public education. I see this therefore as a component of treatment on a broader scale. Let's help our clients and their families by doing all we can to heal the undeserved wound that ignorance creates. Experience, as well as research, teaches us that public education can pave the way to removing stigma associated with a disorder like stuttering. Reeves (chap. 11, this volume) discusses the importance of public education and awareness in stuttering.

Outcome measurement and the effectiveness of treatment

On the final day of the intensive, our clients once again fill out the self-report scales of the *PSI*, *WASSP*, and *OASES*. In addition, we do another videotaped session of an interview and reading.

In the end, use of a particular approach to treating stuttering is only justified by its outcomes. Given the call for Evidence-Based Practice (EBP, see Pietranton, chap. 3, this volume), we now document changes across a variety of domains from baseline (entry into the therapy program) to program end and analyze group performance (as well as individual improvement) statistically to gauge how successful our program is. Given our orientation toward stuttering, we measure a number of potential variables thought to be relevant to our clients. These include behavioral features, such as stuttering rate, as well as cognitive and affective responses to stuttering that are targeted by our program for change. In the following section, we offer some examples of program outcomes. Because our groups can be very heterogeneous in terms of profile, we use nonparametric statistics in measuring group change from pre- to posttherapy assessment. As we note in the following section, after participation in the AIS programs, we see significant changes in both attitude and behavior.

The results of our most recently seen cohort of participants are quite typical of our short-term outcomes. We compiled data from our teen and adult clients who participated in intensive programs from December 2003 through July 2004. During our last several sessions, we saw 23 individuals with a mean age of 22 years. Their average dysfluency rate, calculated in percent stuttered syllables, was 13.7% on entry into the program; stuttering rate declined to an average of only 0.4% on discharge. This difference is highly significant (Mann-Whitney U, adjusted to a Wilcoxon Z value of 4.1977, $p < .000029$), in addition to being quite meaningful in terms of clinical outcome and personal satisfaction with fluency change.

As noted earlier in the diagnostic portion of this chapter, we use the *Perceptions of Stuttering Inventory (PSI*; Woolf, 1967), the *Wright & Ayre Stuttering Self-Rating Profile (WASSP*; Wright & Ayre, 2000), and the *Overall Assessment of the Speaker's Experience of Stuttering (OASES*; Yaruss & Quesal, 2004) to measure aspects of cognitive and affective change as well as clients' self-report of stuttering behaviors. For the same cohort, total *PSI* score on entry into the program was 29.875, which declined to a mean of 8.54 posttherapy (Wilcoxon Sign Rank Test Z = 4.2294, p <.000025). Similarly, for the *WASSP*, the total mean pretherapy score was 98.54, whereas the posttherapy average full-scale score was 43.81 (Z = 4.2576; p <.0022; subscales showed improvement trends that were similar to the total aggregate score). Finally, for the *OASES*, the pretherapy total mean score was 278.4, whereas posttherapy scores declined to a mean of 160.63 (Z = 4.1977, p <.000029).

In summary, such numbers support our program focus on a combination of behavioral, affective, and cognitive goals. Whereas we have not yet performed a large scale assessment of long-range outcomes using similar statistical treatment, this is in progress. As St. Louis (chap. 4, this volume) notes, treatment outcomes and effective means of measuring success continue to be hotly debated issues. Just what do we mean by "success"? I'd like to share with you what my view of success is at this point in time. Because I view stuttering as having many dimensions of impact on the individual and his family, and because treatment has evolved to endeavor to help people effect change on many levels, we need to be able to assess many levels of change. Success can mean different things for different people. We believe that just as the amount of observable dysfluency does not reflect the full extent of the impact that stuttering has on one's life, isolated measures of fluency levels do not necessarily reflect success. And as we well know, speech fluency measurements in stuttering can be difficult to measure due to the potential variability.

To document some of the outcomes that we feel are important in stuttering treatment, some years ago we conducted a survey that was independently prepared by the ICR Survey Research Group on past participants in intensive treatment at the Communications Reconstruction Center in New York, which was the predecessor to the American Institute for Stuttering. These participants had undergone treatment from 1985 to 1988. Ninety-one percent of the 200 past participants surveyed reported that the program was highly worthwhile for them. About 81% reported a substantial increase in self-confidence. No speech samples were collected, as it was simply an opinion survey (Otto & Dimetrosky, 1989).

To personalize the impact of the treatment I describe in this chapter, 2 years after his intensive program, I asked Gianni Jacklone (personal communication), age 25, to write something for our website that he would like others who stutter to see. Gianni is the fellow who snagged that TV commercial. Here are his words.

> *Stuttering is a disability which can manifest itself in many ways, physically, emotionally, cognitively, even unconsciously. It is also a disability which does well to mold itself to the individual that holds this trait; hiding itself at times, seeming inescapable at others, and all the while remaining inconsistent and mysterious as it does what it does best: confound all that come into contact with it. It is no wonder most people who stutter carry with them some sense of imprisonment and helplessness in their battle to come to terms with, understand, and take control of their speaking lives.*
>
> *But you do not have to remain in the dark indefinitely; there are people and places that can help. The American Institute for Stuttering is one such place. Here you will find a treatment program that is both holistic and pragmatic, that addresses the different dimensions that stuttering operates within, that holds the individual's goals and needs above all, and that teaches tools, strategies, and methodologies that can help you take control of your speech in the real world, not just while sitting in a room at home alone. You will leave the program with a deep sense of understanding in what causes stuttering, a superior education in how you can take control of it, and perhaps most importantly, a newly found sense of freedom and the will to tackle challenges and pursue opportunities that you never thought possible.*

Over these past 25 years, my client/teachers have taught me that no matter what one chooses to do, what is important is that the stuttering no longer controls life's decisions. What's important is that one feels free. What's important is that one no longer avoids *anything* because of speech. What's important is that they have some sense of control and management with speech; that the feeling of helplessness no longer exists. What's important is that they feel good about themselves. What's important is that the stuttering is no longer the hub of one's life. It is only a spoke on a most amazing wheel!

Acknowledgments

I feel blessed and privileged to have fallen into work with those who stutter. These are courageous people and they continue to be my teachers. This journey has taken me to many places and to many, many wonderful people including those colleagues with whom I've had the privilege and pleasure of kinship, friendship, and being the beneficiary of their wisdom and knowledge. I thank them all.

I'd like to make specific mention and give thanks to my professional soul mate and dear friend, Adriana DiGrande, whose path I was unknowingly paralleling until connecting with her in Hilton Head in 1994 at the very first Division 4 Conference. We have since become a collaborative team and have traveled the road of integration together. Portions of this chapter have been taken from material that she and I compiled for clinician training workshops.

I would also like to acknowledge Dorv Brietenfeldt, the developer of the Van Riper/Sheehan-based Successful Stuttering Management Program (SSMP). The SSMP takes Van Riper's and Sheehan's work to a new level and has given us all the gift of creating experiential activities to accomplish these goals of treatment. I will be forever grateful for Dorv's work. While initially, carrying out many of these activities was some of the most difficult and emotional work I've ever done as a clinician, they have lead to transformation for both my clients and myself. Finally, I would like to thank Nan Bernstein Ratner and Debbie Livesey, who assisted in our data analysis for the last cohort of Institute participants.

References

Adams, M. R., Conture, E. G., & Freeman, F. J. (1984). Laryngeal dynamics of stutters. In R. F. Curlee & W. H. Perkins (Eds.), *Nature and treatment of stuttering: New directions* (pp. 89–129). Needham Heights, MA: Allyn & Bacon.

Ambrose, N., Yairi, E., & Cox, N. (1993). Genetic aspects of early childhood stuttering. *Journal of Speech and Hearing Research, 36*, 701–706.

Andrews, G. & Harris, M. (1964). *The syndrome of stuttering. Clinics in developmental medicine, No. 17.* London: Spastics Society Medical Education and Information Unit in association with William Heinemann Medical Boosk, Ltd.

Bandura, A. & Cervone, D. (1983). Self-evaluative and self-efficacy mechanisms governing the motivational effects of goal systems. *Journal of Personality and Social Psychology, 45*, 1017–1028.

Blood, G. (2000, November). *The Stigma of stuttering: Centuries of negative perceptions and steroetypes.* Presentation to the annual meeting of the American Speech-Language-Hearing Association, Washington, D.C.

Bloodstein, O. (1993). *Stuttering: The search for a cause and cure.* Needham Heights, MA: Allyn & Bacon.

Bloom, C. & Cooperman, D. (2003). Counseling and disorders of fluency: An overview. *ASHA Perspectives on Fluency and Fluency Disorders, 13*(2), 3.

Bond, J. (1993). *Using visual imagery to help you to achieve your speech goals.* Paper presented at the annual meeting of the Canadian Association for People Who Stutter. Ottawa, Canada.

Breitenfeldt, D. H. & Lorenz, D. R. (1999). *Successful stuttering management program: For adolescent and adult stutterers* (2nd ed.). Cheney Washington: School of Health Sciences.

Cannon, W. B. (1929). *Bodily changes in pain, hunger, fear, and rage* (2nd ed.). New York and London: Appleton and Co.

Cannon, W. B. (1939). *The wisdom of the body.* New York: WW Norton and Company.

Cauchon, C. (1994). Whistler's mutter. *Psychology Today, 27,* 20–22.

Cooke, P. (2000). Turning stuttering from a hub into a spoke. In H-G. Bosshardt, J. S.Yaruss, & H. F. M. Peters (Eds.), *Fluency disorders: Theory, research, treatment and self-help. Proceedings from the Third World Congress of Fluency Disorders in Nyborg, Denmark* (pp. 458–461). The International Fluency Association: Nijmegen University Press.

Cooper, E. B. & Cooper, C. S. (2003). *Cooper Personalized Fluency Control Therapy, 3rd Editions (PFCT-3) for Children and for Adolescents and Adults.* Austin, TX: ProEd.

Dahm, B. (1997). *Generating fluent speech: A comprehensive speech processing approach.* Eau Claire, WI: Thinking Publications.

Drayna, D., Kilshaw, J., & Kelly, J. (1999). The sex ratio in familial persistent stuttering. *American Journal of Human Genetics, 65,* 1473–1475.

De Nil, L. F. (1999). Stuttering: A neurophysiological perspective. In: N. Bernstein Ratner & E. C. Healey (Eds.), *Stuttering research and practice: Bridging the gap* (pp. 85–102). Mahwah, NJ: Lawrence Erlbaum Associates.

De Nil, L. F. (2003, July). *Moving forward a path to solving the crises in clinical practice and research.* Presentation at the Fourthth World Congress on Fluency Disorders, Montreal, Canada.

Feltz, D. L. & Landers, D. M. (1983). The effects of mental practice on motor skill learning and performance: A meta-analysis. *Journal of Sport Psychology, 5,* 25–57.

Foundas, A., Bollich, A., Corey, D., Hurley, M., & Heilman, K. (2001). Anomalous anatomy of speech-language areas in adults with persistent developmental stuttering. *Neurology, 57,* 207–215.

Freeman, F. & Ushijima, T. (1978). Laryngeal muscle activity during stuttering. *Journal of Speech and Hearing Research, 21,* 538–562.

Guitar, B. (1998). *Stuttering: An integrated approach to its nature and treatment.* Baltimore, MD: Williams & Wilkins.

Handly, R. (1985). *Anxiety and panic attacks: Their cause and cure.* New York: Ballantine Publishing.

Helmstetter, S. (1982). *What to say when you talk to yourself.* New York: Simon & Schuster.

Howie, P. (1981). Concordance for stuttering in monozygotic and dizygotic twin pairs. *Journal of Speech and Hearing Research, 24,* 317–321.

Hutchinson, M. (1984). *The book of floating.* Quill: New York

Ingham, R. J. (2001). Brain imaging studies of developmental stuttering. *Journal of Communication Disorders, 34,* 493–516.

Ingham, R., Fox, P., Costello, J., & Zamarripa, F. (2000). Is overt stuttered speech a prerequisite for the neural activations associated with chronic developmental stuttering? *Brain and Language, 75,* 163–194.

Jacobson, E. (1938). *Progressive relaxation.* Chicago: University of Chicago Press.

Jeffers, S. (1987). *Feel the fear and do it anyway.* New York: Fawcett Crest Books.

Kaufman, B. (1977). *To love is to be happy with.* New York: Fawcett Crest Books.

Kaufman, B. (1991). *Happiness is a choice.* New York: Random House.

Kidd, K. (1984). Stuttering as a genetic disorder. In R. Curlee & W. Perkins (Eds.) *Nature and treatment of stuttering* (pp. 149–169). San Diego, CA: College-Hill Press.

Luks, A. & Barbato, J. (1989) *You are what you drink.* New York: Stonesong Press.

Luterman, D. (2001). *Counseling persons with communication disorders and their families.* Austin, TX: ProEd.

Mahoney, M. (1993). Introduction to special section: Theoretical developments in the cognitive psychotherapies. *Journal of Consulting and Clinical Psychology, 61,* 187–193.

Manning, W., Bennett, E., Starkweather, C., & Yaruss, J. (1999, November). *Developing skills for counseling people who stutter and their families.* Presentation to the annual meeting of the American Speech-Language-Hearing Association, San Francisco, CA.

Martin, F. (1926). *Manual of speech training*. Bristol, RI: National Institute for Voice Disorders.

Meichenbaum, D. (1977). *Cognitive-behavior modification: An integrative approach*. New York: Plenum.

Montgomery, C. (1999). The benefits of stuttering: clearing out the roadblocks to recovery. In K. Bakker, L. Rustin, & F. Cook (Eds.), *Proceedings of the Fifth Oxford Dysfleuncy Conference*. (pp. 48–52). London: Rowley.

Montgomery, C. (2002). *Manual for the American Institute for Stuttering Intensive Treatment Program: A comprehensive, integrated treatment process for the person who stutters*. Unpublished manuscript.

Nutt-Williams, E. & Hill, C. E. (1996). The relationship between self-talk and therapy process variable for novice therapists. *Journal of Counseling Psychology, 43*, 170–177.

Otto, C. & Dimetrosky, S. (1988). *CRC follow up study. The ICR Survey Group*. Philadelphia: Unpublished manuscript.

Porter, K. & Foster, J. (1990). *Visual athletics*. Dubuque, IA: Wm. C. Publishers.

Rama, S., Ballentine, R., & Hymes, A. (1979). *Science of breath*. Honesdale, PA: Himalayan International Institute of Yoga Science and Philosophy.

Richardson, A. (1969). *Mental imagery*. New York: Springer-Verlag.

Runyan, C. & Runyan, S. (1999). Therapy for school-age stutterers: An update on the fluency rules program. In R. F. Curlee (Ed.), *Stuttering and related disorders of fluency* (pp. 110–122). New York: Thieme Medical Publishers, Inc.

Sandak, R. & Fiez, J. A. (2000). Stuttering: A view from neuroimaging. *The Lancet, 356*, 445–446.

Sheehan, J. G. (1970). *Stuttering research and therapy*. New York: Harper & Row.

Shugart, Y., Mondorff, J., Kilshaw, J., Doheny, K., Doan, B., Wanyee, J., Green, E., & Drayna, D. (2004). Results of a genome-wide linkage scan for stuttering. *American Journal of Medical Genetics, 124A*(2), 133–135.

Sommer, M., Koch, M., Paulus, W., Weiller, C., & Buchel, C. (2002). Disconnection of speech-relevant brain areas in persistent developmental stuttering. *The Lancet, 360*, 380–383.

Stuttering Foundation of Ameridca. (1997). *Therapy in action: The school age child who stutters* (Video). Memphis, TN: The Stuttering Foundation of America.

Thase, M. & Howland, R. (1995). Biological processes in depression: An updated review and integration. In E. E. Beckham & W. R. Leber (Eds.), *Handbook of depression*. New York: Guilford Press.

Van Riper, C. (1973). *The treatment of stuttering*. Englewood Cliffs, NJ: Prentice-Hall.

Watson, D. & Tharp, R. (1989). *Self-directed behavior: Self-modification for personal development*. Pacific Grove, CA: Brooks/Cole.

Webster, R. (1977). *The Precision Fluency Shaping Program: Speech reconstruction for stutterers—Clinician's program guide*. Roanoke, VA: Communications Development Corp.

Webster, R. (1979). Empirical considerations regarding stuttering therapy. In H. Gregory (Ed.), *Controversies about stuttering therapy* (pp. 209–239). Baltimore: University Park Press.

Woods, D., Twohig, M., Fuqua, R., & Hanley, J. (2000). Treatment of stuttering with regulated breathing: Strengths, limitations, and future directions. *Behavior Therapy, 31*, 547–566.

Woolf, G. (1967). The assessment of stuttering as struggle, avoidance and expectancy. *British Journal of Disorders of Communication, 2*, 158–177.

Wright, L. & Ayre, A. (2000). *Wright & Ayre Stuttering Self-Rating Profile*. United Kingdom: Winslow Press Ltd.

Yairi, E. (1998). Is the basis of stuttering genetic? *ASHA, 40*, 29–32.

Yairi, E. & Ambrose, N. (2002) Evidence for genetic etiology in stuttering. ASHA Special Interest Division Four, *Perspectives on Fluency and Fluency Disorders, 10–14*.

Yaruss, J. S. & Quesal, R. W. (in press). Overall assessment of the speaker's experience of stuttering (OASES): Documenting multiple outcomes in stuttering treatment. *Journal of Fluency Disorders*.

Yaruss, J.S., & Quesal, R.W. (2004). Overall Assessment of the Speaker's Experience of Stuttering (OASES). In A. Packman, A. Meltzer, & H. F. M. Peters (Eds.), *Theory, research, and therapy in fluency disorders* (Proceedings of the Fourth World Congress on Fluency Disorders; pp. 237–240). Nijmegen, The Netherlands: Nijmegen University Press.

— 9 —

Technical Support for Stuttering Treatment

Klaas Bakker
Southwest Missouri State University

Overview

A discussion of all technical options for stuttering therapy would be too broad to be handled in one chapter. Therefore, the following critique is a selection of those clinical technologies most likely to be of interest to providers. It is biased toward discussion of technical features, functionality, and availability of the products. Although a thorough discussion of their clinical implementation would be desirable and much needed at this point, it would not have much meaning without first considering the basic facts about the available tools.

Discipline-wide clinical technical products for speech-language pathology

Compared to many other forms of clinical service, speech-language pathology has always been a fairly nontechnical discipline. Nevertheless, three general forms of clinical technology are prevalent: (1) measurement (or assessment) applications, (2) biofeedback applications (acoustic or physiological), and (3) applications in which communication is augmented, or substituted by alternative means. Another relatively new form of clinical technology assists "distance" speech therapy through long distance communications such as through live (satellite) video, telephone, or the use of computers on the Internet.

Despite the somewhat limited clinical role for technology in speech-language pathology, new technical products and options do continue to emerge each year. As technical products also reduce in size, cost, and complexity for the operator, they become more attractive and practical for clinicians than previously. Although many new products appeal to our understandable desire to keep pace with emerging technology, unfortunately, we usually do not have accompanying data to verify if available technical products lead to desired results, and do so with clinically meaningful validity, accuracy, and reliability. Such information should be the result of clinical research devoted to the possible contributions of technologies to therapeutic outcomes, but this research presently does not keep up with the marketplace.

Future speech language pathologists will need to receive relevant information about the use of certain clinical technical products during their training, or at least bring their knowledge up to a level of preparation that allows them to select among new technologies or those that have yet to appear on the market. Currently practicing clinicians will need opportunities for continued education that help them acquire this type of knowledge and experience. It is clear that developing and implementing this educational component will require time. At this time, research and education regarding clinical technologies is lacking in many ways, leaving the responsibility of choosing among available and emerging technical options to practicing SLPs who often do not feel prepared, and in fact aren't, to make such decisions. At present, in speech-language pathology there does not appear to be an organized support system to assist in this need.

The role of technical solutions for the treatment of fluency disorders

Although the clinical role of technical products across areas of practice in SLP is relatively limited, this appears to be particularly so in the area of fluency disorders. There are some obvious reasons for this. Wendell Johnson once explained (Johnson, 1955) that stuttering is in the ear of the listener and not in the mouth of the speaker. He should have added that this applies to speech fluency as well! In the physical and physiological reality of perceptually fluent speech sound production, there is nearly nothing that deserves to be described as smooth or fluent. Speech fluency ultimately is a perceptual property created in the brain and consciousness of listeners. Thus, machines by nature are not very adept at measuring or remediating speech fluency.

The perceptual nature of speech (dys)fluency forms a significant barrier to the development of technical solutions that are designed for detection, measurement, or improvement of speech fluency. It is unlikely that technologies can ever be perfected for automatically measuring, or providing feedback on, individual speech dysfluency patterns, although preliminary attempts have been made (see Howell, El-Yanif, & Powell, 1987). Despite this, a number of technical developments to facilitate speech fluency have emerged (e.g., Delayed Auditory Feedback (DAF), Fluency Altered Feedback (FAF), and auditory masking (such as used by the Edinburgh Masker)). These same technologies recently have begun to generate interest from clinicians in other specialization areas that are concerned, for example, with the treatment of aspects of dysarthria, apraxia, voice disorders, foreign accents, or even aphasia.

This chapter does not take a position regarding how certain technologies should, or should not, be implemented in existing stuttering therapies. In addition, the specific technologies will change, although the concepts we discuss should remain relevant to new product releases. Thus, the discussion focuses on the current features of available technologies and desirable attributes of technology designed to assist fluency therapy or use of fluent speech. It is hoped that this information can facilitate clinicians in making informed decisions about their use for clinical applications, or their use for improving communication in situations known to be difficult for one's fluency clients. The following section is devoted primarily to the most popular electronic stuttering reduction devices.

Electronic stuttering reduction devices

INTRODUCTION

Recently, the production and sales of devices for reducing or eliminating stuttering, primarily by providing altered auditory feedback about one's speech, appear to have become a profitable market. Despite the fact that these devices are more readily available now than before, they continue to be underrepresented in the stuttering therapy and research literature. Today, a fairly high percentage of persons who stutter (PWS) appear to be willing to "test drive" and spend sizable amounts of money on devices that they hope can make them fluent speakers. Unfortunately, for the most part, they buy these devices without the availability of objective information about their quality, or effectiveness in establishing speech fluency, and usually without the help of speech-language pathologists. Users may be aware of the possible limitations of such technologies, but a powerful attraction of the devices is the ability to *"buy speech fluency"* rather than work at it.

The clinical literature on fluency disorders does not address the growing use and availability of stuttering reduction devices, nor does it systematically address the apparent needs of PWS who buy them. Even the most trusted textbooks on clinical instruments for speech-language pathology (e.g., Baken & Orlikoff, 2000) have virtually no information on such products other than a few paragraphs on the use of delayed auditory feedback.

Because of this paucity of information, most clinicians don't know much about stuttering reduction devices, and are uncertain what to tell their clients should they express an interest in buying one. It would be only logical to assume that clinicians would avoid the issue, or go with their intuition that the client may have false expectations of how these devices affect their speech fluency in the long run. In the absence of informed opinions publicly shared in our discipline, commercial companies, now unopposed, have become quite aggressive in their claims of effectiveness.

The public appeal of stuttering reduction devices today is shaped mostly by attractive-looking commercial websites and multimedia presentations which play strongly into the unrealistic expectations of instantly improved speech fluency. Most stuttering reduction devices today are sold directly to persons who stutter with the purpose of helping them reduce if not eliminate stuttering severity. The reasons why PWS are willing to take chances with the devices may be variable. They may possibly be interested in them to help out in selected communication situations (e.g. professional presentations, sales, teaching). But, perhaps they expect more: a lifelong elimination of their stuttering problem. Importantly, the expectations of the effects of stuttering reduction devices in the eyes of PWS depend on the information available to them, which in most cases is directly from producers, their websites, and popular TV or radio programs. When stuttering reduction devices are sold directly to PWS, the information on which decisions are made is unlikely to come from controlled empirical clinical research or speech-language pathologists.

One product, *SpeechEasy*[1], has received unrivaled attention in recent years through its exposure on a number of popular TV shows. With its introduction, as well as that of the *Fluency Master*[2] a few years earlier, a new distribution system for fluency aids came into existence that depends on mediation by speech-language pathologists. Unfortunately, speech-language pathologists do not typically receive training in, nor do they have sufficient experience with the use, or fitting, of such devices. Particularly in light of this recent change in the service delivery of stuttering reduction devices, it is important to know how such devices work, who can benefit from them, and the data supporting their clinical efficacy, as well as competencies required to fit the devices and train their owners how to use them.

HOW BIG IS THE MARKET OF
STUTTERING REDUCTION DEVICES?

The perspective of persons who stutter

There are no studies, to my knowledge, that have addressed the apparent usage of stuttering control devices in any systematic manner. Fortunately, results of a survey conducted by the National Stuttering Association (summary available in McClure & Yaruss, 2003) provide preliminary insight into the prevalence of stuttering reduction devices being purchased today. The survey was designed to sample the opinions of PWS on a wide range of issues. Thus, the questions regarding use of stuttering reduction devices were among other questions regarding aspects of stuttering therapy in general, and did not address stuttering devices in great detail.

Among the respondents (710 in total), 125 (or 16.6%) reported that they had used a "feedback or speech pacer device such as DAF, masker, *Fluency Master*, *Pacemaster*, etc." at some point in their lives. This implies that about 1 out of 6 PWS NSA members have explored the use of technology in controlling their fluency. If this ratio applies to the entire pop-

[1]*SpeechEasy*[1], a true fluency device. Contact information: Janus Development Group, Inc., 112 Staton Road, Greenville, NC 27834. Phone: (252) 551-9042; Fax: (252) 413-0950. Email: customerserv@janus-development.com; Website: www.speecheasy.com

[2]*Fluency Master.* Contact information: National Association for Speech Fluency, 228 Birch Drive, New Hyde Park, NY 11040-2322. Telephone: (516) 248-8383; Fax: (516) 294-5454. Email: stuttering@net-walk.com; Website: www.stutteringcontrol.com

ulation of PWS (which exceeds 2 million people) we get a sense of how potentially lucrative this market is. Of course, the membership of the NSA could be made up of individuals who are more likely to consider experimenting with the use of stuttering reduction technologies than the general population of persons who stutter in general. On the other hand, the opposite may be true as well: that more active and knowledgeable members of self-help groups are less likely to use stuttering reduction technology. In this case, the potential market for the devices is even larger than estimated.

On the same survey, users reported somewhat mixed experiences with the devices. About 62% of the users of stuttering reduction devices reported only partial success, and 38% reported that their device wasn't successful at all for them. Only 18% of the users reported "complete success" with the use of a stuttering reduction device. However, these same data suggest that stuttering devices could be more prevalent in the lives of persons who stutter than traditional speech therapy. We don't have a good sense of the number of persons who stutter who are receiving therapy (see Manning, chap. 7, this volume). We can't contrast their relative evaluation of the benefits of speech fluency aids that either replace or augment formal speech therapy. Thus, it would not be wise to shun or deny their existence, or the benefits apparently experienced by a number of their users.

The survey did not permit a breakdown according to type of device (and not all available devices were identified in the question). As a result, the composite trend could mask a mixture of positive and negative responses to devices that are very different in nature and may have different effects on the speaker. Furthermore, it isn't entirely clear what the respondents to the question considered "success with using their device" and how this experience might have related to success they might have otherwise experienced following changes through stuttering therapy. Obviously, these are important questions that need to be addressed by our specialization in order to effectively deal with the fact that so many of our potential clients invest in stuttering reduction devices. Also, such research could reveal the potential benefits of implementing the devices for augmentative purposes with fluency clients in addition to therapy. It would seem that even in addition to a successful therapy regimen the need for augmentative fluency devices may still exist.

The perspective of clinicians who work with fluency clients

There is no convincing basis for the belief that the use of stuttering reduction devices produces long-term fluency benefits, although some recent reports are suggesting that this may be possible at least to some degree (Molt, Merson, Kalinowski, & Kehoe, 2003). Clinicians have traditionally used DAF (1) for differential diagnostic purposes to distinguish among fluency disorders (Deal, 1982), (2) in rate reduction strategies (e.g., Curlee & Perkins, 1969), and (3) to elicit or strengthen selected fluency enhancement targets. Among the latter are "continued phonation" (Shames & Florance, 1980) and "gentle voice onsets." These speech changes usually increase speech fluency whether employed volitionally or induced reflexively by the auditory feedback delay.

Delayed Auditory Feeback (DAF)

Delayed auditory feedback involves any technology that returns the speech signal to the ears of a speaker with a predetermined delay setting, generally in a range of 50 to 250 ms. It should be noted that other forms of sensory feedback are not delayed by this method. For example, the auditory feedback which reaches the ear through bone conduction can not be delayed by DAF in any known device. Obviously, other forms of sensory feedback from the speech structures (e.g., tactile and kinesthetic) are not delayed to begin with.

Although a delay of 50 ms appears to the user perceptually as a form of "reverberation," the arrival of speech acoustics 250 ms after the fact creates a clear discrepancy between the speech output and the ability to monitor speech through auditory feedback. It is generally experienced as confusing, and its effects may be partially overcome by slowing down the rate of delivery. Especially in the most extreme settings of DAF, there may be multiple and simultaneous effects on the speaker that directly or indirectly affect speech fluency.

The principle of DAF has been known since the middle of the last century (Lee, 1950). Early investigations employing DAF with normally fluent speakers among others revealed that DAF affects speech by increasing the number of nonfluencies (Lee, 1950), reducing intelligibility (Atkinson, 1954), reducing rate (e.g., Spilka, 1954), increasing intensity (Zalosh & Salzman, 1965), and increasing phonation time of voiced segments (Ingham, 1984). Despite these deleterious effects on speech produced by normally fluent speakers, it was later observed that the presence of DAF often improves speech fluency in persons who stutter (e.g., Chase, Sutton, & Rapin, 1961; Kalinowski, Stuart, Sark, & Armson, 1996). However, these observations have never encouraged clinicians to use DAF strictly for that purpose. In nearly all cases, the fluency enhancing effects of DAF disappear immediately when a device is turned off.

Although DAF has the capability of reducing stuttering in many cases, this is not the reason why clinicians turned to delayed auditory feedback for clinical purposes. Rather, DAF is used as a clinical tool for manipulating aspects of speech that promote fluency through means that do generalize beyond its application. Specifically, DAF was implemented as a tool for manipulating aspects of speech production that are fluency enhancing by themselves. Thus, a range of stuttering therapies over the past quarter century have implemented DAF as a tool for reducing speech rate (e.g., Curlee & Perkins, 1969; Ryan, 1971), or other prolonged speech-related goals such as use of gentle voice onsets or continued phonation (Shames & Florance, 1980). We cover these concepts in more detail in the following section as they can be applied to both stuttering reduction devices and assistive devices for stuttering diagnosis and therapy.

COMMONLY REPORTED EFFECTS
OF DELAYED AUDITORY FEEDBACK

Fluency changes. Although the disruptive effects of DAF interfere with speech fluency in many persons who do not stutter, DAF exposure actually tends to reduce the frequency of dysfluencies in many persons who stutter. Because of this unique differential reaction to DAF by PWS, the effect may be employed diagnostically for differentiating among multiple types of fluency disorders (Deal, 1982), in addition to therapeutic uses discussed later in this chapter. That is, if a client speaks more fluently under DAF than without, this may be used as partial support for the differential diagnosis of stuttering. This because many other fluency-disordered speakers (e.g., those who clutter, or have a neurogenic speech and/or language disorder) appear to be more dependent on auditory feedback for correct speech production than are PWS, and thus are prone to breaking down in the presence of the aberrant feedback. Research using DAF with persons who are verbally apraxic, however, has suggested a potential benefit to this population as well (Goldberg, Stokes, & Richards, 2002), although the evidence is mixed.

Unfortunately, not all PWS experience fluency facilitation under DAF. Additionally, the fluency-enhancing effect of DAF is not the same for all clients who stutter, or in some cases may not be there at all. If one were to examine if DAF can lead to a reduction in stuttering (e.g., in terms of the number of dysfluencies or stuttering duration), the only definitive way to find out is simply to test this out with each individual client. If the fluency-enhancing effect is clearly present at maximum delay settings, it may be expected to be present with relatively short delay settings as well. In most cases, a relatively small delay setting would be preferable, as the disruptive effects of DAF (such as, for example, the effects of being exposed to it for long periods of time, or disruption of expression in a linguistic/pragmatic sense) are not as strong with short delay settings.

Speech rate changes. Both immediately as well as over time, users of DAF find out that slowing down speech helps them to adapt to its disruptive effect. Some speakers do this spontaneously, but others may need instruction that rate reduction will make speaking easier and more fluent while under DAF. This is a potentially vulnerable aspect of using DAF for spontaneous stuttering reduction. The client who uses DAF for slowing down in difficult daily living situations may forget about this instruction and begin to ignore the effect altogether. In my experience this is not an irreversible effect, and the effect can return upon the instruction to pay attention to the DAF stimulus and let it affect one's speech again as before.

Often DAF is implemented to target speech rate reduction with fluency clients, especially when the client does not respond to clinician instruction to slow down speech. DAF in these cases can be a more forceful method for reducing rate, as with clients where an involuntary and rapid speaking rate is considered an aspect of the fluency problem. Persons who clutter, for example, often accelerate speech involuntarily, and may not slow down easily merely following instructions by the clinician. DAF is more forceful in establishing rate reduction in these cases. (Although cluttering doesn't improve under DAF during diagnostic evaluations, DAF may be used to help produce a lower rate of speech production during therapeutic intervention.) Here, too, the effects of DAF aren't the same for all clients. I have personally used DAF in a research attempt to control speech rate systematically in normal speakers, only to find out that none of the subjects varied rate in a systematic way relative to the extent of delay. Although the majority of the participants reduced their rate, they did so unequally, while one participant was entirely unaffected by the presence of DAF in any delay setting. DAF implemented merely as a regulator for speech rate is not very reliable, as any university instructor who has exposed students to it during instruction about its nature and use can testify.

DAF, clinically speaking, may be a helpful tool for "nudging" speakers into the right direction for achieving a targeted rate, but its use is indicated only if other voluntary methods (e.g., modeling and instruction) fail. The dependence on DAF for establishing a desired rate reduction would appear counterproductive for later attempts to generalize the effect to natural speaking conditions.

Additional effects of DAF. In addition to speech rate manipulation, DAF can be helpful in instilling other speech changes thought to enhance speech fluency, such as continued phonation, the use of gentle voice onsets, or soft articulatory contacts or approximations. These targets are usually established through modeling and instruction, but may be facilitated further through the use of DAF.

Summary of DAF effects. DAF represents the most widely used and evaluated stuttering reduction device. It offers multiple potential benefits for stuttering therapy. If one expects to work with fluency cases more than occasionally, it does make sense to purchase a system, especially one that is flexible enough to be useful for most potential uses.

In addition to assisting in stuttering therapy, DAF is also among the longest existing stuttering reduction devices available today (perhaps secondary only to the Edinburgh Masker). The populations for which DAF is considered useful have expanded in recent years, and now include persons who clutter, or who demonstrate the clinical signs of dysarthria, apraxia, and even aphasia.

Technical features of available DAF systems

Although the first DAF machines used loops of magnetic recording tape, all current forms of DAF employ digital electronic conversion and manipulation to establish the feedback delay. This change in producing DAF devices has made it possible to make miniature DAF units that can be inconspicuously carried and worn. In addition to reducing the size of devices and making them less noticeable, digital processing has opened new avenues of control over the type of feedback that is presented to the speaker. Among the manipulations available on some devices are the option of frequency altered feedback (FAF), the ability to boost the "vocal tone" or fundamental frequency of one's voice (Fluency Master), or to shift the frequency bands of resonation (formants) of the speech signal, as well as generic sound quality improvements such as digital noise reduction applied to the feedback signal.

In my opinion, it is advisable for clinicians who work with fluency-disordered clients to have at least one form of DAF system available in one's practice. For reasons that I will specify, a DAF version that contains the option to provide FAF would be preferable. The DAF component alone serves multiple clinical needs, and can be important for making differential diagnostic decisions, in supporting components of existing treatment procedures, and in helping to evaluate the possible effectiveness of a DAF/FAF instrument as an augmentative communication device for a client. However, the clinician's needs for using a DAF system are clearly different than those of PWS, who primarily want to use the device for achieving speech fluency in selected communication situations. This difference in need brings with it different preferences for features of the device. For example, PWS prefer that a device is relatively unnoticeable to others. The PWS will generally not find it necessary to change the settings of a device, while the clinician, on the other hand, needs a device that is adaptable and may be used for a range of clinical purposes.

Practical considerations in using DAF

As noted, PWS users will typically prefer smaller and less conspicuous instruments. These devices tend to be "pricey" for most users. Therefore, it is important to verify that a company offers arrangements for returning a DAF if it doesn't turn out to be effective or satisfying for a particular client. In many cases, lack of satisfaction with DAF can be averted by testing the effects of a clinician's DAF device on the client first. This not only avoids the need to return an instrument, but can avoid costs associated with an audiological exam and the need to make a mold for fitting DAF devices that are worn like a hearing aid. Such costs cannot be reimbursed when a custom-made device is returned.

Most companies, fortunately, offer fairly specific return policies, but there are no data that reflect how well companies follow up on their return policy promises, or how hard it may be for a person who stutters to return a device and be fully reimbursed to the extent promised by the company. Monitoring of such policies would be useful to consumers.

FREQUENCY ALTERED FEEDBACK (FAF)

As noted, some DAF devices come with an FAF option. Under FAF, either the fundamental frequency of one's voice, or all of the speaker's speech frequencies are shifted upward or downward to produce an acoustic result in which speech remains intelligible but essentially loses its personal character. Some readers may have seen this technology used in the media for cases where individuals wished, or needed, to conceal their identity during interviews on radio or TV. In other words, most of us have at one point been exposed to the type of distortion FAF produces. The effects of FAF are sometimes described as "Darth Vader" speech (from the movie *Star Wars*) when the frequencies are shifted downward, or as "Minnie Mouse" (or "helium talk") if the frequencies are shifted upward. Because FAF exposure does not interfere with the temporal organization of speech, to others, the user's speech should sound natural, and not slowed or prolonged as would be the case with speech produced under DAF. FAF, as a relatively new clinical technology known to have stuttering reducing benefits, has probably been insufficiently researched. Moreover, whatever data are available in large part come from a group of researchers who are commercially connected with a popular DAF/FAF device currently on the market.[3] These data, of course, should gain meaning if replicated by independent research groups.

It is possible to experience the type of speech quality that FAF produces, with the help of a computer program (the *DAF/FAF Assistant*©) produced by "ArtefactSoft."[4] This software produces good quality FAF (and DAF) from current PC computers at low cost. It may be downloaded directly from the company at relatively low cost or for free for a limited trial period (at least at the time this chapter was prepared). The ArtefactSoft *DAF/FAF Assistant* may be the ideal choice for clinicians who want to have their clients try out DAF, or FAF, or combinations of both

[3]The researchers who invented *SpeechEasy*, and are associated with its production, have a comprehensive bibliography of their research efforts available on the following website: www.ecu.edu/csd/speecheasy/researchdata.htm

[4]The *DAF/FAF Assistant*©. Contact information: ARTEFACT, LLC, 2381 Rolling Fork Circle #106, Herndon, VA 20171. Fax: (509) 984-3022. Email: support@artefactsoft.com; Website: www.artefactsoft.com

(note 4 explains how to order the software, whereas the program itself is discussed in more detail later in this volume). Recently, ArtefactSoft has begun to sell a version of the program that works on palm top computers as well. Interested users for the palm top version should carefully consider certain performance differences in the program compared to the full PC version. Also, running this type of program frequently depletes the batteries of a palm top. Devices specifically devoted to FAF (with or without DAF) do not have this limitation to the same extent.

Because FAF does not interfere significantly with linguistic or temporal speech processing, there is no need for the speaker to change much about speech at all. The user will not naturally slow down speech, nor has evidence surfaced that speech is changed in any other unnatural way. The distractive sensation of hearing oneself with a distinctly different speech sound quality seems to be the only active factor associated with why some PWS speak more fluently under FAF. But, of course, that by itself does not explain the effect.

In fact, the fluency-enhancing effect of FAF is not well understood at this time and currently lacks sufficient empirical support. An intuitive explanation for the effect has been suggested by Kalinowski and Dayalu (2002), who explain that FAF modified speech is perceived by the speaker as the presence of an additional speaker, thus producing the same effects as shadowing, or choral reading, commonly referred to in our literature. Although a reasonable explanation, it should be noted that this simply pushes the mystery of how FAF achieves its ends one step further back, since it is not clear why choral reading or shadowing are fluency facilitating, either.

As is the case with DAF, FAF does not affect stuttering similarly for all clients, while it may not work at all for others. The only way to determine the actual fluency-enhancing potential of FAF for a client is to simply try it out in different configurations using a clinic-based DAF/FAF device. The researchers associated with the invention of *SpeechEasy* have reported data suggesting that a shift of merely a quarter octave is sufficient for producing an optimal FAF-induced stuttering reduction (Stuart, Kalinowski, Armson, Stenstrom, & Jones, 1996). These data are currently in need of independent replication.

Apparently, the stuttering reduction acquired by FAF, if it can be demonstrated to exist in a particular client, is at least to some extent unique and independent from that obtained through DAF. This causes a combination of DAF and FAF to be even more effective than either feedback mode alone. In other words, in case a client wishes to use an augmentative fluency device, there are now a number of options in which DAF and FAF are combined in one unit, most of which are small enough to be unobtrusive and convenient to use.

TECHNICAL SPECIFICATIONS FOR DAF AND FAF SYSTEMS

As there currently are few conclusive explanations of the stuttering reducing effects obtained with either DAF or FAF, it is difficult to judge what characteristics of these technologies are important for maximizing the effect. This makes it difficult to recommend specifications for the devices. With this limitation in mind, the following preliminary technical features and specifications will be suggested for devices intended for frequent use in daily communication situations. The needs of clinicians who wish to use a device for multiple clinical reasons, and across different clients, will be considered as well.

The Microphone. Any effects of a DAF/FAF system begin with the microphone, which picks up the speech signal before delaying it or altering its spectral properties. Each device should have a microphone that has the ability to pick up a strong signal from the speaker while, as much as possible, separating it from environmental background sounds. Generally, a unidirectional microphone, positioned relatively close to the mouth (but not in front of it!) should produce optimal results. Only devices that permit a microphone to be oriented in the direction of the speaker's mouth can benefit from a unidirectional microphone. Certain hearing aid-type devices with the microphones built in cannot be unidirectional and must depend on other noise reduction schemes inside the processor to accomplish a reasonable signal-to-noise ratio. How a system handles noise is very important, as the user will hear background sounds through the device even when not speaking. Moreover, such background noise could potentially be loud enough to be delayed and frequency shifted by the device as well, causing listener discomfort.

When purchasing a DAF/FAF device, one is not necessarily limited to a microphone delivered with the system (unless the microphone is built in, as with in-the-ear models). With the specifications provided, it should be possible to find alternatives that may work better, or are more pleasing, for the user. In order to match microphones with one's DAF/FAF system, several specifications are critical:

1. The impedance of the microphone should match that of the unit.

2. The microphone should reflect the speech frequency range reasonably (frequency range equaling or exceeding 80 to 8000Hz).

3. A system that uses microphone-headphone sets avoids cable clutter, and, of course, a wireless system avoids this altogether.

4. The connector plug should match the input of the device (but in many configurations this can be changed by the user if needed).

To a client who wants to purchase a system for use in selected daily communication situations, it is usually important how visible a microphone/headphone set is to others. In addition to in-the-ear models, wireless microphone/headphone combinations are now available as a result of developments in the cell phone industry. There is a good chance that most of these sets are compatible with portable DAF/FAF units, but this should be checked in each case.

In portable applications, a microphone is physically connected to the speaker, and this connection itself can be a source of unwanted noises (e.g., movement, rubbing against clothes). In choosing a microphone system, one should check to see if it is vulnerable to the effects of electromagnetic interference (e.g., neon lights, computers, and monitors) or wind. Wireless versions reduce some of these interference sources and free the user from connection cords. For PWS, these are important issues of convenience as well as cosmetic appeal. Still, there are some possible drawbacks that should be considered. There is the possibility that a wireless system compromises one's privacy. There could be other communication devices within the specified range that would receive signals on the same frequency. Usually, it is possible to determine from the specifications of a wireless set what is the maximum radius within which this possible invasion of privacy can occur. Also, the device could have built-in options for ensuring that one's conversations remain confidential. Finally, wireless sets require power, creating the need to frequently change batteries.

The (DAF or FAF) unit. When a device is not of a hearing-aid type, the processing unit must be worn on the body. This makes size and weight of the unit an issue that should be considered. For example, the

Kay Elemetrics *Facilitator*[TM] (to be discussed in the next section) would be too big to be carried in one's pocket and is worn in a waist pack, making it quite noticeable. The models discussed below all have in common that the physical dimensions are clearly specified.

Any portable electronic device depends on the use of batteries. Potential users of devices that are meant to be carried around and used for long durations should be prepared for frequent recharging or replacing batteries, and because of this should check battery cost and availability. In other words, it is an advantage to have a system that uses commonly available batteries, and also has the option to use an adapter for avoiding battery use where possible (as in using the device in one's home or office during phone calls). Shoppers should also investigate typical run-time for a device when fully charged. Rechargeable batteries usually have a slightly lower voltage compared to alkaline equivalents, and don't have the same durability, and this may be an issue for particular devices for which an exact voltage is important, or devices that use a relatively high amount of current. There is little known about how these issues impact the relative benefits of available devices, and publication of the results of independent comparisons of the most common devices is clearly needed at this point. We note that the current popularity of digital cameras and cell phones has stimulated the development of a new type battery (NiMH) that, over time, could provide a solution to battery life problems if devices can be designed to work well at a slightly lower voltage.

The settings of DAF/FAF units that are meant to be worn in routine daily communication situations are typically kept the same from day to day (e.g., DAF delay, type and amount of frequency shifting in FAF) although there may be some need to adjust volume depending upon setting. In clinical applications, on the other hand, setting changes are quite common. This raises questions about how convenient it is to change the relevant settings of a system. The smallest versions of DAF/FAF, such as hearing aid-type devices, tend to be least convenient as far as changing settings are concerned. For clinical applications, then, one should consider how convenient it is to operate the controls.

Specifically important for DAF is the range of possible delays. Traditionally, the most common settings have been 50, 100, 150, 200, and 250 ms. With newer, more flexible electronic designs, it became possible to adjust the delay with greater precision, and sometimes greater ranges of delay are available than those used in traditional clinical and research applications (e.g., the *Facilitator* and Auditory Feedback Tool of Kay Elemetrics allow DAF settings up 500 ms). However, from a practical point of view, the longest delay settings aren't as useful (virtually no research has investigated use of DAF at a delay longer than 250 ms), while shorter settings (e.g., 25 ms) may be all that is needed for many speakers to create a significant fluency-enhancing effect without the disruptive effects common to the longest delays. Thus, a shorter but effective DAF setting is advantageous to PWS who wish to use the device throughout much of the day. In contrast, longer delay settings are of most value to therapies which prescribe speaking tasks to be produced initially under the longest delay settings and generalizing to the shorter, more natural, DAF effects after reaching preset therapy goals for fluency or other speech changes are worked on.

The digital manipulation of auditory feedback delays may affect the effective frequency range passed by the system. This is an issue for the digital manipulation in the frequency domain for FAF as well. In other words, slower analog to digital conversions do not permit passing of the highest frequencies. This makes it relevant to determine for an application which of the speech-related frequencies survive the digital electronic conversion. Although the resulting feedback following a delay or frequency alteration can affect the ultimate frequency band of the signal passed, we do not know whether this is relevant clinically. As stated earlier, the mechanisms by which FAF/DAF enhance fluency are still uncertain; however, they should ultimately dictate the specifications DAF/FAF systems in order for them to be optimally clinically effective.

The digital manipulation of the frequency shifting in FAF is potentially more demanding for a processor than merely delaying the auditory signal. This is why the FAF effect is sometimes produced with certain "short cuts." There are different forms of FAF. FAF is made possible by merely shifting the fundamental frequency of the speech signal and leaving all other frequencies unchanged. This produces a somewhat distorted but intelligible representation of speech that is perceptually more normal than the effect of frequency shifting across an entire frequency spectrum. The *DAF/FAF Assistant* program, which is a computer-hosted system, offers the user the option to use "Fast FAF," which reduces processor overhead by merely shifting the fundamental frequency of phonation.

According to the vendor, this option was created for those who wish to use the program on older computers that would not be able to keep up with the demands of a full spectrum signal shift. It is possible that either FAF effect produces the same degree of fluency enhancement, but this has not been subject to investigation so far.

Finally, for both DAF and FAF applications, it is relevant to consider the dB SPL output that is presented to the listener's ears. After all, if the feedback is going to be needed for long durations, it would not be healthy to be exposed to feedback that is relatively loud. Also, as speech volume is a continuously variable feature, there is a chance that with amplification some of the intensity peaks reach unacceptably high intensity levels, and so a device should be protected from producing these levels, as many hearing aids of today are. Obviously, the risk of overloading the hearing system is not so great with DAF or FAF as these applications require little amplification (suggested volume settings are described as ranging from the same sound level as the speech signal all the way up to about 90 dB SPL). Unfortunately, many devices are designed in a way that the output cannot be conveniently checked and calibrated.

The Headphone(s). The headphones which will present the delayed and/or frequency altered signals to the ears are also important. First, because they are the most visible part of a DAF/FAF system, many users wish to have headphones that are minimally visible for cosmetic reasons and the convenience of not having to deal with the wires to the unit. Although it is easier to produce high quality headphones that are relatively large and surround the ears entirely, good earphones are now available that are much smaller and thus less visible. As noted earlier, a recent device (*SpeechEasy*) offers small hearing aid type devices (behind the ear, in the canal, and even completely in the canal). Its earphone part matches the technology of current hearing aids and thus provides a similar signal quality. For most consumer purposes, today the major difference between devices that are bulkier and those that are less conspicuous, such as *SpeechEasy,* is one of price.

There are several headphone-related issues that are specific to certain devices and potentially affect the degree of fluency enhancement obtained. One issue is whether DAF/FAF should be monaural or bilateral. Most traditional systems provide bilateral feedback, while some current systems—among which the most expensive ones—provide monaural feedback. The reason for this shift was mostly to avoid the excessive costs associated with (1) needing to have two separate DAF/FAF devices, or (2) two separate wireless microphone/headphone pieces. Some preliminary evidence suggests that monaural feedback is not significantly much less effective than DAF/FAF to both ears (Stuart, Kalinowski, & Rastatter, 1997), although there is some difference. These research data, however, come from researchers directly linked to the production of the monaural *SpeechEasy* device. There is a strong need to systematically evaluate the differential effectiveness of monaural and bilateral feedback on stuttering, both for DAF and FAF.

Yet another issue related to headphones is to what extent they allow the user to hear other speakers during a conversation. Earphones that completely cover the ears (such as those on the Kay Elemetrics *Facilitator*, or those that accompany their *AFT* or *Visipitch* program) block the speech coming from other speakers, including the clinician. In the canal (ITC) type earphones, or others outside the canal that do not completely cover the ears, do not block other speakers to the same extent, but of course, pass some of the extraneous feedback, which could reduce the effectiveness of DAF/FAF to some extent, although there are no published studies on this question.

Finally, there is an issue that is specific to FAF. As one setting of FAF (down-shifting the frequencies) produces speech at frequencies lower than those usually carried over headphones, regular headphones aren't always as effective in passing these frequencies effectively to a user. For this reason, Casa Futura Technologies has traditionally sold a headphone set with DAF that amplifies the lower frequencies to attempt to compensate for a possible loss in passing the lowest frequencies produced by downshifted signal (e.g., one octave down) during FAF. This should not be an issue for users that prefer the upward shifted frequency manipulation.

Consumer Protection Concerns. When deciding on a brand of DAF/FAF device, PWS who are intending to use it as an augmentative device for daily communication situations should know the return policies in place for that product, particularly if they wish to buy such a product without the help of a speech-language pathologist. DAF, FAF, or even the combination of the two may not be effective for all users. Further, the degree to which a device works may not be satisfactory to the user. Trying out use of DAF or FAF with a speech-language pathologist before making a purchase can avoid the need to return a device whose effect is not exactly what one was hoping for.

Any electronic device used for long durations is prone to encounter technical difficulties. With the costs involved for DAF/FAF devices, one should expect the availability of a strong and technical support system. A reputable company should indicate what support is available, and through what means this support can be obtained (phone, mail, local representatives). With the in-the-canal type devices, interested users should be prepared for long-term maintenance issues, including ear wax entering the aid. Thus, it is not surprising that devices which are worn often may need to be serviced on a regular basis, of course raising its overall cost.

Finally, there is the issue of potential side effects of wearing a feedback device for long sustained periods. Headphones and earpieces can lead to local discomfort, while the continued presence of delayed or frequency manipulated feedback may not be tolerated well by other users. Moreover, the possibility that the central nervous system acclimatizes to frequency distorted feedback and in the long run either ignores it, or even affects all of hearing with the exposed ears (even when the device is turned off), has not be researched. Obviously, this possibility is in need of investigation. Despite many short-term demonstrations of the effects of DAF and FAF, virtually nothing is known about possible long term side effects. In this respect it is important to consider that users of in-the-ear canal hearing aids, similar like in the canal-type DAF and FAF devices sold today, experience problems with ear wax penetrating their aids. There are no published materials that objectively describe to what extent users of DAF/FAF devices experience these inconvenient side effects and what are costs associated with servicing the devices.

Description of commercially available DAF/FAF systems

THE *DAF/FAF ASSISTANT*© PROGRAM

As was suggested before, the *DAF/FAF Assistant* (see note 4) is an inexpensive and quality system for producing a range of DAF or FAF effects and settings (and their combinations) on one's computer. Although the program limits social use (that is, one is confined at a computer), the program contains highly desirable features for speech-language pathologists who want to evaluate whether DAF, FAF, or a combination, are going to have the desired effect on clients who want to pursue this technology for improving speech fluency in daily living situations. The program has additional uses in difficult differential diagnostic evaluations, or as a system for promoting speech rate changes, or other changes effectively induced under DAF or FAF.

Two sliding scales allow the user to manipulate DAF delay and extent of FAF across the entire clinically relevant ranges (a simple side-tone, a complete absence of delay, is not possible, perhaps due to the processing requirements for a system that needs to be capable of providing DAF and FAF simultaneously). The FAF effect ranges from minus one octave to plus one octave shifting. An option for "Fast FAF" with reduced computational demand allows the program to operate on fairly old computers as well. Some listeners could prefer this option, as "Fast FAF" involves a less extreme sound quality manipulation which may be less distracting to the user as well. An adapted but somewhat limited version of the software is now available for use with PDA's.

Unfortunately, when recording sound on computers, a user should be prepared, on occasion, to have to change the settings of the computer sound board. Moreover, different programs may manipulate these settings without one's knowledge and leave them unchanged after use causing other programs to experience difficulties. Among these difficulties are failure to record or poor sound quality (in which case the board's sampling rate, bit rate, or other settings were changed and not reset). Clinicians should be expected to be able to counsel clients about such issues, and troubleshooting sound problems with computers. These are desirable competencies for SLPs in the new millenium.

CASA FUTURA TECHNOLOGIES DEVICES

Casa Futura Technologies (CFT)[5] has been devoted to producing stuttering reduction devices, at relatively low cost, since 1992. Because it targets sales to PWS directly, the emphasis has been on portable devices, with the majority of them providing DAF, FAF, and some rudimentary

---

[5]Casa Futura Technologies products. Contact information: Casa Futura Technologies, 720 31st Street, Boulder, CO 80303-2402. Phone: (888) FLU-ENCY or (303) 417-9752; Fax: (303) 413-0853. E-mail: sales@casafuturatech.com; Website: www.casafuturatech.com

form of masking. Among additional available options are connections for using them during telephone conversations, wireless microphone ear-phone sets, and wireless transmission to a user's hearing aid.

At press time, both the product line and pricing have been changing dynamically. One of the most interesting devices for speech-language pathologists appears to have been discontinued (the *Desktop Fluency System*^{TM}, or DFS). Another desirable model for SLPs, the School DAF system, is still available in its original form and at the original and low pricing level (roughly $295). It appears that Casa Futura Technologies is beginning to focus on products designed to appeal to PWS who looking for devices that are portable, optimally convenient, and minimally notice-able to others. As this involves features that aren't needed for typical applications in speech-language pathology, these products have become too pricy for that purpose.

The CFT devices currently listed offer DAF (full range of delay) and FAF (varies between +/− 1 octave). Both DAF and FAF work in a "voice triggered" mode, similar to VOR (Voice Onset Recording) on cassette recorders. The most expensive devices have an additional option for mask-ing. However, the masking option in Casa Futura Technologies devices has historically consisted of a 104Hz tone manually triggered by the user. This is consistent with the philosophy of the manufacturer that masking should be used as a last-resort "panic button" for suppressing stuttering.

The high end Casa Futura Technologies models can all be connected to telephones, thus allowing users to conveniently use DAF/FAF during phone calls with the altered speech signal only audible to the user. This, of course, facilitates use of DAF/FAF in situations where phone calls need to be frequently made.

Specifications for the sound quality output are not available, and per-haps have not been determined. In the author's experience, feedback qual-ity of the CFT products is perceptually good. As with all devices, the quality depends on the microphone and headphone used in an applica-tion, and both items can be replaced with alternatives to improve quali-ty if desired. The CFT devices are approved by the FDA as "anti-stam-mering devices" that are safe and effective. FDA approval is uncommon for many other similar products.

At press time, the *Ultimate Fluency System* ($3,795 to $3,995) is the most advanced of the Casa Futura products. It provides the same DAF,

FAF, and masking options as those previously available in the DFS, but housed in a small pocket-size unit. The *Basic Fluency System* ($1,995 to $2,495) provides DAF and FAF, but does not contain the masking button. As noted earlier, both models connect to the telephone and have multiple options for reducing unwanted background noise. Although the best results should be obtainable with binaural presentation, and a unidirectional microphone pointed at the mouth, this is also the most visible option. Therefore, users may prefer the monaural version for cosmetic reasons, even though this configuration may not lead to optimal results in terms of fluency enhancement. The microphone of the wireless set is not directional and thus more prone to background noise than a more visible but directional microphone. The transmission range of the wireless set is up to 30 feet and so conversations may not be confidential within that range. Frequent need for battery replacement is an added concern with the wireless version.

SPEECHEASY©

SpeechEasy is a very recent hearing aid-size option for Delayed Auditory Feedback (DAF) and Frequency Altered Feedback (FAF). As with hearing aids, it is custom made for individuals and thus primarily designed for use as an augmentative fluency device rather than a clinical evaluation or training tool. *SpeechEasy* devices are available behind the ear (BTE), in the canal (ITC), and completely in the canal (CIC). This extent of miniaturization is a cosmetic improvement over other devices which leave a microphone, headphone/earphone, and unit visible to varying degrees. As a programmable digital hearing aid, *SpeechEasy* can approximate the sound quality of such hearing aids and thus has a specified performance.

Compared to earlier feedback technology, *SpeechEasy* is relatively expensive. At press time, the models were priced in the $3,600 to $4,900 range, which includes an appointment with an audiologist for an ear mold and a session with a speech-language pathologist to receive training in its usage. It should be noted that digital hearing aids without the special functions offered by *SpeechEasy* are not much lower in price. The additional cost is at least in part related to the unique software adjustments needed to produce the DAF and FAF effects.

SpeechEasy is now available in both basic and advanced configurations. The advanced configuration has added a number of new features:

Maximum DAF delay is extended from 120 to 220 ms. The sound output can now be shaped in 16 (as opposed to eight) frequency bands. This offers interesting options for users who have coexisting hearing problems that reduce auditory response in selected frequency ranges. Software for controlling the settings of an advanced configuration is upgradable.

The advanced version of *SpeechEasy* implements an advanced noise reduction scheme. This is necessary as the microphone to the system is in, or near, the ear canal, and thus cannot be directional. The resulting inevitable increased sensitivity to background noise is handled with INAS (intelligent noise attenuation strategy), which systematically favors the frequencies that belong to speech while reducing the intensity of frequencies likely to be associated with noise. Although no objective data documenting the benefits of the INAS inclusion are available, it would appear that noise reduction is essential to ensure proper functioning of this particular type of device. Further control over noise comes in the form of an external volume control in the BTE and ITC models. In contrast, most CIC models are controllable only by use of a computer and a transmission system that communicates with the device; thus, they don't have an easy option for situation-based volume adjustments. Finally, as *SpeechEasy* produces FAF/DAF response to all incoming sound, it does this for some competing signals as well. This problem is avoided in the advanced unit by implementing EVAT (effective voice activation technology), which effectively creates a voice switch for turning the DAF/FAF process on and off, based on an algorithm that determines whether the signal is likely to be originating from the speaker as opposed to an external source.

A potential concern with *SpeechEasy* is whether or not the device should be considered a hearing aid with amplification and thus subject to FDA approval for this purpose. The level of amplification required for the DAF/FAF effect is minimal and should not exceed a conversational speaking level by much, thus, the need for FDA hearing-aid approval may not be needed for that reason. However, as clients do have the ability to increase volume of the device and are likely to use it for lengthy periods of time, this issue merits attention, as any users of an amplified feedback system could affect their hearing by misusing this option. Users need to be made aware of the consequences of certain volume settings. Importantly, speech-language pathologists who are involved in dispensing *SpeechEasy* to customers need to understand potential liability in the event that changes in hearing thresholds can be linked to feedback signals produced by *SpeechEasy*. The possible use of *SpeechEasy* with children, furthermore, opens up a range of other possible liabilities if a device is not properly cleared by the FDA, as regulation of devices to be used with children is much stricter than that with adults.

THE *FACILITATOR*™ (KAY ELEMETRICS)

The *Facilitator* is a clinical tool that incorporates five distinct modes of auditory feedback. It was designed primarily to augment a range of voice therapy procedures. Some of the options in the *Facilitator* are also relevant for aspects of stuttering therapy, either for use as a portable stuttering reduction device or for specific therapeutic applications.

The available feedback options are (1) amplification, (2) looping, (3) DAF, (4) masking, and (5) metronome/pacing. The last three of these feedback options are typically of interest to those who work with fluency clients, which is why these options are reviewed in some detail. The reader may already have a *Facilitator* for use with voice clients, or for clients with motor speech disorders.

The DAF delay settings of the *Facilitator* vary between 10 ms and 500 ms in increments of 10 ms; use of delays beyond the 250 ms mark, however, would appear unnecessary for stuttering therapy. The very short delays, however, are interesting and potentially beneficial for clients who demonstrate fluency enhancement under DAF. If a client responds well with DAF, they are likely to maintain their benefits with short delays that are minimally distracting and cause little interference to the speaker. As noted, some evidence suggests that delays as short as 25 ms can be very effective in producing the fluency enhancing effect in PWS.

In addition to DAF, the *Facilitator* provides masking, which is considered another fluency enhancing manipulation of audition (e.g., Cherry, Sayers, & Marland, 1955). The type of masking produced by the *Facilitator* is speech range masking, which is presented binaurally to the user. Speech noise does not require the amplitude of other forms of masking (either white or pink) to reach the same effect. Within the effective speech range frequency band, the noise provided is true noise. The masking option in the *Facilitator* provides for approximately 26 dB of level adjustment in 3 dB (or finer) adjustments around a desired setting. This range is certainly sufficient for finding the most effective setting of the masker for achieving fluency enhancement. Masking can be either continuous or voice-activated. The Adjust button on the *Facilitator* allows the user to toggle between these two types of masking. Obviously, the voice-triggered option is important when used in conversational settings, when there is the need to be able to hear others.

The metronome/pacing option in the *Facilitator* produces a click that can be adjusted in 5 beats per minute increments (range: 50 to 150 clicks per minute). Depending on the stuttering speaker, this may be sufficient, or slightly too fast to produce benefits. For example, some stuttering treatments start out at severely prolonged speech rates at the "2-second stretch" level which would require a rate of 30 clicks per minute. On the other hand, normal speaking rates in syllables per minute average between 180 to 200 SPM, which would be beyond the settings of the *Facilitator*. When the number of words per minute metric is used, 150 beats per minute is usually sufficient. Clinically, the use of a metronome for rate manipulation may produce unnatural speech rhythm, an outcome to be avoided.

RELEVANT SPECIFICATIONS

Although the *Facilitator* is marketed as a portable product, it is still larger than many other available devices. As a result, it needs to be carried in a waist pack. The headphones and microphone are quite visible and thus may limit continued use by children, or in professional settings. It is, of course, quite sufficient for generalizing skills to outside situations on a temporary basis.

As the *Facilitator* was primarily designed to be used in speech therapy, the controls needed to be flexible. Although straightforward for clinicians, they aren't exactly friendly to daily users, especially young ones or those with cognitive limitations, and practice in using the controls may take some time. Another limitation of the *Facilitator* is the fact that it uses built-in rechargeable batteries, which create availability and cost concerns. Although an adapter avoids these problems, it limits mobility of the user.

Manufacturer acoustic specifications indicate that the device operates in a frequency band ranging from 70 to 7800 Hz (dB range: 26 dB variation relative to the volume setting at startup). Sixteen-bit processing furthermore assures a fairly good sound quality. Unfortunately, this device has no option for FAF. Although more conspicuous and more limited than some competing devices, it is also priced more reasonably.

Auditory Feedback Tools® (AFT; Kay Elemetrics)

Kay Elemetrics[6] markets a software program, *Auditory Feedback Tools,* that replicates all of the *Facilitator* functions within the PC environment. It is available as an option for Kay's *CSL* and *Multi-Speech* speech analysis modules and is one of the standard modules within the *Visi-Pitch III* and *IV,* and *Sona-Speech* programs. Time-warping is an added function to these systems, which allows a recorded speech signal to be played back in a compressed (fast) or prolonged (slow) way without affecting the quality of the signal in other ways. The time-warp function may be useful for allowing patients to hear their own speech at a relatively slow or rapid pace. In my experience, the time-warp manipulation is not completely without "glitches." Nevertheless, time warping offers an interesting option for demonstrating targeted speech rates to the client, while having the benefit of demonstrating the result using the client's own speech!

As was the case with the *Facilitator,* these products do not provide FAF as a feedback option. At the time of development, there didn't seem to be sufficient empirical demonstration of the benefits of FAF on fluency (Kay Elemetrics, corporate communication).

The Fluency Master

In the words of the producer of the *Fluency Master,* it "fosters better hearing of the natural vocal tone associated with speaking." A contact microphone picks up the bone-conducted speech signal (especially voice-related vibrations) and adds it to amplified side-tone while affecting a phase shift. Thus, the *Fluency Master* does not provide feedback that is similar to DAF or FAF, although some delay of a much smaller magnitude than typically implemented in DAF is applied. The delay is limited to the fundamental frequency of phonation and is probably merely a phase shift of this wave, although technical specifications are unavailable.

---

[6]Kay Elemetrics Corp. Contact information: Kay Elemetrics Corp., 2 Bridgewater Lane, Lincoln Park, NJ 07035. Phone: (800) 289-5297 or (973) 628-6200; Fax: (973) 628-6363. Email: info@ kayelemetrics.com; Website: www.kayelemetrics.com

Feedback produced by the *Fluency Master* is only minimally perceptually different from that normally perceived by speakers and thus is not distracting to the user. This is, of course, one of its advantages. Wearing the aid for prolonged periods is feasible to the same extent as would be a hearing aid of the same make and type.

Currently, the *Fluency Master* comes with a money-back, satisfaction guarantee. People who purchase the *Fluency Master* are encouraged by the company to use it in all speaking situations, especially those in which stuttering is most likely. If the results are not satisfactory during a trial period, the device can be returned for a substantial (but not complete) refund. The refund cannot include a participating clinician's professional fee or the costs associated with a custom ear mold.

The *Fluency Master* is not a system designed to augment stuttering therapy, such as is the case with DAF. Documentation volunteered by the vendor describes the use of the *Fluency Master* solely for the purpose of stuttering reduction. Empirical information about the efficacy of this system is virtually absent at this point in time, and is limited to uncontrolled observations described in an anecdotal report. Although the involvement of speech-language pathologists in the purchase and use of the device is encouraged by the manufacturer (see note 2), the apparent lack of efficacy data means that it is not possible for speech-language pathologists to make informed decisions about the potential utility of the *Fluency Master* as an augmentative fluency enhancement device. Although the device could well work, or have partial benefits, this potential is in need of independent and objective verification in peer-reviewed outlets.

In sum, the only claimed benefit of the *Fluency Master,* fluency enhancement in an augmentative sense, is not effectively supported at this time. To date, the extent to which the *Fluency Master* improves fluency has not been independently verified. The only data I was able to obtain were presented by Webster (1991). The original experimental procedure involved various degrees of phase shifting of vocal tone, which produced variable and mixed results in only a few PWS. Webster, the original holder of the patent for this technology, has since sold the rights to a hearing aid company which now manufactures the *Fluency Master*.

In my contacts with the company in preparing this chapter, I was also unable to obtain the necessary technical details to be able to meaningfully discuss how the device works and what specifications it meets. The producer claimed to have added "proprietary technologies" that could not be disclosed for commercial reasons. The apparent lack of publicly known specifications is another weakness that limits the ability for SLPs to recommend its use, although the system is widely marketed to both professionals and potential consumers.

The ethics and practice of working with anti-stuttering devices

This chapter has presented a number of important concepts that arise in the use of anti-stuttering devices, including their documented efficacy, differential effects on fluency from person to person, potential side effects, financial ramifications of purchase and upkeep, and programming requirements, to name a few.

It is a clinician's responsibility to make clients aware of the existence of electronic anti-stuttering devices, explain what can reasonably be expected from their use, and why therapy is still nearly always needed. It would seem unprofessional to deny the stuttering-reducing effects of the devices for some persons who stutter. There is nothing wrong with a person who stutters wanting to use a device or experiment with it in order to find out what it does to one's stuttering, as long as its effects aren't interpreted as an exclusionary alternative to treatment. Whether or not a particular device is going to be effective is something that needs to be individually determined on a case-by-case basis. The result of the evaluation could demonstrate that a device does not have the targeted benefit and thus should not be used by a client.

The role and usefulness of stuttering reduction devices are currently in debate, and for many their use remains controversial. There probably is no unified answer about their utility that is shared by all fluency specialists, although it would be helpful to develop one. With an increasing number of clinicians now becoming dispensers of these products in association with companies who produce them, it is in the interest of the specialization to recognize this, approach the use of stuttering reduction devices in an objective manner, and promote objective information supported by empirical clinical research. Foremost, it is in the interest of our specialization to understand and potentially regulate what is freely made available to PWS in the marketplace. Education can assist clinicians in helping avoid PWS' inordinate expenditures on devices that may not have the intended effect.

Without support of a clinician, PWS could find themselves at a disadvantage in trying to return devices that do not work for them.

Future challenges for the increased implementation of effective technology in speech-language pathology practice

There is an important role for the professional organizations, such as the American Speech-Language-Hearing Association and its Special Interest Divisions, in providing guidance to clinicians and assuming responsibility for controlling and monitoring the quality of clinical technologies employed in therapy. The American Speech-Language-Hearing Association, so far, has not invested resources in examining or controlling the quality of technical products available to speech-language pathologists, even those that are intended to be used in clinical settings. Thus, clinicians cannot be expected to be able to determine reasonable and objective minimal standards for the clinical instruments they intend to use with clients.

There are a number of negative side effects to the current lack of minimal standards for the technical education of speech-language pathologists which have consequences for all participants in the clinical process. Companies interested in producing clinical technologies, for example, find little or no direction or guidance in preparing their products for the anticipated customers they target. As a result, it may well be that available technologies do not meet the needs of practicing clinicians, or are produced to minimal technical standards to keep development and production costs low. In the absence of defined minimal standards, it is possible also that well-designed and potentially beneficial products find unreasonable resistance in the professional community based on unfounded suspicion or rumor.

The availability of reasoned, and researched, minimal standards would affect the development and production of new technologies. With defined minimal standards available, products that don't meet them would not be viable in the market place. Importantly, the availability of defined performance criteria forms a protection for all potential users. That is, clinicians would not have the burden of sorting out for themselves if a product meets the minimal standards that apply to available equipment designed for specific clinical needs. For developers, it would become attractive to raise the bar for their products, as this gives leverage in positioning quality products in a competitive marketplace. That is, companies could market based on the fact that their product meets or exceeds defined minimal standards. Finally, and most importantly, clients would be better protected, as they wouldn't be exposed to treatment technology that does not meet adequate specifications, or that has not been properly tested in terms of clinical efficacy.

ASHA currently requires that clinicians meet minimal standards and competencies to be certified and maintain clinical certification. This demand should be extended to the use of technical products for diagnostic or treatment-related purposes. Although a laudable goal, as one could imagine, this is potentially a complex issue and involves more than merely establishing these specifications. For example, standards should reflect issues of safety (proper approval by agencies that determine if a product is safe) and hygiene, as well as procedural aspects of how equipment is used with clients, and if operators of the technologies can be considered capable of using the technologies in the way intended. Obviously, this means that this content should be available in the training of competent clinicians by instructors familiar with the technology in question, and also become a scope of clinical research.

A Few Final Words

This chapter reviewed the most common anti-stuttering devices sold to many persons who stutter, and recently also to some speech-language pathologists who work with fluency clients on a regular basis. Of course, it could not cover all available models, but some important issues were raised that apply beyond the specific devices discussed.

In my opinion, there is nothing wrong if a person who stutters shows interest in purchasing an antistuttering device as long as they are aware of all the options and what can be reasonably be expected from each of them, including the need for concomitant therapy. Although there are multiple ways in which DAF may be used in the assessment and treatment of fluency disorders, antistuttering devices are more commonly sold directly to persons who stutter and often without the involvement of speech-language pathologists or audiologists. This can have costly consequences. Moreover, the devices available on the market are usually not tested for safety or effectiveness. The long-term effects of their use, or possible misuse, are in most cases not known.

Because few speech-language pathologists are knowledgeable about anti-stuttering devices, persons who stutter are most likely in today's market to simply take their chances and help themselves. Prices of the devices have gone up tremendously in just a few years whereas minimal technological improvements have emerged. It is time that our specialization gets involved in this market by conducting controlled empirical clinical studies, by enforcing minimal standards and specifications for devices, and by speaking out against the appalling and unnecessary price hikes seen in recent years.

A recent development is that speech-language pathologists, acting as dispensers for manufacturers, have begun to dispense anti-stuttering devices to persons who stutter. This is a form of clinical practice not currently covered in the training of SLPs, nor is it specifically addressed by the code of ethics. Although the involvement is a positive sign that speech-language pathologists are finally getting involved in this market, they may expose themselves to unknown liabilities at this time. This is mostly because the devices dispensed are usually not FDA-approved, and the certification of SLPs has little meaning with regard to this form of clinical practice. Using amplified auditory feedback over long time frames could have currently unknown consequences for hearing for which SLPs may be liable as well.

Our specialization in fluency and fluency disorders should accept its responsibility for looking into the booming market of anti-stuttering devices. Initiatives are needed that ultimately protect PWS who are interested in the devices, clinicians, and reputable producers of antistuttering devices. Such initiatives could entail recommending specifications and minimal standards for these technologies, promoting proper training and adequate research into the use of these devices, and examining, promoting, and publishing issues relating to their safety, hygiene, ethics, and liability.

References

Atkinson, C. J. (1954). Some effects on intelligibility as the sidetone level and the amount of sidetone delay are changed. *Proceedings of the Iowa Academy of Science, 61*, 334–340.

Baken, R. J. & Orlikoff, R. F. (2000). *Clinical measurement of speech and voice, 2nd edition.* Vancouver: Singular.

Chase, R. A., Sutton, S., & Rapin, I. (1961). Sensory feedback influences on motor performance. *Journal of Auditory Research, 1,* 212–223.

Cherry, C., Sayers, B., & Marland, P. M. (1955). Experiments on the complete suppression of stammering. *Nature, 176,* 874–875.

Curlee, R. F. & Perkins, W. H. (1969). Conversational rate control therapy for stuttering. *Journal of Speech and Hearing Disorders, 34,* 245–250.

Deal, J. L. (1982). Sudden onset of stuttering: a case report. *Journal of Speech and Hearing Disorders, 47,* 301–304.

Goldberg, L., Stokes, B., & Richards, N. (2002, November). *Effects of DAF on apraxia of speech in adults.* Annual National Meeting of the American Speech and Hearing Association, Atlanta, GA.

Howell, P., El-Yaniv, N., & Powell, J. (1987). Factors affecting fluency in stutterers when speaking under altered auditory feedback. In H. F. M. Peters & W. Hulstijn (Eds.), *Speech motor dynamics in stuttering* (pp. 361–369). Nijmegen: Nijmegen University Press.

Ingham, R. J. (1984). *Stuttering and behavior therapy: Current status and experimental foundations.* San Diego, CA: College Hill Press.

Johnson, W. (1955). A study of the onset and development of stuttering. In W. Johnson & R. T. Leutenegger (Eds.), *Stuttering in children and adults.* Minneapolis: University of Minnesota Press.

Kalinowski, J. & Dayalu, V. (2002). A common element in the immediate inducement of effortless, natural-sounding, fluent speech in stutterers: "The second speech signal." *Medical Hypotheses, 58,* 61–66.

Kalinowski, J., Stuart, A., Sark, S., & Armson, J. (1996). Stuttering amelioration at various auditory feedback delays and speech rates. *European Journal of Disorders of Communication, 31,* 259–269.

Lee, B. S. (1950). Effects of delayed speech feedback. *Journal of the Acoustic Society of America, 22,* 824–826.

McClure, J. A. & Yaruss, J. S. (2003). Stuttering survey suggests success of attitude-changing treatment. *ASHA Leader, 8,* 19.

Molt, L. F., Merson, R., Kalinowski, J., & Kehoe, R. (2003, November). *Assistive devices for stuttering management: Clinical forum.* Annual Convention of the American Speech-Language-Hearing Association, Chicago, IL.

National Stuttering Association (2003). *The experience of people who stutter: A survey by the national stuttering association.* New York: Author.

Ryan, B. (1971). Operant procedures applied to stuttering therapy for children. *Journal of Speech and Hearing Disorders, 36(2),* 264–280.

Shames, G. H. & Florance, C. L. (1980). *Stutter-free speech: A goal for therapy.* Columbus, OH: Merrill.

Spilka, B. (1954). Some vocal effects of different reading passages and time delays in speech feedback. *Journal of Speech and Hearing Disorders, 19,* 37–47.

Stuart, A., Kalinowski, J., & Rastatter, M. P. (1997). Effects of monaural and binaural altered auditory feedback on stuttering frequency. *Journal of the Acoustical Society of America, 101,* 3806–3809.

Stuart, A., Kalinowski, J., Armson, J., Stenstrom, R., & Jones, K. (1996). Fluency effect of frequency alterations of plus/minus one-half and one-quarter octave shifts in auditory feedback of people who stutter. *Journal of Speech and Hearing Research, 39,* 396–401.

Webster, R. L. (1991). Manipulation of vocal tone: implications for stuttering. In H. F. M. Peters, W. Hulstijn, & C. W. Starkweather (Eds.), *Speech motor control and stuttering. Proceedings of the 2nd International Conference on Speech Motor Control and Stuttering* (pp. 535–545). Amsterdam, The Netherlands: Excerpta Medica.

Zalosh, S. & Salzman, L.F. (1965). After effects of delayed auditory feedback. *Perceptual and Motor Skills, 20,* 817–823.

— 10 —

Neuropharmacology of Stuttering: Concepts and Current Findings

Christy L. Ludlow

Laryngeal and Speech Section, National Institute of
Neurological Disorders and Stroke, National Institutes of Health

The purpose of this chapter is to provide readers with an overview of the issues regarding neuropharmacological treatments for stuttering. A first issue is what evidence is needed for determining whether or not a new treatment is effective. The types of research designs required to provide evidence of benefit for a treatment will be reviewed and then used as a frame of reference in evaluating the research to date on the effects of different neuropharmacological agents on stuttering. Second, how neuropharmacological agents (drugs) work in the central nervous system will be reviewed. The principles of neurotransmission and how drugs can alter neurotransmission between neurons in the brain will be discussed. The third part of this chapter reviews the data available on the effects of different classes of drugs on stuttering and their side effects. Finally, the fourth part will be a discussion of the current status of the neuropharmacology of stuttering, what neurotransmitter types seem to worth pursuing, and what types of research are needed to explore the possibilities of using drugs to assist persons who stutter.

Research designs required to demonstrate the effectiveness of new pharmacological treatments

CLASSIFYING RESEARCH EVIDENCE

Different classification systems are used to evaluate the evidence of treatment benefit; this review follows the framework employed by the American Academy of Neurology Therapeutics and Technology Assessment Subcommittee, September 1999 (Goodin & Edlund, 1999) that was used in a recent evidence-based review (Sataloff, Mandel, Mann, & Ludlow, 2004). Class I refers to the gold standard in treatment efficacy research—a randomized controlled trial (RCT). Such studies usually involve investigators at multiple centers, and are referred as Phase III Clinical Trials by the Food and Drug Administration (FDA). A couple of successful Phase III clinical trials meeting the Class I standard are usually required before a new drug will be approved for market as a treatment for a disorder by the FDA. *Class I evidence* must depend on trials that are:

1. prospective;
2. have randomized assignment of patients between control and experimental treatment groups;
3. use masked (blinded) measures of effectiveness;
4. assess outcomes reflecting a patient's ability to meet their needs for daily living at baseline and with treatment;
5. have adequate statistical power and account for drop-outs;
6. control sources of bias;
7. and use inclusion/exclusion criteria to define a large representative sample of the patient population.

   Class II evidence depends on prospective trials with a matched control group cohort in a representative population with masked outcome assessment where:

(a) primary outcomes are clearly defined;
(b) exclusion/inclusion criteria are clearly defined;
(c) adequate accounting for drop-outs and cross-overs with numbers sufficiently low to have minimal potential for bias, and;
(d) relevant baseline characteristics are presented and substantially equivalent among treatment groups or there is appropriate statistical adjustment for differences.

   Class II evidence may also include randomized controlled trials (RCT) in a representative population that lack one criterion from a to d.

   Class III evidence includes all other controlled trials (including well-defined natural history controls or patients serving as own control) in a representative population, where outcome assessment is independent of patient treatment.

   Class IV evidence is from uncontrolled studies, case series, case reports, or expert opinion.

   Class I evidence can establish a treatment as beneficial. Class II evidence can determine that a treatment is probably beneficial. Class III evidence can only determine that a treatment might possibly be useful. Class IV evidence can only indicate that the effects of a treatment are unknown.

CLINICAL TRIAL METHODS FOR TESTING NEW TREATMENTS

Research aimed at developing a new treatment usually follows different phases. Each phase addresses different questions regarding the treatment. Phase I trials are usually small, uncontrolled, and aimed at determining whether or not a drug or device is safe to use in humans. If the drug or device already has been found effective for other disorders, then a Phase 1 trial is aimed at determining whether or not it is safe to use in the new indication. That is, if the drug is established as effective for depression, then a Phase 1 trial may examine whether or not is it safe to use in people who stutter but are not depressed, which would be a new "off-label" indication. Phase I trials are small, usually only have 10 to 20 participants, are usually not blinded, and are inherently biased. Sources of bias include: both the patients and the investigators usually are eager to have the new treatment be beneficial; the measures are not made independently from the investigators; and there is no control condition or group. Such studies do not provide evidence regarding treatment benefit and contribute only Class IV evidence; however, they report on side effects and any adverse effects of the treatment.

Phase II trials are usually aimed at determining an effective dose for using the new treatment. Participants may be compared at different drug dosages, with a baseline or placebo condition. The same individuals can be compared at the different dosages, within a subject crossover design, or different groups of individuals may receive different drug dosages, a between subjects design. For safety reasons, the participants may be blinded but not the investigators, so that if the high dose condition/group has significant side effects (adverse events) then the high dose arm of the study can be stopped. Phase II trials usually only contribute to Class III evidence because they are not well controlled. However, they may include a nontreated comparison group/condition, blinded measurement, an independent data safety monitoring committee, and a sample size of between 20 and 40.

Phase III are prospective trials aimed at comparing a new treatment with the established treatment for a disorder. These may be multicenter trials to include a large sample size of a representative population of between 100 and 500 patients. Because both the patients and the investigators are blinded, an independent Data Safety Monitoring Committee is *essential* for monitoring the study. The aim is to determine how effective the new treatment is relative to the best treatment currently available for the disorder, which, in stuttering, would be speech therapy. Surprisingly no neuropharmacological studies in stuttering have compared the effects of neuropharmacological treatments with the gold standard, behavioral treatments for adult stuttering. To date, studies in this area are either small Phase II trials with various level of control or Phase I uncontrolled studies reporting on individual subjects' responses to a medication.

How neuropharmacological agents can modify neurotransmission in the central nervous system

Neurotransmission in the central nervous system

The purpose of this section is to provide the reader with a general overview of how neurotransmission occurs in the central nervous system, as a basis for understanding the various actions of different neuropharmacological agents. This is a vast literature that covers both a large scope and a great depth of knowledge and is constantly being revised as new discoveries occur almost daily. This introduction will only cover the general principles and may be outdated as new knowledge develops. The following overview is drawn heavily from two sources, chapter 8 in *Fundamental Neuroscience* (Deutch & Roth, 1999) and *Goodman & Gilman's The Pharmacological Basis of Therapeutics* (Hardman & Limbird, 2001).

Neurotransmission is the communication between two neurons at synaptic junctions. A neuronal cell membrane has a negative resting potential, referred to as hyperpolarization, which is negative on the inside relative to the extracellular space (Fig. 10-1). An action potential in the axon rapidly changes the charge across the membrane of the axon, allowing ions to enter the cell, making the inside of the membrane positive for a short time before it returns to hyperpolarization. In excitatory synapses, when an action potential reaches the synaptic ending, a neurotransmitter is released by the presynaptic neuron and binds to the postsynaptic junction, resulting in membrane changes allowing for calcium influx through ion channels in the postsynaptic membrane. This produces a small depolarization in the postsynaptic membrane referred to as an excitatory postsynaptic potential (EPSP). In inhibitory synapses, there is influx of negatively charged ions, such as chloride, across the postsynaptic membrane resulting in a small further inhibitory postsynaptic potential (IPSP) (Fig. 10-1).

Neurotransmitters are endogenous substances released by a presynaptic nerve terminal into the synaptic junction in response to calcium influx over the presynaptic membrane in response to an action potential (Fig. 10-2). When these neurotransmitters are released into the synaptic junction, they are free to bind to receptors on the postsynaptic membrane. Such receptor binding results changes the postsynaptic membrane to allow for ion transfer across the membrane.

There are many ways in which neurotransmitter release can be augmented or interfered with as illustrated in Figure 10-2. Neurotransmitters

FIGURE 10-1

Schematic diagram illustrating membrane polarization and ion transfer due to action potentials in presynaptic axons, and exitatory postsynaptic potentials and inhibitory postsynaptic potentials. (See text for further details.) Adapted from Hardman & Limbird, 2001.

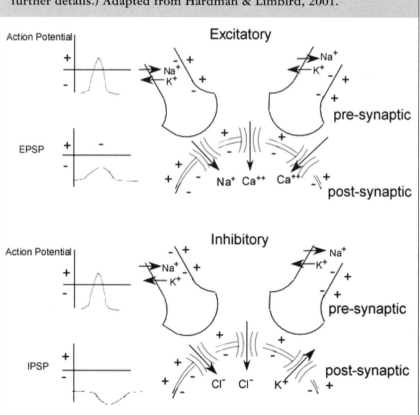

enter vesicles (4) and become stored in vesicles in the presynaptic cyto-
plasm (5). These vesicles move to the presynaptic membrane (6) and dock
or fuse to the presynaptic membrane (7). After calcium influx due to an
action potential in the presynaptic neuron (8), a vesicle releases neurotransmitter into the synaptic junction, which is referred to as exocytosis (9).
Certain proteins refereed to as docking proteins must be present for vesicle
docking and membrane opeing to release neurotransmitter into the synaptic junction. Neurotransmitter synthesis in the presynaptic axon (2)
involves several processes: some neurotransmitters or precursors are trans-
ported from the cell body down the axon (3); others re-enter the axonal
ending by endocytosis (1); while some re-enter the presynaptic neuron by
re-uptake from the synaptic junction via transporter molecules (11). Non-
neuronal glial cells may take up amino acids that function as excitatory
(glutamate) or inhibitory (γ-aminobutyric acid) neurotransmitters, and
resynthesize them. Several mechanisms are involved in regulating the level
of neurotransmitter in the synaptic junction. If certain enzymes are not
present either in the synaptic junction or the glia, then neurotransmitters
may not be broken down and can accumulate. Similarly, if postsynaptic
receptors do not bind the neurotransmitter (10) then the neurotransmitter
may accumulate in the synaptic junction. Finally, if transport molecules
required for neurotransmitter re-uptake into the presynaptic neuron are
absent or not functioning, then neurotransmitter can accumulate in the
synaptic junction and increase the excitability of the postsynaptic neuron.

   If neurotransmission is interfered with, there are both immediate and
long term changes which can alter neurotransmission in different ways.
For example, if a postsynaptic receptor is inactivated then the postsynaptic neuron is less likely to fire, resulting in a reduction in neurotransmission. However, if less neurotransmitter is bound, it can accumulate in the
synaptic junction and can then alter postsynaptic excitability and perhaps
presynaptic neurotransmitter synthesis in the long term.

   Neuropharmacological agents, or drugs, influence neurotransmission
through a variety of actions. Neurotransmission can be enhanced by increasing the amount of neurotransmitter precursor for synthesis that is available.
It can be interfered with by a postsynaptic receptor blocking agent. On the
other hand, blocking neurotransmitter re-uptake will increase the level of a
neurotransmitter in the synaptic junction and therefore increase the excitation of the postsynaptic neuron leading to increased neurotransmission.

FIGURE 10-2

Schematic diagram illustrating neurotransmission involving exocytosis of neurotransmitter into the synaptic junction, postsynaptic receptor binding, and mechanisms of re-uptake, endocytosis, synthesis, axonal transport, and vesicle formation for neurotransmission. (See text for further details.) Adapted from Deutch & Roth, 1999.

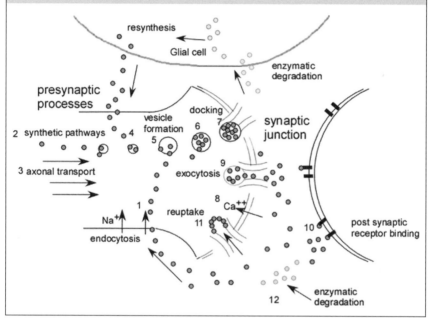

Some neurotransmitters are excitatory, such as glutamate, thus increasing their levels will increase neurotransmission, whereas others such as GABA (γ-aminobutyric acid) are inhibitory, reducing neurotransmission. Finally, as shown in Figure 10-1, ion transfer across membranes is essential for changes in polarization across neuronal membranes. Some drugs, known as channel blockers, can interfere with ion transfer, reducing neurotransmission.

Evidence on the degree of benefit and side effects from use of different types of neuropharmacological agents in stuttering

DOPAMINE D2 RECEPTOR BLOCKERS

Dopamine (dihydroxyphenylethylamine) is contained in specific neurons in the central nervous system. Dopamine is part of the catecholamine system which also includes norepinephrine and epinephrine. Dopaminergic neurons are found in the substantia nigra in the midbrain and project to parts of the basal ganglia, the caudate, and the putamen. The loss of dopaminergic neurons in the substantia nigra in Parkinson disease and the treatment of this disorder by administration of L-Dopa, a precursor to dopamine synthesis, is well recognized.

Clinical studies of changes in speech fluency secondary to the administration of levodopa (Sinemet®) have suggested that increases in the level of dopamine neurotransmission may induce stuttering. Anderson et al. (Anderson, Hughes, Rothi, Crucian, & Heilman, 1999) reported increased stuttering during periods following levodopa therapy in a man with Parkinson disease, while Louis et al. (Louis, Winfield, Fahn, & Ford, 2001) reported on two patients with Parkinson disease whose stuttering increased with levodopa therapy.

These reports suggest that a reduction in dopaminergic neurotransmission might benefit stuttering, a hypothesis that was addressed in the 1970s by many investigators in a large number of Phase II trials. To reduce dopaminergic neurotransmission, agents that block the postsynaptic dopaminergic receptor will block neurotransmission in dopaminergic neurons. There are several different types of postsynaptic receptors for dopamine, labeled D_1 through D_5. Neuropharmacological agents that block two receptors, D_1 and D_2, have been developed for treating psychotic illness. Haloperidol (Haldol®) has been used for decades to treat schizophrenia. This is a D_2 receptor blocker known to reduce neurotransmission in dopaminergic neurons in the striatum, frontal cortex, medulla, and midbrain. Seven double-blinded studies, which would qualify as Class II evidence, are reviewed in Table 10-1.

These studies demonstrated benefits: all showed statistically significant increases in speech rate and some improvement in fluency. The dropout rate averaged at 16.9% and three studies reported that only 37% of persons remained on the treatment past the study with limited benefit. The main reason for the poor long-term results were the side effects experienced by the participants that included involuntary movements (dyskinesia), fatigue, dry mouth, blurring vision, drowsiness, anxiety, depression, and facial tics.

Side effects have been the major limitation in using D_2 receptor blocking agents in stuttering. In the 1990s, more selective D_2 receptor blocking agents were developed and used in adults who stutter; however, some have had significant side effects. Pimozide (Orap®) was found to induce depression in a double-blind cross-over study of adults who stutter (Bloch, Stager, Braun, & Rubinow, 1997). Prior to the study, all eight participants had normal motor function and did not demonstrate depression; at the conclusion of the study, one participant had been noncompliant, four of seven developed depression (four major, one minor depression), one developed akathesia (inability to sit still), and three developed mild Parkinsonism. The authors concluded that the adults who stuttered might have been predisposed to depression and had increased sensitivity to antipsychotic medications.

Tiapride, a selective D_2 blocker available in Germany (Rothenberger, Johannsen, Schulze, Amorosa, & Rommel, 1994) was used in an open trial with 10 adolescents with severe stuttering and was reported to benefit speech in various situations.

Fewer abnormal movements are induced by some of the more recent D_2 blockers such as risperidone (Risperdal®), which involves not only

TABLE 10-1

Double-blind studies of the effects of haloperidol on stuttering.								
Author	Year	Control	Blind	Fluency Change*	Rate	Placebo	Dropout	Follow-up & Rx
T.J. Murray, Kelly, Campbell, & Stefanik, 1977	1977	cross	double	61%	inc	no	31%	27.7% 1/26
Rantala & Petri-Larmi, 1976	1976	cross	double	ns	inc	20%	12%	
Rosenberger, Wheelden, & Kalotkin, 1976	1976	cross	double	NS 50%	inc	27%	0%	
Wells & Malcolm, 1971	1971	cross	double	P=.01	83%	no	33%	10/36
Burns, Brady, & Kuruvilla, 1978	1978	cross	double	P=.05	80%	–	0%	
Swift, Swift, & Arellano, 1975	1975	yes	double	85%	P=.05	0%	13.6%	57%
Prins, Mandelkorn, & Cerf, 1980	1980	cross	double	P=.04	P=.009	–	29%	

*Either measured as percent increase in fluency or the statistical probability (P) of the change measured is provided.

dopamine blockade but also alters serotonin (5-HT) levels. Two studies were reported by Maguire and his associates in 1999 and 2000 (Maguire, Gottschalk, Riley, Franklin, Bechtel, et al., 1999; Maguire, Riley, Franklin, & Gottschalk, 2000). The 1999 study was a Phase II study; although 21 subjects were randomized to a control and an experimental group, the investigators were not blinded. Speech improved in the experimental group but data were not gathered on the side effects in the long term. The second study involved random assignment and blinded measures with significant improvement in speech fluency and rate and 30% sedation side effects. More recently, olazapine (Zyprexa®) (Maguire, Riley, Franklin, Maguire, Nguyen, et al., 2004), which is both a serotonin2 and dopamine D_1-D_4 receptor blocker, was found beneficial on three speech measures in a place-bo-controlled double-blind trial involving 24 adults. No significant side effects were reported, indicating that further research would be warranted.

Curiously, however, some case studies have reported that stuttering can be induced by some of the same dopamine receptor antagonists. One case study reported that stuttering was induced in a schizophrenic adult by the fifth day after starting on risperidone. Stuttering increased as the dosage was increased but after 1.5 months both the stuttering and the schizophrenia abated while the patient was still on the medication. Clozapine (Clozaril®), which interferes with D_1-D_5 receptors and is also an adrenergic, cholinergic, histaminergic, and serotinergic antagonist, induced stuttering in four different reports. In one case, stuttering occurred with dystonia (Thomas, Lalaux, Vaiva, & Goudemand, 1994); in two, it occurred with seizures (Duggal, Jagadheesan, & Nizamie, 2002; Supprian, Retz, & Deckert, 1999), and in a fourth case without other disorders (Ebeling, Compton, & Albright, 1997).

Given the multiple blinded controlled studies showing some stuttering benefit with dopamine receptor blockade, the Class II evidence suggests that these agents may possibly benefit stuttering. Although statistical significance has been reached on measures of stuttering and speech rate with these agents, the clinical significance of these speech changes to participants' lives and communication abilities is still unclear. The degree of clinical benefit relative to the side effects may predict the numbers of persons who will continue on these medications and whether adults who stutter will find them to be viable treatment options. Reports of long term treatment outcomes are needed to examine these issues in future studies of dopamine receptor blockade effects on stuttering.

NOREPINEPHRINE REUPTAKE INHIBITORS

Norepinephrine is another catecholamine neurotransmitter contained in specific neurons in the central nervous system as well as in postganglionic sympathetic neurons in the peripheral nervous system. Reuptake inhibitors for norepinehrine were developed as antidepressants and have been used in a few studies in adults who stutter. Imipramine and desipramine are two examples of this drug class. Desipramine (Norpramin®) was used in a blinded study comparing two agents with placebo (Stager, Ludlow, Gordon, Cotelingam, & Rapoport, 1995a). Following treatment, no significant changes were found in syllables stuttered per second or in percent fluency on speech communication tasks; only six out of 16 reported that they were improved from baseline, but few experienced side effects. Given this poor result, it is unlikely than this class of medications will be proven beneficial in the treatment of stuttering.

SEROTONIN SELECTIVE REUPTAKE INHIBITORS (SSRI)

These medications interfere with the action of plasma membrane transporter molecules which are needed for the reuptake of serotonin from the synaptic junction. Because re-uptake is blocked, serotonin increases in the synaptic junction leading to increased postsynaptic neuronal excitation. Examples of this drug class include Clomipraine (Anafranil®), paroxotine (Paxil®), and fluoxetine (Prozac®). A double-blind controlled study of an SSRI included a comparison of both clomipraine (Anafranil®) and desipramine with placebo (Gordon, Cotelingam, Stager, Ludlow, Hamburger, et al., 1995). Seventeen subjects underwent a baseline and placebo phase before being randomly assigned to one of two medication orders, 5 weeks of one medication, 2 weeks of placebo washout, and 5 weeks of the other medication. This provided a crossover comparison of the two medications. Clomipramine had a significant improvement over desipramine on: subjects' visual analogue scales indicating their perceived stuttering severity, thoughts about stuttering, resistance to stuttering, judgment of others' reactions to their stuttering, and expectancy of stuttering. Added measures were made of speech rate. Fifty percent of the subjects (8/16) chose to continue on clomipramine after the study. Five of these subjects were followed up for 7 and 10 months with a modest benefit that was less than the initial 6-week benefit (Stager, Ludlow, Gordon, Cotelingam, & Rapoport, 1995b).

The Gordon study (Gordon et al., 1995) provided an excellent model of measuring outcomes relevant to the participants' daily communication needs. By using visual analogue scales to determine the degree to which subjects thought about stuttering and perceived that it interfered with their daily living, the measures reflected the impact of stuttering on participants' daily life.

Paroxetine (Paxil®) is an SSRI that produced such significant adverse effects in adults who stuttered that an investigational study of the medication had to be stopped for safety reasons (Bloch, Stager, Braun, & Rubinow, 1995). During withdrawal from paroxetine, two men who had previously had brief episodes of minor depression had significant mood changes. In one, hypomania, hyperactivity, aggression, optimism, and talkativeness occurred between 2 days and 1 week after withdrawal. The other developed suicidal impulses, became irritable, dizzy, short-tempered, and homicidal 2 weeks after withdrawal. These symptoms abated after 2½ weeks. The authors interpreted them as reactions to depletion of central serotonin after re-uptake was no longer blocked.

On the other hand, paroxetine benefited acquired stuttering and depression in a few case reports (Schreiber & Pick, 1997). In two cases of acquired stuttering and depression after brain injury, paroxetine benefited both after 3 to 4 weeks. In another case posthemorrhage, both tics and stuttering were alleviated. Case studies have also found that paroxetine benefited patients with both obsessive-compulsive disorders and stuttering (Boldrini, Rossi, & Placidi, 2003; M.G. Murray & Newman, 1997).

Some SSRIs, however, have been reported to have induced stuttering. Both Sertraline (Zoloft®) and fluoxetine (Prozac®) have induced stuttering in individual cases (Christensen, Byerly, & McElroy, 1996; Guthrie & Grunhaus, 1990).

Only a few studies have evaluated SSRIs in a controlled fashion in stuttering (Gordon et al., 1995). Using the limited evidence available, many from case studies, altering serotonin re-uptake can both decrease and induce stuttering, suggesting that levels of serotonin may modulate stuttering. However, the significant side effects with some of these agents (Bloch et al., 1995) suggest that caution must be used in persons who stutter. Some of the more successful D_2 dopamine receptor blockers in stuttering also have actions blocking serotonin, such as risperidone and olanzapine, which are both dopamine and 5-HT2 receptor antagonists. A combination of both D_2 and 5HT2 antagonists may have some effect in stuttering with somewhat fewer side effects than D_2 dopamine receptor blockers alone.

GABA AGONISTS

As mentioned earlier, γ-aminobutyric acid (GABA), an amino acid, is the major inhibitory neurotransmitter in the brain. There are at least two different types of GABA receptors, GABA$_A$ and GABA$_B$. The GABA$_A$ receptor contains the chloride ion channel resulting in the influx of this negatively charged ion following neurotransmission. Benzodiazepines modulate GABA$_A$; some examples are diazepam (Valium®) and Xanax®, both well-known medications used for anxiety disorders. Baclofen (Lioresal®) is a GABA$_B$ receptor agonist affecting G proteins, is known to increase inhibition of motor neurons and have been used to treat spasticity. To date, there are no well-controlled studies of the use of GABA receptor agonists in stuttering.

CHANNEL BLOCKERS

Medications that block ion channels are used as antiarrhythmics for cardiac disorders. Examples are beta blockers that affect sodium (Na$^+$) channels. When propanolol (Inderol®), a beta blocker, was used in an uncontrolled study in adults who stuttered (Cocores, Dackis, Davies, & Gold, 1986), it reduced both stuttering and anxiety.

Calcium channel blockers were examined in the 1980s in stuttering. An initial single-blind controlled trial included 70 subjects and reported that 84% had greater improvement than placebo, although no quantitative speech measures were used (Zachariah, 1980). One subsequent double-blind placebo controlled study reported more modest improvement with only two participants continuing on the medication over 30 months (Brady, Price, McAllister, & Dietrich, 1989). Another Phase II trial, however, found no significant benefit (Brumfitt & Peake, 1988).

Overall, the few well-controlled trials of calcium channel blockers have not had beneficial results and too few studies have been conducted on beta blockers to reach any conclusion.

Conclusions

GENERAL TRENDS IN THE NEUROPHARMACOLOGICAL LITERATURE ON THE TREATMENT OF STUTTERING

This review found Class II evidence suggesting that dopaminergic D$_2$ receptor blockade may have a possible benefit in stuttering. It has yet to be determined, however, if adults who stutter choose to remain on these medications for the long term outside of controlled trials for management of their stuttering. Side effects and limited improvements in participants' concerns about stuttering and speech fluency in everyday life may be the basis for limited long-term benefits.

Overall, although the results of single case studies in the literature have been encouraging, similar benefits are usually not seen when groups of adults who stutter participate in well controlled trials. This may be because the case studies often involved a person who stuttered who was placed on a medication because of another disorder, such as obsessive-compulsive disorder, and treating this disorder also benefited their stuttering. When large studies are conducted in persons who stutter who do not have these other disorders, less benefit occurs.

Finally, some of the serious mood alterations and worsening of stuttering reported subsequent to use of certain selective serotonin re-uptake inhibitors (Bloch et al., 1995), suggest caution should be used with these medications in adults who stutter.

DIRECTIONS FOR FUTURE RESEARCH ON NEUROPHARMACOLOGICAL TREATMENT OF STUTTERING

Thus far, the selection of agents for study in the treatment of stuttering has not been theoretically based. Data are needed on possible differences in activity in various neurotransmitter systems in stuttering to determine if there are abnormalities in levels of specific neurotransmitters in the brain of persons who stutter. One example was the study by Wu and associates (Wu, Maguire, Riley, Lee, Keator, et al., 1997) using positron emission tomography (PET) with 6-FDOPA as a marker for presynaptic dopaminergic activity. Their finding of higher levels of 6-FDOPA uptake in subjects who stuttered in several brain regions provided the basis for their subsequent studies evaluating the use of D_2 receptor blockers in stuttering (Maguire et al., 2000; Maguire et al., 2004). One approach might be to identify those individuals who stutter who have abnormalities in particular neurotransmitter systems as participants for experimental treatment studies.

Few Phase I studies aimed at first determining whether or not a medication is safe to use in adults who stutter and the best dosage level. Such studies should be conducted first to avoid the costly and more risky Phase II studies of agents not previously used in persons who stutter. All of the medications used to date were developed and approved for use in persons with other disorders, such as depression or psychosis. Research studies evaluating them in stuttering are examining an "off-label" use and should be reviewed by the FDA before the study is initiated.

All of the neuropharmacological trials to date have used medication alone in their designs, rather than examining whether such agents might interact with cognitive and/or behavioral fluency training in adults who stutter. Treatment trials comparing speech therapy alone versus speech therapy combined with medications might be useful. For example, low levels of D_2 receptor blockade in combination with speech therapy might be more beneficial than either therapy alone.

Finally, most studies have measured speech fluency in the clinical setting, where stuttering is less frequent. Measuring participants' perceived impairment that stems from worrying about stuttering and speech experiences in daily living might be more relevant. Visual analogue scales, as were used by Gordon et al. (1995), could provide more relevant outcome measures, particularly in long-term studies examining whether participants continue to find a treatment beneficial in daily life activities.

References

Anderson, J. M., Hughes, J. D., Rothi, L. J., Crucian, G. P., & Heilman, K. M. (1999). Developmental stuttering and Parkinson's disease: The effects of levodopa treatment. *Journal Neurol Neurosurg Psychiatry, 66*(6), 776–778.

Bloch, M., Stager, S., Braun, A., Calis, K. A., Turcasso, N. M., Grothe, D. R., et al. (1997). Pimozide-induced depression in men who stutter. *Journal Clinical Psychiatry, 58*(10), 433–436.

Bloch, M., Stager, S. V., Braun, A. R., & Rubinow, D. R. (1995). Severe psychiatric symptoms associated with paroxetine withdrawal [letter]. *Lancet, 346*, 57.

Boldrini, M., Rossi, M., & Placidi, G. F. (2003). Paroxetine efficacy in stuttering treatment. *International Journal Neuropsychopharmacology, 6*(3), 311–312.

Brady, J. P., Price, T. R. P., McAllister, T. W., & Dietrich, K. (1989). A trial of verapamil in the treatment of stuttering in adults. *Biological Psychiatry, 25*, 626–630.

Brumfitt, S. M. & Peake, M. D. (1988). A double-blind study of verapamil in the treatment of stuttering. *British Journal of Disorders of Communication, 23*, 35–40.

Burns, D., Brady, J. P., & Kuruvilla, K. (1978). The acute effect of haloperidol and apomorphine on the severity of stuttering. *Biological Psychiatry, 13*, 255–264.

Christensen, R. C., Byerly, M. J., & McElroy, R. A. (1996). A case of sertraline-induced stuttering. *Journal Clinical Psychopharmacology, 16*(1), 92–93.

Cocores, J. A., Dackis, C. A., Davies, R. K., & Gold, M. S. (1986). Propranolol and stuttering. *American Journal of Psychiatry, 143*(8), 1071–1072.

Deutch, A. Y. & Roth, R. H. (1999). Neurotransmitters. In M. J. Zigmond, F. E. Bloom, S. C. Landis, J. L. Roberts & L. R. Squire (Eds.), *Fundamental neuroscience* (pp. 193–234). New York: Academic Press.

Duggal, H. S., Jagadheesan, K., & Nizamie, S. H. (2002). Clozapine-induced stuttering and seizures. *American Journal of Psychiatry, 159*(2), 315.

Ebeling, T. A., Compton, A. D., & Albright, D. W. (1997). Clozapine-induced stuttering. *American Journal of Psychiatry, 154*(10), 1473.

Goodin, D. & Edlund, W. (1999). *Process for developing technology assessment.* St. Paul, MN: American Academy of Neurology.

Gordon, C. T., Cotelingam, G. M., Stager, S., Ludlow, C. L., Hamburger, S. D., & Rapoport, J. L. (1995). A double-blind comparison of clomipramine and desipramine in the treatment of developmental stuttering. *Journal of Clinical Psychiatry, 56,* 238–242.

Guthrie, S. & Grunhaus, L. (1990). Fluoxetine-induced stuttering [letter]. *Journal of Clinical Psychiatry, 51,* 85.

Hardman, J. & Limbird, L. (Eds.). (2001). *Goodman & Gilman's the pharmacological basis of therapeutics.* New York: McGraw Hill.

Louis, E. D., Winfield, L., Fahn, S., & Ford, B. (2001). Speech dysfluency exacerbated by levodopa in Parkinson's disease. *Movement Disorders, 16*(3), 562–565.

Maguire, G. A., Gottschalk, L. A., Riley, G. D., Franklin, D. L., Bechtel, R. J., & Ashurst, J. (1999). Stuttering: Neuropsychiatric features measured by content analysis of speech and the effect of risperidone on stuttering severity. *Comprehensive Psychiatry, 40*(4), 308–314.

Maguire, G. A., Riley, G. D., Franklin, D. L., & Gottschalk, L. A. (2000). Risperidone for the treatment of stuttering. *Journal of Clinical Psychopharmacology, 20*(4), 479–482.

Maguire, G. A., Riley, G. D., Franklin, D. L., Maguire, M. E., Nguyen, C. T., & Brojeni, P. H. (2004). Olanzapine in the treatment of developmental stuttering: a double-blind, placebo-controlled trial. *Ann Clinical Psychiatry, 16*(2), 63–67.

Murray, M. G. & Newman, R. M. (1997). Paroxetine for treatment of obsessive-compulsive disorder and comorbid stuttering. *American Journal of Psychiatry, 154*(7), 1037.

Murray, T. J., Kelly, P., Campbell, L., & Stefanik, K. (1977). Haloperidol in the treatment of stuttering. *British Journal of Psychiatry, 130,* 370–373.

Prins, D., Mandelkorn, T., & Cerf, F. A. (1980). Principal and differential effects of haloperidol and placebo treatments upon speech disfluencies in stutterers. *Journal of Speech & Hearing Research, 23,* 614–629.

Rantala, S. L. & Petri-Larmi, M. (1976). Haloperidol (Serenase) in the treatment of stuttering. *Folia Phoniatrica, 28,* 354–361.

Rosenberger, P., Wheelden, J. A., & Kalotkin, M. (1976). The effect of haloperidol on stuttering. *American Journal of Psychiatry, 133,* 331–334.

Rothenberger, A., Johannsen, H. S., Schulze, H., Amorosa, H., & Rommel, D. (1994). Use of tiapride on stuttering in children and adolescents. *Perceptual & Motor Skills, 79*(3), 1163–1170.

Sataloff, R. T., Mandel, S., Mann, E. A., & Ludlow, C. L. (2004). Practice parameter: laryngeal electromyography (an evidence-based review). *Otolaryngology Head & Neck Surgery, 130*(6), 770–779.

Schreiber, S. & Pick, C.G. (1997). Paroxetine for secondary stuttering: further interaction of serotonin and dopamine. *Journal of Nervous & Mental Disease, 185*(7), 465–467.

Stager, S. V., Ludlow, C. L., Gordon, C. T., Cotelingam, M., & Rapoport, J. L. (1995a). Fluency changes in persons who stutter following a double blind trial of clomipramine and desipramine. *Journal Speech & Hearing Research, 38*(3), 516–525.

Stager, S. V., Ludlow, C. L., Gordon, C. T., Cotelingam, M., & Rapoport, J. L. (1995b, August). Maintenance of fluency following long term clomipramine treatment. *Proceedure 1st World Congress on Fluency Disorders,* pp. 516–519.

Supprian, T., Retz, W., & Deckert, J. (1999). Clozapine-induced stuttering: epileptic brain activity? *American Journal of Psychiatry, 156*(10), 1663–1664.

Swift, W. J., Swift, E. W., & Arellano, M. (1975). Haloperidol as a treatment for adult stuttering. *Comprehensive Psychiatry, 16,* 61–67.

Thomas, P., Lalaux, N., Vaiva, G., & Goudemand, M. (1994). Dose-dependent stuttering and dystonia in a patient taking clozapine. *American Journal of Psychiatry, 151*(7), 1096.

Wells, P. G. & Malcolm, M. T. (1971). Controlled trial of the treatment of 36 stutterers. *British Journal of Psychiatry, 119,* 603–604.

Wu, J. C., Maguire, G., Riley, G., Lee, A., Keator, D., Tang, C., Fallon, J. & Najafi, A. (1997). Increased dopamine activity associated with stuttering. *Neuroreport, 8*(3), 767–770.

Zachariah, G. (1980). Verapamil in the management of stuttering. *Antiseptic, 77,* 87–88.

—11—

The Role of Self-Help/Mutual Aid in Addressing the Needs of Individuals Who Stutter

Lee Reeves
National Stuttering Association

Stuttering is a speech disorder that has plagued mankind for thousands of years. From its earliest known depictions in ancient Egypt to the sophisticated technology of PET scans and fMRIs, the cause of this frustrating and potentially handicapping condition has remained elusive. Treatments for stuttering have had an equally long, frustrating, and, in many instances, tragic history (Bobrick, 1996; Van Riper, 1973). Although researchers have studied a multitude of factors believed to either cause or aid in the resolution of stuttering, very little attention has been given to the role that self-help groups or consumer-based support organizations play in improving the lives of those affected by stuttering. In addition, the relationship between the professional community and such groups appears to be undervalued, and therefore has not been studied. In this chapter, I will suggest that the future of effective long term stuttering treatment as well as sustained scientific investigation into the etiology of stuttering may lie not only in a better understanding of self-help groups, but also in the dynamic of their relationship with professionals.

The concept of self-help is not unique to stuttering. In fact, the only thing that is unique to stuttering in the world of self-help is the disorder itself. This is not to say, of course, that the development of the self-help phenomenon within the stuttering community does not have a rich and unique history. Indeed, the events and personalities within both the stuttering and professional communities that constitute the development of the stuttering self-help movement make for very interesting reading. However, the focus of this chapter is on self-help groups and organizations in general as they relate to various disorders, including stuttering. Hopefully, the knowledge gained from other disciplines will be helpful in forging a positive future for those who stutter.

A historical perspective on the self-help movement

It is generally accepted that the original concept of self-help for those unable to be "cured" by traditional professional treatment originated in 1935 with the formation of Alcoholics Anonymous (Adamsen & Rasmussen, 2001; Borkman, 1999). Since then, self-help/support groups or "mutual aid groups," as some have referred to them, have grown dramatically across both national borders and social/political systems (Adamsen & Rasmussen, 2001). It has been estimated that in the United States alone, over 500,000 self-help groups exist and that over 60 million people have participated in a self-help group at some point in their lives (Reissman, 2000). There are now self-help groups established for every condition or disorder recognized by the World Health Organization (Banks, 2000).

Several definitions of self-help/mutual aid groups have been offered (Adamsen & Rasmussen, 2001), but the one developed by Katz and Bender (1976) is probably the definition most used and is the one recognized by the World Health Organization. They define self-help groups as:

> ... *voluntary, small group structures for mutual aid and the accomplishment of a special purpose. They are usually formed by peers who have come together for mutual assistance in satisfying a common need, overcoming a common handicap or life-disrupting problem and bringing about desired social and/or personal change. The initiators of such groups emphasize face-to-face social interactions and the assumption of personal responsibility by members. They often provide material assistance, as well as emotional support; they are frequently 'cause' oriented, and promulgate an ideology or values through which members may attain an enhanced sense of personal identity.* (p. 141)

The self-help phenomenon began as an alternative for "hopeless alcoholics" whose attempts at recovery utilizing a traditional medical model had been unsuccessful (Oka & Borkman, 2000). Soon, their "12 Step" philosophy was adopted by others suffering from or living with those suffering from addictions. By the mid-1950s and early 1960s, self-help organizations had emerged for a number of physical and mental health disorders and were based on a variety of organizational and operational models.

From relatively recent and narrow roots, the self-help movement grew rapidly in the mid-1960s. Some viewed the movement as more of a social than a medical phenomenon (Adamsen & Rasmussen, 2001; Emerick, 1996; Vattano, 1972). Others concluded that most groups lacked the organizational structure, ideology, or desire to be a "social movement," and were best viewed as an attempt to meet individual needs (Borkman, 1990; Katz & Bender, 1990). In the 1970s, as health care became less personalized, more specialized and technical, and gated by health care providers (Borkman, 1997; DamenMortelmans, & Van Hove, 2000), individuals needing support encountered more frustration and there appeared to be an upsurge in antiprofessional sentiments held by many seeking professional services. Such negative attitudes and beliefs continued to grow at the same time that self-help groups began to broaden in scope and activity. Professional services and self-help groups increasingly were viewed as exclusionary and polarized options for individuals seeking help for disabling conditions.

Thus, it is not entirely strange that descriptions of self-help groups as "strange subcultures of deviants" and "strictly anti-professional" (Borkman, 1970; Damen et al., 2000) began to appear in the professional literature. These descriptions were probably an accurate assessment of the beliefs held by many in the professional community and, unfortunately, by some even today. However, that attitude only served to support the negative belief held by most of the self-help community regarding professionals. That belief was probably best expressed by former United States Surgeon General, Dr. C. Everett Koop, who stated "... many professionals still believe that transformation, change, and healing are the prerogative of an elite who possess knowledge and techniques bestowed by specialized training" (in Bradberry, 1997, p.393.). Attitudes and beliefs such as these contributed to an atmosphere of "mutual disrespect" that served as a barrier to the development of any meaningful relationship between these seemingly disparate communities. Fortunately, things began to change in the 1980s.

Recognizing the growth and importance of the self-help/support group movement, Surgeon General Koop sponsored a National Workshop on Self-Help and Public Health in 1987. The workshop was

attended by large numbers of both consumers and professionals. Its proceedings concluded that "health providers alone could not ease the suffering of people who are physically or mentally ill or addicted." It was recommended that educational programs and practice settings provide practitioners with an increase in knowledge and a change in attitudes about
self-help and self-help groups. Specifically relevant to stuttering, the
speech pathology community was also urged to pay attention to the validity of self-help groups by the American Speech and Hearing Association's
Director of Consumer Affairs when Koop wrote, a few years later, that:

> *Consumers are becoming more interested in taking charge of their own lives.*
> *Professionals need to recognize this trend and acknowledge the potential bene-*
> *fits of self-help.* (Diggs, 1990, p. 32)

The role of professionals in self-help/support groups

Since then, slow but steady progress has been made between many self-
help groups and their respective professional communities. Distinctions
and legitimacy of both experiential and professional knowledge began to
be explored (Borkman, 1976, 1990). More recently, researchers have
begun to study the structure of different groups and organizations as well
as the roles that professionals might play within those structures to maximize their effectiveness (Ben-Ari, 2002; Wituk, Shepherd, Slavich,
Warren, & Meissen, 2000).

In a recent study conducted to assess the involvement of professionals in different types of self-help groups, Ben-Ari (2002) concluded that
attitudinal constructs and age of participants were a critical factor. On a
continuum that would place mutual collaboration with professionals on
one end, and completely separate roles for the two on the other, he found
that 12-step-based groups and groups with a majority of participants
under the age of 30 were less likely to choose collaboration with professionals than health-oriented groups composed of more mature participants. This is not surprising, given the history and structure of 12-step
programs. It is also not surprising that younger people would be more
inclined to prefer a more "closed" model. The fact that they have joined
a self-help group may indicate that traditional modes of therapy have not
been effective for them and they may be resentful that professionals could
not "fix" them. Relevant to stuttering, this has certainly been my person-

al experience as well as my observations over the course of 30 years within the stuttering self-help community.

On the other hand, self-help members who were over the age of 30, had higher education, and/or had more experience with self-help were more likely to value collaboration with professionals working in the area of their health concern. This group also had a better understanding and appreciation for the different but equally legitimate roles of self-help and professional intervention. This "open" approach (inclusion of those seeking support and information as well as those who are professionals in the field) has become the more desirable model for most groups (Adamsen & Rasmussen, 2001; Ben-Ari, 2002).

As groups developed a more open approach, questions about the role of professionals in self-help associations began to surface. Through the years, professionals have assumed a variety of roles in the development and maintenance of self-help groups, ranging from original organizer to consultant/advisor (Ben-Ari, 2002; Bradberry, 1997). The level of involvement of professionals is often related to the nature or philosophy of the group. For example, as noted, a 12-step model is less likely to accept professional involvement than a more open health-oriented group (Ben-Ari, 2002). Some groups prefer professionals to be fully integrated participants, while others prefer them to take a less active or consultant role (Adamsen & Rasmussen, 2001). Over the years, studies have shown that professional involvement is on the rise (Ben-Ari, 2002). One study (Adamsen & Rasmussen, 1992) found that 84% of participants in self-help actually request professional involvement. For those working in the area of stuttering, it is interesting to note that these findings are consistent with a survey of members of the National Stuttering Association (formerly the National Stuttering Project), in which 85% of respondents felt that professionals as well as "others" should be invited to participate in meetings and other association activities (Krauss-Lerhman & Reeves, 1986).

Still, there is active discussion about the role that professionals should play in an "open" self-help group or organization. To some it appears that debating this issue in the general context of self-help or within a specific group is not unlike debating the appropriate treatment of stuttering itself. There does not appear to be a "one-size-fits-all" model. Some groups have been established by a professional who has helped encourage and guide the group toward more autonomy and self-leadership, whereas others have been established solely by nonprofessionals, yet encourage professional attendance and participation. It is important to note that the level of professional involvement is not only dependent upon the attitudes of self-helpers. Some professionals themselves feel uncomfortable in self-help meetings and prefer to take a more distant role as an available consultant (Gregory, 1997). Others appear much more comfortable in meetings, and gain insight while still being available to provide information as appropriate. However, professionals need to guard against the potential for inappropriate levels of participation that can turn a group meeting into "group therapy."

Although some professionals still view the relationship with self-help groups as antagonistic (Adams, 1990), most see it as a positive and rational progression in the evolution of health care (Jacobs & Goodman, 1989; Kurtz, 1990; Reissman & Carroll, 1995). Some have even speculated that in 10 to 20 years, self-help groups will become the most favorable choice of treatment for many psycho-pathologies and non-psychiatric illnesses, or "life predicaments," as some have called them (Adamsen & Rasmussen, 2001; Goodman & Jacobs, 1994).

In the end, it is not a question of whether or not professionals should be involved in self-help groups, but to what extent and in what capacities. Each organization and each group within an organization has certain unique characteristics and needs. Although most self-help/support groups are organized and facilitated by peers, it is not essential. This is less important to label or restrict roles than it is to understand the goals and needs of the individual group and how self-helpers and professionals can work together to achieve those goals. The key factor is whether the focus is on the sharing of experiential knowledge and support rather than professionally directed therapy.

A closer look at the value and efficacy of self-help groups

The positive value and role of self-help for stuttering has been voiced by many, particularly in texts devoted to stuttering treatment or clinician training (Bloodstein, 1995; Manning, 2001; Shapiro, 1999; Starkweather & Givens-Ackerman, 1997; and Yaruss & Reeves, 2002, to name a few examples). However, there have been few empirical data available to support these assertions specific to stuttering (Krauss-Lehrman & Reeves, 1986; Yaruss et al., 2002). Fortunately, there is a significant body of research on self-help groups outside of stuttering that spans many years. This literature has demonstrated positive outcomes of self-help group involvement on a variety of different conditions, diseases and disorders.

For example, Kyrouz, Humphreys, and Loomis (2000) conducted an extensive review of the research literature on the effectiveness of self-help/mutual aid groups that addressed mental health problems, weight loss, addiction-related recovery, bereavement, diabetes, the welfare of caregivers and the elderly, cancer patients, and those with chronic illnesses. They reported on 37 different studies across the range of disorders mentioned earlier. Their review is significant because they concentrated exclusively on longitudinal studies that compared self-help participants to nonparticipants (controls). Thus, they were able to directly contrast benefits of self-help participation.

Although all of the studies showed consistently positive results, one that involved individuals affected by scoliosis, a developmental disorder resulting in an abnormal curvature of the spine, is of particular interest. The condition can be potentially disabling due to pain or physical limitations. Though there is no cure for scoliosis, there are treatments available that help manage the condition. In addition, because of the physical deformity and need for bracing that can only be partially hidden with loose fitting clothing, the disorder can also be emotionally handicapping. Thus, given the social stigma felt by many who suffer from this chronic and currently incurable condition, scoliosis seems particularly appropriate for comparison with stuttering. Kyrouz, Humphreys, and Loomis (2000) summarized the results of the study, conducted by Hinrichsen, Revenson, and Shinn (1985) as follows:

> *Adults with scoliosis who had undergone bracing or surgery and participated in a Scoliosis Association self-help group (N = 33) were compared to adults with similar treatment who did not participate in the group (N = 67). Compared to nonparticipants, group participants reported (1) a more positive outlook on life, (2) greater satisfaction with the medical care they received, (3) reduced psychosomatic symptoms, (4) increased sense of mastery, (5) increased self-esteem, and (6) reduced feelings of shame and estrangement. (p. 84)*

Another study that involved individuals with diabetes found that patients who attended two or more peer-led support group meetings in a year showed significantly better control of their diabetes than those who did not. In addition, attendees showed significantly greater knowledge about their condition (Simmons, 1992). Many other studies in this review had similar outcomes.

With the increasing numbers of self-help groups and the mounting evidence of positive outcomes for participants, it would seem that there would be a natural synergy between these groups and the providers of health care services. Although there is clear evidence of a trend toward more understanding and cooperation (Adamsen & Rasmussen, 2001; Ben-Ari, 2002), there remains a disconnect between the two cultures— one emphasizing the "health" side of the equation and the other emphasizing the "care" side (Banks, 2000).

The call for attitudinal changes and incorporation of training programs made by the National Workshop on Self-Help almost 30 years ago has not made much progress in the United States. Wituk et al. (2000) reported that the incorporation of self-help groups into the training and practices of human services professionals has not reached its full potential. In one study, 50% of graduate students in social work and psychology did not think that self-help groups were an appropriate management setting for mental illness. In another study involving forensic mental health professionals (Lee, 1995), it was noted that while 94% of respondents referred patients to AA or NA, only 2% referred to Recovery, Inc, a well-established mental health self-help organization. Many professionals acknowledge that self-help groups are underused (Toseland & Hacker, 1985).

This is in contrast to the growing number of self-help groups and organizations (Reissman, 2000) and mounting evidence of their value in improving the lives of people who suffer from any number of diseases and/or disorders. The disconnect may in part be the result of attitudes and beliefs that the two communities—self-help and professional—developed about each other in the years during which self-help first developed as a movement. It may also be due in part to the lack of understanding by both sides of the complimentary roles that each can play in the "health" and "care" of those affected by personal challenges. Regardless of the underlying cause, it remains apparent that professional education regarding the value of self-help remains a critical strategic need (Constantino & Nelson, 1995).

The history of stuttering self-help in the United States

The history of self-help in the stuttering community has generally followed the path of other self-help organizations described above, with the exception of the early 12-step programs. Though there are early reports of people who stutter gathering together to share concerns and offer support for one another (see Fraser, 2005), it was not until the 1960s that the stuttering self-help movement as we know it today had its roots (Gregory, 1997; Krauss-Lehrman & Reeves, 1989).

The group generally acknowledged as the first stuttering self-help organization was The Council of Adult Stutterers in Washington, D.C. in 1965. The intent of this group was expressed by one of its founders, Michael Heffron, who said that:

> *I would like to form a group of stutterers—or join a group that already exists in which the members want to help themselves and to help other stutterers. ... I would seek to make stutterers proud, not that they stutter, for only a fool can take pride in affliction, but that they are doing something to help themselves.*
> (Van Riper, 1973, p. 169)

The group was initially formed with the help and support of a professional, Eugene Walle, a speech-language pathologist at Catholic University. The National Council of Stutterers (NCOS) met regularly and attracted a wide variety of individuals from all walks of life. They explored the impact that stuttering had on their own lives and the lives of others. This was a revolutionary concept in stuttering that was much different than group therapy, something some members had previously experienced. They discussed openly some of the tough issues—often and not surprisingly with a little edge. For example, here is an excerpt from the editorial page of one of their journals dated March–April, 1968:

> *... Discussion at a recent Council meeting of the proposition 'once a stutterer always a stutterer' touched off some strong feelings on both sides of that question. We objected to being labeled something bad, and being told it was our fate for life. ... On the other hand some said it is a familiar psychological truth that a powerful trauma in early years will have its effect forever. That's why even the big shot stuttering therapists still stutter!* (Guitar, 1968, pp. 1–2)

Within a short time other groups began to emerge in North Carolina, Georgia, and Florida (National Council of Stutterers, 1966). Although structured as independent and autonomous groups, they formed a loose federation and had annual conferences. These early groups, although creating a forum for support and encouragement, were also a safe place to express concerns and frustrations. Some of that frustration was understandably directed at the profession of speech-language pathology for its lack of an effective treatment for stuttering. Members also expressed frustration toward family members, teachers, employers, and society in general. However, there were also humorous stories and poems presented that reflected positive attitudes about life and each other. Eventually, each of the NCOS groups declined in membership and the organization disbanded. Most of the early groups were formed with the assistance, support, and participation of professionals. What changed the spirit of cooperation between those who stutter and professionals seen in those very early groups?

A major factor was that the nature of the self-help movement for stuttering began to change. Prior to 1977, self-help groups were small, local, and only loosely connected or not connected at all. That began to change in 1977 with the creation of Speak Easy International and the National Stuttering Project (Gregory, 1997). Although both groups maintained the basic mission of providing a forum for people who stutter to come together to help themselves and to help each other, they expanded on the basic concept by creating a general membership structure, a network of connected self-help groups, and added the goal of advocacy to their efforts. They wanted to raise public awareness and empower people who stutter (PWS) to begin to stand up for themselves and be heard. It was important to somehow get the message out that PWS do not have to be handicapped. Their position was that there was nothing wrong with people who stutter other than the fact that they happen to stutter, and that being labeled as a "stutterer" was inappropriate. Speak Easy International remained a regional organization, whereas the NSP was to become the first truly national consumer-based organization for people affected by stuttering.

One of the unique characteristics of this effort was that it was not a joint venture with speech pathologists. According to one of the NSP's founders, Michael Sugarman (personal correspondence), the idea was not to alienate professionals but to establish peer-facilitated self-help groups as an additional and viable option for helping those who stutter.

As groups became more organized, began to communicate more frequently, and gather for joint meetings, participants quickly realized that they were not alone in their struggle with stuttering. They also found that they were not alone in their experiences with speech therapy. Although it was reassuring and comforting to find others who shared common experiences, it was also disturbing to learn that many had fallen through the cracks in the delivery system for speech therapy services. Many participants, including some in leadership roles, had significant feelings of hostility directed at the professional community. There was a common feeling that most SLPs knew very little about stuttering or how to treat it and even less about the impact that it had on the daily lives of those affected by the disorder. Many studies confirmed the validity of many of their feelings. For example, many SLPs held negative stereotypical and biased views about PWS, did not feel confident treating stuttering, and did not view stuttering as easily responsive to therapy (Shapiro, 1999).

It was also commonly felt that the profession was not taking any responsibility for failed therapy, but instead tended to blame the client for "not trying hard enough." Consumers were left to feel solely responsible and guilty for continuing to stutter. This hostility, combined with what many consumers perceived as a lack of interest in addressing these concerns or issues, led to a diminished appreciation of the potential role of speech-language pathologists in consumer organizations. Even though joint meetings were arranged to bring stuttering groups and professionals together, the attitudes and feelings expressed by some of the consumer leadership caused many professionals to maintain a distance (Gregory, 1997). The negative attitudes and feelings, however, were not limited to consumer leadership. Some SLPs who attended some support group meetings admitted that it was difficult for them to observe severe stutterers who in their opinion "do not take constructive action" and feared that potential clients attending these meetings would not seek professional help (Gregory, 1999). The proclamation from those within the self-help movement that "it's OK to stutter" reinforced the assumption of some SLPs that self-help groups for stuttering were "anti-therapy" and "anti-SLP."

However, in a survey of the National Stuttering Project (now the National Stuttering Association) conducted by Krauss-Lehrman and

Reeves (1988), this assumption was not substantiated. Rather than viewing self-help groups as the only option open to those who felt that traditional speech-language pathology had failed them, those responding to the survey viewed self-help/support groups as meeting very different needs than those provided by traditional speech therapy. In fact, 75% of NSP members felt that their therapy had been mildly or very successful. Thus, it seems fair to say that while many professionals view successful therapy in terms of percentages of overt stuttered utterances, many who stutter have a much different view of how successful therapy should be measured (Krauss-Lehrman & Reeves, 1988; Yaruss et al., 2002; Yaruss & Quesal, 2004). Only 25% felt therapy had been unsuccessful. In addition, 64% indicated that they considered the expertise of their personal SLP to be fair or good, whereas 14% rated their therapist as "excellent." Only 20% felt the expertise of their SLP was poor. Of particular interest is the finding that 75% of respondents felt that their therapy was successful, even though they still had varying degrees of stuttering! As discussed by St. Louis (chap. 4, this volume), it seems imperative in this era of outcomes-based treatment (see Pietranton, chap. 3, this volume) that we should be asking PWS more about what they consider to be treatment goals, and how they would define successful therapy (see also Manning, chap. 7, this volume).

It seems fair to say in comparing surveys such as that by Krauss-Lehrman and Reeves (1988) and Yaruss, Quesal, and Murphy (2002) that, while many professionals viewed successful therapy primarily in terms of percentages of overt stuttered utterances, many who stutter had a much different view of how successful therapy should be measured. As many authors in this volume note, this important concept may dramatically alter how SLPs establish treatment goals, address symptoms of concern to PWS, and measure progress to establish evidence-based treatment guidelines. Continued and expanded cooperation between self-help stuttering groups and professionals working in the area of stuttering may dramatically improve therapy outcomes for those who stutter.

In the past several years there have been a few "watershed" moments that have threatened such continued and expanded cooperation. Leaders of the self-help movement were dismayed when the American Speech-Language-Hearing Association did not join the consumer-driven effort to establish a national day to recognize and increase awareness about stuttering. When that grassroots effort culminated in 1988 with President Reagan signing a proclamation establishing National Stuttering Awareness Day, no representative from ASHA was present. Then in 1993, when prior requirements for fluency classwork and clinical experience were dropped from SLP clinical certification standards, it appeared that the profession had given up on those who stutter altogether. A tangible result of those changes was a national trend for graduate programs to reduce or even remove the requirements for academic knowledge and clinical experience with stuttering (Yaruss & Quesal, 2002). Revisions to certification standards in 2002 may further threaten the educational and clinical training of SLPs in the area of fluency disorders.

On the other hand, there have been some very positive events and experiences that brought professionals and self-help groups closer together. One such event was the very successful 1996 "Year of the Child Who Stutters" program, jointly sponsored by ASHA, the National Stuttering Association, and the Stuttering Foundation of America. Since that time there have been numerous initiatives and programs established by both consumer and professional organizations (Bradberry, 1999; Gregory, 1997; Yaruss & Reeves, 2002). Led by a number of individuals representing both constituencies, professional associations are reaching out more to include consumers in a variety of programs and policymaking committees, reciprocating similar efforts by consumer organizations.

Self-help in the new age

It is important to note that the development and growth of self-help for stuttering is not a phenomenon limited to the United States. As with other conditions, the concept of self-help for stuttering knew no geographical, socioeconomic, or political boundaries. One has only to conduct a brief Internet search of the International Stuttering Association to find numerous organizations throughout the world that have similar missions of helping people who stutter, educating the general public, and working with the professional speech-language pathology community. In addition, the creation of the International Fluency Association as an organization that embraces both professional and consumer membership and issues has done much to strengthen the alliance worldwide between the two communities.

Future challenges and opportunities for stuttering self-help groups

It seems apparent that there is no longer a need to debate either the need for or the value of self-help groups or self-help organizations. The role that self-help/support organizations play in improving the lives of those who stutter and their families is now well established. It is also evident that self-help/support is viewed by participants as complementary to various forms of professional therapy, rather than its alternative. Although much progress has been made in the last few years to close the gap between the self-help and professional communities, there is still work to be done. As Diggs (1990) stated over a decade ago:

> *Self-help and professional treatment can be compatible approaches to a problem, but danger exists when either group believes that it can do the work of the other.* (p. 33)

A successful and synergistic relationship will occur if both communities continue to develop an honest mutual respect and understanding for the benefits and limitations of the other. In order for this to occur, I believe there has to be a basic shift in the thinking of both groups. I personally believe that at the root of this shift must be a change in the notion by both consumers and professionals that speech-language pathologists can "fix" a person who stutters. This does *not* mean that consumers or professionals should view therapy as useless. Far from it. They simply need to reconceptualize its goals. SLPs can no more fix stuttering than an orthopedist can fix a broken bone. An orthopedic surgeon can diagnose a fractured bone, evaluate and respond to concomitant issues that may impact healing, stabilize the fracture site selecting from a a variety of methods (e.g., pins, plates, screws, casts, splints, etc.), and can educate the patient and/or family about the nature of broken bones and the environment needed to optimize healing. However, the only person who can produce new bone and therefore heal the fracture is the patient.

The treatment of stuttering is no different. A SLP can diagnose stuttering, identify, evaluate, and manage concomitant factors, use a variety of methods to stabilize the production of speech, and educate the client and/or family about the nature of stuttering and the environment needed to optimize fluency. However, the only person who can actually "heal" the stuttering, regardless of age, is the person affected.

It is this basic set of distorted expectations that, in my opinion, has been and continues to be the foundation for misunderstandings and animosity between consumers and professionals. The self-help movement in stuttering was begun by individuals who felt that they had not been "fixed" by speech therapy and were searching for a way outside of traditional modes of therapy to address their needs. Speech pathologists were arguably trained to "fix" stuttering, but were unable to do so in the vast majority of cases. There was bound to be a collision between the two; a population of consumers and parents that expected themselves or their children to be fixed by someone else and a population of professionals who expected to and felt responsible for providing that "fix."

In the coming years, we must rise to the challenges that face the stuttering community as a whole—professional training, appropriate and adequate delivery of services, public awareness, and research. It is my opinion that not only is it advantageous for us to work together, it is imperative. The power of consumer advocacy cannot be overstated, as evidenced by the successful establishment of National Stuttering Awareness Day. Although many professionals may feel uneasy or threatened by consumers or self-help organizations strongly advocating for better training and treatment for stuttering, it is time for them to understand that advocacy need not be taken personally. It should be clear by now that self-help groups and organizations can be allies for those who care about improving the lives of people who stutter. Consumers have been a powerful and positive force in moving the profession toward better training, specialization, and more public awareness and education.

It is tragic but evident that the once prominent stature of stuttering continues to decline within the larger scope of speech pathology. The quantity and quality of professional training has steadily dropped since 1993 (Yaruss & Quesal, 2002). This has occurred even in the face of numerous studies pointing to the fact that many SLPs do not feel comfortable in being asked to treat stuttering (ASHA Omnibus study, 2001; Cooper & Cooper, 1996). A number of these undertrained and ill-equipped (yet "certified") SLPs are then employed by public school systems, a setting in which they are required to treat a condition that they have had little—if any—training in, and are discouraged from referring to those more qualified (see Bernstein Ratner & Tetnowski, chap. 1, this volume). This has been a major concern of consumers for many years. The professionals within the stuttering community have not been able to reverse this trend within the profession at large.

Consumers have been at the forefront in advocating for better training and specialization for the treatment of stuttering for many years. If these efforts are to be successful, professionals who are committed to helping those who stutter and consumer based self-help organizations must work together to develop joint strategies to improve training and continuing education. Two sets of voices will make themselves heard more loudly than either one alone.

Positive steps have already been made on the national level by making provisions for self-help advocates and professionals to serve on policy-making boards of each of the respective organizations. Examples include the boards of the National Stuttering Association and the Speciality Board for Fluency Disorders, the recently created ASHA effort to issue postgraduate credentials (certificates of Fluency Specialization) for those with specific expertise in the treatment of stuttering. These efforts have not only provided an opportunity for knowledge and information exchange but also for the two cultures to learn more about each other. In addition, joint presentations have been invited and presented at both professional and self-help national meetings. These efforts can only move an emerging mutual agenda forward.

The future may already be here: Model cooperative self-help programs

To paraphrase Tip O'Neill, "All progress is local"—at least at first. On the local level, there have been numerous examples of ways in which self-help groups and graduate training programs for communication disorders can work together. One example is the longstanding partnership between the University of Texas at Dallas and the Dallas chapter of the National Stuttering Association. Although the self-help group is independent and autonomous, it was created with the assistance and support of the university. The group has held monthly meetings at the university clinic for over 20 years. Hundreds of students, clinicians, and educators have benefited from the numerous joint programs developed through a mutual desire to increase knowledge and understanding about the nature of stuttering. Members of the chapter are routinely invited to speak to graduate classes, and students have been required to attend at least one self-help meeting. A program in which members of the group volunteered to be "interviewed" by students as potential clients has met with very positive responses from students, educators, and participants. Jointly sponsored weekend workshops designed to bring adults and children who stutter, family members, and professionals together have made it possible for those in the community to meet others who share a common concern, learn more about stuttering, and become aware of the many resources available to them.

A summer fluency program has been developed by the university for children and parents that incorporates volunteers from the self-help group and is a practical learning experience for graduate students. The summer program was a catalyst for an ongoing monthly support group for children and parents facilitated by clinical staff and graduate students. Once again, adults from the local chapter of the NSA are frequent participants and guests. Members of the self-help group have also participated in distance learning classes and programs at other nearby university programs. Feedback from self-help members who participate in these "teaching" programs has been overwhelmingly positive. Participants report feelings of personal satisfaction, accomplishment, and purpose by helping young potential SLPs develop a better base of knowledge and understanding about stuttering. They also report feelings of improved self-confidence and self-esteem by being able to speak more openly and frankly about their own speech. Feedback from graduate students has been equally positive. Students report an appreciation for the willingness of those who stutter to share their personal stories. They also report that experience gained from the variety of learning opportunites is simply not possible through a traditional teaching model.

With the new ASHA Certification Standards requiring both knowledge and skills in fluency disorders, programs may want to consider fostering the development of a self-help group on their campus, in their clinic, or in their community. In addition, because of the range of ages, socioeconomic, and cultural backgrounds of individuals participating in self-help groups, graduate programs that incorporate these kinds of learning experiences for students can more easily comply with the new ASHA Standard IV-F that requires experience with diverse populations. There are other examples of university programs working with local self-help groups, but unfortunately they are the exception rather than the rule.

With over 250 accredited graduate programs for speech-language pathology in the United States, only a handful are known to sponsor their own or have an association with a local self-help group for stuttering. With a reported population of people who stutter within each community of approximately ¹/₂–1% (Bloodstein, 1995), sponsoring or promoting a self-help group could also help to achieve a university's mission of community outreach. The long-term advantages of fostering this kind of partnership benefits students, clinicians, those affected by stuttering, and the community.

Other challenges in our future

Improved training for speech-language pathologists is only one of the challenges facing members of both self-help groups and the profession as a whole. Delivering appropriate professional services to those who need it is another. The expanding scope of practice coupled with increasing case loads have created in schools a situation in which children who stutter (CWS) often fall through the cracks. The 2000 United States Census reported that there were 64,928,734 children in the United States between the ages of 3 to 18. Using the accepted professional prevalence of stuttering at 1% would estimate the potential number of children needing clinical services in a school setting at 649,287. In that same year, ASHA conducted a Special Schools Survey (2000) in which it was reported that of the 85,425 ASHA-certified SLPs, 54.6% were employed in a school setting and of those, 84.4%, or roughly 39,365, provided clinical services. In that same survey, it was stated that 2.6 students with fluency disorders were served per clinician. Using the ASHA Survey data would estimate that only 102,349 (2.6 times 39,365) or 39% of children who stutter are being diagnosed and/or treated in schools!

There may be several explanations for this severe gap in the number of children who stutter and those being served. Not all states or school systems require a certified SLP to treat children with speech and language disorders. In addition, many school districts interpret the IDEA in a manner that denies children access to services if they are performing at academic grade level. These two issues along with a lack of understanding about stuttering by teachers may result in fewer teacher referrals. It is also possible that some older children simply do not want therapy and some parents may have their children enrolled in private therapy. In addition there is always the possibility of statistical error. However, even if all of these factors are taken into account, there is still an unacceptable number of children who "fall between the cracks."[1]

Along with professionals, consumer organizations can help to encourage schools to require certified SLPs for the treatment of speech and language disorders, encourage higher salaries for well-trained professionals, and help to educate parents about their rights under the IDEA. In addition, it is important to educate parents of CWS, as well as "educators," about stuttering in general, different approaches to therapy, and how to best advocate for CWS. Self-help groups and organizations are playing an important role in providing parents with both education and support. Providing information to parents in the form of written materials, directing them to appropriate websites on the internet, making referrals to professionals knowledgeable in childhood stuttering, and connecting them with other parents who have been "through it before" are some of the ways self-help groups and organizations are helping parents to realize that they too are not alone. Putting parents who are trying to obtain services for their children in touch with others who have successfully advocated for their own children has been very helpful in many instances in securing appropriate services. The NSA and Friends: The Association for Young People Who Stutter both have programs that address these important issues. In addition, the Stuttering Foundation of America, the oldest non-profit organization for helping those who stutter, produces numerous written, audio, and video materials that educate parents and assist in referrals.

In a recent survey of parents attending an NSA conference (Yaruss et al., 2001) it was determined that almost 25% had received inaccurate or inappropriate information about their child's stuttering from professionals, including pediatricians as well as speech-language pathologists. Clearly, more education is also needed for allied professionals.

To address these concerns, both the Stuttering Foundation of America and the National Stuttering Association have produced informational materials for pediatricians. In addition, both have developed programs and materials (including pamphlets, videos (SFA) and lay and professional educational seminars) to increase awareness and education for teachers, employers and the general public. An emerging group, Friends: The

---

[1] I am extremely grateful to Charles Diggs of the American Speech-Language-Hearing Association for his help in attempting to detangle these complex estimates of children needing and receiving services.

Association of Young People who Stutter, is positioned to add to these resources.

Insurance coverage for stuttering therapy continues to be a challenge. Although some efforts have been made through the ASHA Division 4 (Fluency and Fluency Disorders) and the SFA to get this situation changed (SFA Resource Brochure: see www.stutteringhelp.org/insuranc.htm), little has been done to rally consumer support for insurance coverage changes. Working together and using the power of the consumer through self-help organizations, there may be a better chance to get stuttering treatment included in insurance coverage. In addition, self-help organizations are helping educate parents about the need to seek early specialized evaluation and treatment for their children who are at risk for chronic stuttering. Working as allies to improve the training of SLPs, helping to promote appropriate treatment, and assisting in efforts to get speech therapy services covered by insurance will help future generations of those affected by stuttering.

Equally important to training, public education, and service delivery is research. There is a crisis in attracting bright young students to research track doctoral programs for stuttering and speech-language pathology in general (Donaher & Eldridge, 2002; Oller, 2002). Exposing more students to the fascinating world of stuttering through participation in self-help meetings is one way to increase the odds of attracting some into research careers. Having the opportunity to meet and interact with current researchers at self-help conferences, workshops, and conventions is another. Paired with this decline in the potential number of researchers has been a decline in available research funding, particularly for therapy efficacy research (Ingham, 2003).

Obtaining funding for stuttering research has become increasingly more difficult. Although the Stuttering Foundation of America has provided some small grants for research, consumer-based organizations until recently have shown little interest in this aspect of advocacy for those who stutter. Hopefully, that too is changing. With the creation in 1998 of the National Stuttering Association Research Committee, the first steps were taken to establish a mechanism for researchers to work with a large self-help organization. This was followed in 2001 by the first joint symposium of consumers, clinicians, and researchers. This unique symposium was sponsored by the NSA, with educational grants from ASHA and the Eli

Lilly Company. Both of these efforts have been well received by both the consumer and professional communities (Yaruss & Reeves, 2002). With increasing competition for public funding, researchers may need to begin seeking more private sources of funding. Working together with self-help organizations to inform and encourage participation in stuttering research will not only increase the appreciation for research but may also open new avenues for funding through the private sector. Such cooperation will also facilitate research enrollment of PWS, an important improvement in a discipline where study participants have been historically difficult to locate in large numbers.

Conclusion

Stuttering is part of the human condition. Throughout the ages, professionals and those affected have struggled with trying to find the cause of what Aristotle referred to over 2,300 years ago as a condition resulting from an "apoplexy" or a seizing of one's ability to speak; he noted perceptively that it was likely to cause a "melancholic" or emotional state. We have been chasing the holy grail of the condition he described ever since.

New technology today may bring us closer to understanding the source of that "apoplexy." But in the words of Lee Travis (1927), the esteemed researcher and founder of the profession of speech pathology:

Scientists are still learning about stuttering, so that what is said today will be subject to modification tomorrow. (p. 527)

However, even if that source is found it will not help the millions of individuals and families currently affected by stuttering. In addition, there is clearly no single mode of treatment or "program" that has been shown to effectively and consistently "fix" stuttering for all people. The father of the profession of speech pathology understood this as well when he wrote,

In handling the stuttering child, it must be first borne in mind that each stutterer is an individual different from every other individual and must be handled on such a basis. (Travis, 1927, p. 537)

Although nothing will replace the professional speech-language pathologist as the primary service provider for those who stutter, it is clear that traditional modes of therapy do not meet many of the needs of people who stutter or their families. It is also clear that participation in a self-help/support group or organization can provide a number of positive outcomes for many affected by stuttering. Working together, professionals and self-help groups have the opportunity to provide a better future for those affected by stuttering.

References

Adams, R. (1990). *Self-help, social work, and empowerment.* London, Macmillan.

Adamsen, L. & Hertz, E. (1992). *Self-help groups under the social development program of Denmark and contiguous domains: A summary of research results.* Copenhagen: Academic Press.

Adamsen, L. & Rasmussen, J. (2001). Sociological perspectives on self-help groups: Reflections on conceptualization and social processes. *Journal of Advanced Nursing, 35*(6), 909–917.

ASHA Omnibus Study (2001). Rockville, MD: American Speech-Language-Hearing Association.

Banks, E. (2000, Summer). *Self-help and the new health agenda. Self-help 2000. The Newsletter of the National Self-Help Clearing House.*

Ben-Ari, A. T. (2002). Dimensions and predictions of professional involvement in self-help groups: A view from within. *Health & Social Work, 27,* 95–104.

Bloodstein, O. (1995). *A handbook on stuttering.* San Diego: Singular.

Bobrick, B. (1995). *Knotted tongues: Stuttering in history and the quest for a cure.* New York: Simon & Schuster.

Borkman, T. (1976). Experiential knowledge: A new concept for the analysis of self-help groups. *Social Science Review, 50,* 445–455.

Borkman, T. (1990). Self-help groups at the turning point: Emerging egalitarian alliances with the formal health care system? *American Journal of Community Psychology, 18,* 321–332.

Borkman, T. (1997). A selective look at self-help groups in the United States. *Health and Social Care in the Community, 5,* 357–364.

Borkman, T. (1999). *Understanding self-help/mutual aid: Experiential learning in the commons.* New Brunswick, NJ: Rutgers University Press.

Bradberry, A. (1997). The role of self-help groups and stuttering therapy. *Seminars in Speech and Language,18,* 391–399.

Constantino, V. & Nelson, G. (1995). Changing relationships between self-help groups and mental health professionals: Shifting ideology and power. *Canadian Journal of Community Mental Health, 14(2),* 55–70

Cooper, E. B. & Cooper, C. S. (1996). Clinician attitudes towards stuttering: Two decades of change. *Journal of Fluency Disorders, 21,* 119–135.

Damen, S., Mortelmans, D., & VanHove, E. (2000). Self-help groups in Belgium: Their place in the care network. *Sociology of Health and Illness, 22,* 331–348.

Diggs, C. C. (1990). Self–help for communication disorders. *ASHA, 32(1),* 32–34.

Donaher, J. & Eldridge, K. A. (2002, November). *Summit of doctoral students in stuttering: Findings and suggestions.* Miniseminar presented at the Annual ASHA Convention, Atlanta, GA.

Emerick, R. E. (1996). Mad liberation: The sociology of knowledge and the ultimate civil rights movement. *Journal of Mind and Behavior, 17,* 135–160.

Fraser, J. (2005). *The Stuttering Foundation of America: A history.* Memphis, TN: Stuttering Foundation of America.

Goodman, J. & Jacobs, M. (1994). The self-help, mutual-support group. In A. Fuhriman & G. Burlingame (Eds.), *Handbook of group psychotherapy: An empirical and clinical synthesis* (pp. 489–526). New York: Wiley.

Gregory, H. (1997). The speech-language pathologist's role in stuttering self-help groups. *Seminars in Speech and Language, 18,* 401–409.

Hinrichsen, G., Revenson, T., and Shinn, M. (1985). Does self-help help? An empirical investigation of scoliosis peer support groups. *Journal of Social Issues, 41,* 65–87.

Ingham, J. C. (2003). Evidence-based treatment of stuttering: I. Definition and application. *Journal of Fluency Disorders, 28*(3), 197–207.

Jacobs, M. K. & Goodman, D. (1989). Psychology and self-help groups: Predictions on a partnership. *American Psychologist, 44,* 536–545.

Katz, A. H. & Bender, E. I. (1976). *The strength in us: Self-help groups in the modern world.* New York: New Viewpoints.

Katz, A. H. & Bender, E. I. (1990). *Helping one another: Self-help groups in a changing world.* Oakland, CA: Third Party Publishing.

Krauss-Lehrman, T. & Reeves, L. (1989). Attitudes toward speech-language pathology and support groups: Results of a survey of members of the National Stuttering Project. *Tejas, Vol. XV, 1,* 22–25.

Kurtz, L. F. (1990). The self-help movement: Review of the past decade of research. *Social Work with Groups, 13,* 101–115.

Kyrouz, E., Humphreys, K., & Loomis, C. (2002). A review of research on the effectiveness of self-help mutual aid groups. In B. J. White & E. J. Madara (Eds.), *American self-help clearinghouse self-help group sourcebook (7th Ed.).*

Lee, D. T. (1995). Professional Underutilization of Recovery, Inc. *Psychiatric Rehabilitation Journal, 19*(1), 63–70.

Manning, W. (2001). *Clinical decision making in fluency disorders.* Vancouver: Singular.

Oka, T. & Borkman, T. (2000). The history, concepts and theories of self-help groups: From an international perspective. *The Japanese Journal of Occupational Therapy, 34,* 716–722. (Summary available from www.Selfhelp.org.uk/links.htm)

Oller, D. K. (2002, April). *Quantitative background on the shortage of research doctorates in communication sciences and disorders.* Proceedings of the annual conference of the Council of Academic Programs in Communication Sciences and Disorders, Palm Springs, CA. Text retrieved from www.capcsd.org/proceedings/2002/talks/dkoller2002.pdf

National Stuttering Association Joint Symposium for Scientists and Consumers (2002). *Pioneering research in the 21st century. Summary report and proceedings.* National Stuttering Association, New York.

Ramig, P. & Bennett, E. (1997). Considerations for conducting group intervention for adults who stutter. *Seminars in Speech and Language, 18,* 343–355.

Reissman, F. (2000). Self-help comes of age. *Social Policy, 30,* 47–49.

Reissman, F. & Carroll, D. (1995). *Redefining self-help: Policy and practice.* San Francisco: Jossey-Bass.

Shapiro, D. A. (1999). *Stuttering intervention: A collaborative journey to fluency freedom.* Austin, TX :Pro Ed.

Simmons, D. (1992). Diabetes self help facilitated by local diabetes research: The Coventry Asian Diabetes Support Group. *Diabetic Medicine, 9,* 866–869.

Starkweather, C. W. & Givens-Ackerman, J. (1997). *Stuttering.* Austin, TX: Pro-Ed.

Support groups are growing rapidly. (2000, September/October). *Futurist, 34,* 7–10.

Surgeon General Workshop on Self-Help and Public Health. (1998). *U.S. Department of Health and Human Services, Public Health Services, Health Resources and Services Administrations, Bureau of Material Health and Child Health Resources and Development Publication no. 224–25.* Washington D.C.: U.S. Government Printing Office.

Toseland, R. W. & Hacker, L. (1985). Social workers' use of self-help groups as a resource for clients. *Social Work, 30,* 232–237.

Travis, L. (1927). *Stuttering.* Chicago, IL: The Class Room Teacher, Inc.

Van Riper, C. (1973). *The treatment of stuttering.* Englewood Cliffs, NJ: Prentice-Hall.

Van Riper, C. (1982). *The nature of stuttering.* Englewood Cliffs, NJ: Prentice-Hall.

Vattano, A. J. (1972). Power to the people: Self help groups. *Social Work, 17,* 7–17.

Wituk, S., Shepherd, M., Slavich, S., Warren, M., & Meissen, G. (2000). Topography of self-help groups: An empirical analysis. *Social Work, 45,* 157–166.

Yaruss, J. S. & Quesal, R. W. (2002). Academic and clinical education in fluency disorders: An update. *Journal of Fluency Disorders, 27,* 43–63.

Yaruss, J. S. & Quesal, R. W. (2004). Partnerships between clinicians, researchers, and people who stutter in the evaluation of stuttering treatment outcomes. *Stammering Research, 1,* 1–15.

Yaruss, J. S., Quesal, R. W., Reeves, L., Molt, L., Kluetz, B., Caruso, A. J., Lewis, F., & McClure, J. A. (2002). Speech treatment and support group experiences of people who participate in the National Stuttering Association. *Journal of Fluency Disorders, 27,* 115–135.

Yaruss, J. S., Quesal, R. W., & Murphy, W. (2002). National Stuttering Association members' opinions about stuttering treatment. *Journal of Fluency Disorders, 27,* 227–241.

Yaruss, J. S., Quesal, R. W., Tellis, C., Molt, L., Reeves, L., Caruso, A. J., McClure, J., & Lewis, F. (2001). The impact of stuttering on people attending a National Stuttering Association convention. In H-G. Bosshardt, J. S. Yaruss, & H. F. M. Peters (Eds.), *Fluency disorders: Theory, research, treatment, and self-help (proceedings of the Third World Congress on Fluency Disorders;* pp. 232–236). Nijmegen, The Netherlands: Nijmegen University Press.

Yaruss, J. S. & Reeves, L. (2002). *Pioneering stuttering in the 21st century: The first joint symposium for scientists and consumers (Summary Report and Proceedings).* Anaheim, CA: National Stuttering Association.

— Author Index —

282

AUTHOR INDEX

Florance, C. L., 211, 212, *237*
Ford, B., 246, *254*
Foster, J., *204*
Foundas, A., 161, *203*
Fox, P. T., 12, *16,* 89, *97,* 188, *203*
Franke, P., 40, *44*
Franklin, D. L., 248, *254*
Franklin, J. A., 72, *80,* 84
Fransella, F., *157*
Freeman, F. J., 106, *123,* 162, 184, *202,*
203
Freund, H-J., *98*
Fuhriman, A., *276*
Fujiki, M., 29, *44*
Fujino, H., 40, *45*
Fuqua, R., 162, *204*
Futurist, 277

G

Gabel, R. M., 132, *155*
Gateley, G., 113, *122*
Gazzaniga, M., *44*
Givens-Ackerman, J., 71, *83,* 260, *277*
Glass, T., *97*
Gleitman, H., 106, *123*
Gleitman, L., 106, *123*
Glenn, K., 74, *81*
Gold, M. S., 251, *253*
Goldberg, L., 212, *237*
Goldberg, S. A., 132, *156*
Goldman-Eisler, F., 131, *156*
Gondo, K., 40, *45*
Goodin, D., 239, *254*
Goodman, D., *276*
Goodman, J., 260, *276*
Gordon, C. T., 249, 250, 253, *254*
Gottschalk, L. A., 248, *254*
Gottwald, S., 101, 111, *123*
Goudemand, M., 248, *254*
Gould, S. J., *16*
Graham, C., 36, 37, 41, *44*
Green, E., 161, *204*
Gregory, H. H., 64, 69, 74, *81, 204,*

260, 263, 264, 265, 267, *276*
Grimes, C., *81,* 84
Gronhovd, K. D., *81,* 83
Grossman, M., 38, *43*
Grothe, D. R., *253*
Grunhaus, L., 250, *254*
Guitar, B. E., 7, *15,* 26, 33, 34, 41, *44,*
64, *81,* 84, 95, 96, 100, 103, 105,
106, 107, 115, 117, *122, 124,* 126,
133, 139, 142, *156,* 162, 168, 171,
174, *203,* 263
Gutherie, E., 33, *44*
Guthrie, S., 250, *254*

H

Hacker, L., 262, *277*
Haight, W., *122*
Hall, A., *44*
Hall, N. E., 29, *44,* 77, *81*
Ham, R. E., 64, 69, *81*
Hamburger, S. D., *254*
Hammer, C., 74, *80, 124*
Hancock, K., 41, *44,* 88, *97, 156*
Handly, R., 165, 189, *203*
Hanley, J., 162, *204*
Hanson, B. R., *81,* 83
Hardman, J., 242, 243, *254*
Harris, M., 89, 91, *97,* 161, *202*
Harris, V., 112, 118, *122*
Harrison, E., 64, *82,* 96, *97,* 107, 109,
122, 123, 126, 133, *156, 157*
Hartfield, K., 38, 41, *44*
Hartsuiker, R., *45*
Harvey, J. H., *158*
Hayden, D., 6, *16*
Healey, E. C., 5, *15, 16, 45,* 74, 75, *80,*
82, 123, 145, *156, 157, 158, 203*
Heilman, K., 161, *203, 246, 253*
Held, B., 151, *156*
Helmstetter, S., 186, *203*
Henderlong, J., 114, 117, *122*
Herbert, J. D., 136, 137, *156*
Hertz, E., *276*

Y

Z

— Subject Index —